Ken Sobol
and
Julie Macfie Sobol

Looking for Lake Erie

TRAVELS AROUND A GREAT LAKE

VIKING

VIKING
Published by the Penguin Group
Penguin Books Canada Ltd, 10 Alcorn Avenue, Toronto, Ontario,
Canada M4V 3B2
Penguin Books Ltd, 27 Wrights Lane, London W8 5TZ England
Viking Penguin, a division of Penguin Books USA Inc.,
375 Hudson Street, New York, New York 10014, U.S.A.
Penguin Books Australia Ltd, Ringwood, Victoria, Australia
Penguin Books (NZ) Ltd, 182-190 Wairau Road, Auckland 10, New
Zealand

Penguin Books Ltd, Registered Offices: Harmondsworth, Middlesex,
England

First published 1995

10 9 8 7 6 5 4 3 2 1

Printed and bound in Canada on acid free paper ⊗

Canadian Cataloguing in Publication Data

Sobol, Ken
    Looking for Lake Erie : travels around a Great Lake

ISBN 0-670-85389-5

1. Sobol, Ken - Journeys - Erie, Lake, Region. 2. Sobol, Julie Macfie,
1936-   - Journeys - Erie, Lake, Region. 3. Erie, Lake, Region -
Description and travel. 4. Erie, Lake, Region - History. 5. Erie,
Lake - History. I. Sobol, Julie Macfie, 1936 -   . II. Title.

F555.S73 1995   977.1'2   C94-932842-1

For
Jane, Corry and Greg & Company,
and John and Annie

AUTHORS' NOTE

Looking for Lake Erie is based on a series of excursions to the various parts of the lake during the summer and fall of 1993. Most readers will quickly realize that we must have passed through many of the places we describe more than once and that our accounts are sometimes amalgams of several visits; the larger cities on the American side in particular demanded a number of trips to fix in our minds just what it was we were seeing. In case anyone wonders.

Writers customarily use this space to acknowledge their gratitude to people who have helped them along their way. One such person was our unfailingly thoughtful and supportive editor, Meg Masters. Most of the others are mentioned in the text. The fact that we weren't kidding when we said we would put them in a book may come as a shock to some, but there they are. (A small number preferred to remain anonymous, so we thank them anonymously.)

We ploughed through a lot of reading in the course of our research, including tourist brochures, regional histories, local newspapers, newsletters and sometimes even thick academic monographs. Since the subject of all of them was the lake, we found them all interesting, if not invariably sparkling or completely reliable, but two books stand out as works that we returned to repeatedly: *Lore of the Lakes* by Dana Thomas

Authors' Note

Bowen and *True Tales of the Great Lakes* by Dwight Boyer.

We would also like to pay our respects to Dervla Murphy and Bill Bryson, two writers we've never met and who probably wouldn't recognize Lake Erie if they fell into it, but whose books were always there to remind us, in quite different ways, of the potential of travel literature.

The International Joint Commission for the Great Lakes and the Ontario Ministry of Natural Resources provided useful technical material. To our lay person's surprise, however, we discovered that no two scientists can seem to agree about anything regarding the Great Lakes. The most basic statistics may vary wildly from source to source, and to ask a slightly complicated question, something for example on the order of why the loon population on the Grand River is increasing, will open a Pandora's box of strongly held opinions ranging from climate shifts to changes in the food chain to cleaner water to doubt that they are to a firm denial that there are now or ever have been loons on that stream. The fact that we chose what seemed the most commonsensical of the competing theories and figures will probably get us in trouble with everyone.

Ken Sobol/Julie Macfie Sobol

CONTENTS

Prologue
The Idea of a Lake

Although we now live in Ontario, both of us grew up close by the American shore of Lake Erie; the Macfies made their home outside Detroit, the Sobols in Cleveland. But no two families could have been more dissimilar in their relationship to the massive body of water they lived near than ours.

A generation after their fathers had humbled the British in the Revolutionary War, the early Everetts and Greenes started west with the first wave of American pioneers. (This was Julie's mother's family; her father's family, the Macfies, arrived in the New World much later.) Along with many of their fellow New Englanders, that initial batch drove and pushed their carts along the ruts of western New York State to Buffalo where they thankfully boarded schooners and sailed the two hundred and forty miles of the lake and disembarked at Detroit to begin carving out farms in the Michigan wilderness. This was the longest voyage on open water they would ever take, and a glorious memory to be treasured and related to the children and grandchildren.

Another group came over from Ireland in the 1830s. These latecomers suffered through weeks of cramped quarters as they traversed the North Atlantic, but once they reached the Promised Land of America conditions improved; they had the luxury of travelling west by way of the newly opened Erie

Canal, then catching one of the early packet steamers and negotiating the lake in relative comfort, with time to sun themselves on deck and wave to passengers on the numerous other vessels flitting by.

The Soblowitz and Titiefsky clans (soon to become Sobols and Tempkins), from Lithuania and the Ukraine respectively by way of Hamburg, would remember their once-in-a-life-time sea voyages with less enthusiasm. When, around the turn of this century, they climbed out of steerage, blinked in the bright sunlight, pointed excitedly to the Statue of Liberty on another little piece of land not far away and streamed down the gangplanks at Ellis Island, most of them swore never to get near water again.

After struggling uptown amid scenes of wild linguistic confusion, disintegrating cardboard luggage and hysterical children, they jammed themselves into a New York Central railcar that would hopefully take them to a place called Cleveland, where other relatives might or might not await them. (Not, as it turned out, but they stayed anyway.) It is likely that they did not see the Great Lake, or even learn there was such a body of water on their doorsteps, until months after their arrival.

All that took place long before we were born, of course, but the pattern continued into our time. The Lake Eries each of us knew as children in the forties and fifties bore almost no resemblance to each other.

KS: The lake is a thing of evil in my earliest memory. Rather than the sparkling, shifting skein of dancing blue and white the uninitiated might have perceived, I knew it to be a boundless depth of malign pollution. "You'd have to be crazy to stick as much as a toenail in that sewer," chorused my parents whenever the liquid horror slipped into view.

Everyone in Cleveland Heights, the suburb where I grew up, seemed to be in agreement that ignoring the lake when possible, and trashing it when not, was the only sensible approach. Not only was Lake Erie filthy, it was, even worse, somehow gentile. People we knew, our crowd, neither swam in it nor sailed its surface.

As immigrant children in the early part of the century, many of my parents' generation had cavorted happily on the beaches and thrown themselves off the piers, oblivious to worries about undertows or pollution, but that ended with the move to the suburbs after World War Two. With the assumption of bourgeois respectability and its accompanying horror of dirt and germs, such lower-class diversions were relegated to the realm of "what we used to do when we were poor."

Even the whitefish that were dredged out of the lake's murky waters had to be cured before they were fit to grace our delicatessen display cases: cured not only of the sin of freshness but apparently of any trace of their marine origin. The wrinkled creatures that ended up on Sunday morning brunch plates looked like old leather mittens with eye sockets, the kind of thing Picasso might have fastened onto an early cubist collage.

Most of Cleveland's other ethnic and immigrant groups seemed to share our suspicions of the lake. Men in faded grey suits who looked vaguely like Bela Lugosi could sometimes be seen fishing off remote piers and on the breakwaters, but not in great numbers, and although I kept an eye out for colourful Italian families seining out seafood dinners and groups of elderly blacks harmonizing their way toward a traditional catfish fry, I never did come across any on my occasional forays along the shoreline.

There must have been yacht clubs on Lake Erie back then. And marinas, tackle and gear stores, pierside restaurants and all those other "Popeye the Sailor Man" accessories. After all, Cleveland has its share of citizens with too much money—more than its share, in fact—and wherever there's wealth and water there are usually fleets of tanned, martini-mixing mariners wearing silly caps and striped jerseys. If they did exist, however, they weren't part of the ethos of the city. Cleveland was on the lake, all right, but the lake was never really part of Cleveland. At least not during my childhood.

The river that flowed into Lake Erie was something else, however. The Cuyahoga enters the city from the south and eventually oozes through the old industrial wasteland known as the Flats to empty its countless gallons of slag and chemical residue into the lake at a point just west of downtown. The river in fact divides the city into its East and West sides, although bizarrely the first nine West streets (not all of them currently extant) are located on the East side.

This, my father would patiently relate, was because the numbering system began at Public Square, which is nine streets to the west of the river. At which point I, logically enough it seemed to me, would ask why they hadn't started numbering at the river itself. This always struck my father as a hostile reflection on the fair city where he had chosen to pass his entire life, and since he was a passionate defender of any status quo, as a veiled attack on him as well. "Shut your mouth," he would then explain, or words to that effect.

In the Flats the river resembled nothing so much as a black worm as it twisted lethargically past the grime-coated steel mills and scrap-yards. Dead fish and condoms occasionally floated by on the oily scum, but beneath the surface all was impenetrable darkness. I worked one summer at a camp nestled along the fresh, clear headwaters of the Cuyahoga where it rises in the foothills of eastern Ohio, and you could stand waist-deep in the water and see below your knees. In the lower river the beam of a powerful searchlight would have been extinguished a quarter inch under the surface.

The Flats themselves, however, were inspirational. The path of the Cuyahoga forms a kind of canyon, on either side of which the rest of the city hovers. Magnificent suspension bridges, memorials to the boisterous engineering aesthetic of Cleveland's glory days around the turn of the century, cross it high above the river bed. Down below, Jones & Laughlin, U.S. Steel and the rest of their fraternity had erected gigantic blast furnaces that turned the entire valley as black as the hearts of their upper management.

Tucked into the shadows of the big boys were ten-foot-wide luncheonettes, sawdust bars, missions, whorehouses, hardware stores, haberdasheries stocked with shelves of Steel Tips and OshKosh B'Gosh overalls, a union hall or two, body shops, deformed little frame houses, junk yards and the rest of a colourful Edward Hopper America that, by the start of the fifties, was quickly becoming little more than a picturesque anachronism.

I would wander down the crooked, crumbling, grease-encrusted streets, stand by the tiny drawbridge watching it grind open to let barges pass, drink a beer in one of the grungy Polish bars where no one cared about your age, ogle the streetwalkers and loiter under the lee of the J&L plant, gazing up at its overpowering bulk. It seemed a monument as significant as one of the Pyramids, at least to my teenaged eyes.

Cleveland of the river was the only part of that insular and declining metropolis that seemed to have any connection with the overall pattern of history, that allowed a romantic misfit like me to escape into another world in the moments I spent there. Curiously, I don't recall ever actually following the river out to the point where it entered the lake, although it could only have been a few hundred yards from the places I wandered around.

Not that there would have been anything but industrial waste to see. It was all closed off to the public, anyway, and nobody seemed to care one way or another. As far as I could tell no citizen of Cleveland ever gave a thought to the lake. It was little more than an embarrassment to a people in love with the emerging miracle of superhighways, shopping centres and Uncle Miltie.

JMS: On the front page of the *Tri-County News* (dateline Grand Rapids, Ohio, July 14, 1933), the editor was waxing philosophical: "Way down deep, we're all still explorers and adventurers. That's why we're always glad to kick off work and listen to a fellow human being who has decided to match his wits, courage and strength against time and elements."

He wasn't talking about Lindbergh or Admiral Byrd. The elements in question were the winds and waves of the Detroit River, Lake Erie and, continuing south into Ohio, the Maumee River. And the human being he referred to was my father, a quiet, twenty-nine-year-old tool-and-die worker by trade, dreamer and adventurer by avocation, by the name of John Macfie. He had just paddled into town, beached his homemade fourteen-foot canoe along the riverbank and headed down Grand Rapids' main street for an exchange of views with what he might have called, in his typically high-Edwardian way, the local "gentlemen of the press."

The fact that our white frame farmhouse was located hundreds of miles from the nearest ocean and increasingly surrounded by the gas stations and bungalows of Detroit's overflow population never deterred him from regularly breaking into John Masefield's "I must go down to the sea again, to the lonely sea and the sky" as he descended the stairs for breakfast. So when the Great Depression really set in and he, like many of our neighbours, found it impossible to turn up even part-time work, he did what for him was the next logical thing. He built a boat out of spare sheet metal and went to sea—the sea in this case being Lake Erie, the nearest substantial body of water.

Enlisting a relative with a delivery truck to carry him to the river, he slid the canoe into the water somewhere near Ecorse, a few miles downstream of the Detroit city limits, and pointed south. Although nearly swamped shortly afterwards by the swell of a large passenger boat, he struggled on toward his first landmark, the point ten miles on where the river opens out into the Great Lake. He camped for the night on one of the small islands south of Grosse Isle.

The next morning he reached Lake Erie and the great odyssey really began. A couple of days later, crossing Maumee Bay, at the turn of the lake in Ohio, one of Erie's notorious squalls suddenly blew up and he barely escaped being overturned. He watched in horror as a rowboat near him foundered and sank in the tempest and sighed with relief when its passengers managed to swim to shore.

A firm believer in letting the wind blow him where it may, he continued on up the Maumee River, gliding under the bridges of industrial Toledo and past sleepy riverfront hamlets with names like Rossford and Perrysberg, then losing half his supplies when he hit the rapids at Waterville. Eventually he arrived at Grand Rapids, where the first few days of his voyage were recorded for posterity in the *Tri-County News.*

This all occurred years before my birth, and while I heard snippets of stories about the trip, I never really got straight where he went after Grand Rapids. He was not a talkative man at best, and I often tuned out when my parents reminisced about the past.

It's possible that my father reversed his path and continued around the lake, as he often seemed to mention places along the Ohio shore with an I-saw-it-with-my-own-eyes knowingness. On the other hand, he came home one day with a recording of "The Banks of the Wabash," which he played until it disintegrated. Since he was completely tone-deaf and I knew he only bought records when they had some particular meaning for him, it seems just as likely that he continued on up the Maumee, somehow got a ride over to the nearby headwaters of the Wabash and then paddled his way down that river by the light of the Indiana moon. Or did both.

Sailing the lake remained his dream. A succession of boats cluttered up the property over the years, particularly a decrepit cabin cruiser that he purchased through an ad in the *Detroit Free Press* and that sat in drydock in our side yard for twenty-five years. There never seemed to be enough money or time to get it shipshape, or a family crisis would intervene just as things looked good for a voyage, and he never went to sea again in the same way as he had in 1933.

But every time I saw him glancing out the kitchen window at the boat, or entering its cabin with yet another replacement part that he had ordered from some mysterious source in the hope of getting the engine operating, I knew my father's heart was on the lake, and that he would have been happiest living within walking distance of ships and sailing men, and maybe being one of them himself.

Our family did manage one major nautical outing every summer—our annual voyage to Boblo Island on the sumptuous international excursion ship *Ste. Claire.* ("International" because Boblo is actually in Canada and to get there we would have to cross the invisible watery border that runs through the centre of the Detroit River.)

A palpable excitement filled the air of the narrow parking lot along Detroit's waterfront, just in the shadow of the Vernor's Ginger Ale bottling plant, from the moment my father turned off our car's motor and we looked around for our first glimpse of the huge white boat.

We strode up the wide, awning-shaded gangplank behind him, jostled good-naturedly by the other holiday picnickers, keeping his lean, blue-suited figure in sight (this was before fathers started wearing the same clothing as their children on family outings). Once settled on board we kids took off, climbing down the aft staircase, up the fore staircase, down again to a sort of balcony on the lowest level, where we leaned over a railing to watch the huge brass pistons moving up and down with an alarming clamour. We would then finish off our ritual exploration of the boat with a visit to the snack bar and the washrooms before returning to the upper deck to find our parents and the other adults who seemed, strangely enough, happy just to sit.

The captain blew two long blasts on the whistle, making enough noise to lift a small child's feet off the deck, and we were off on our two-hour journey to Canada. Passengers relaxed as the band launched into "Sentimental Journey," and everyone began talking animatedly as the dance floor filled up.

As we left the skyscrapers of Detroit behind us, my parents occasionally pointed out landmarks along the shore: to starboard, the imposing houses of Grosse Isle and the mouth of the stream that gave its name to Ford's sprawling River Rouge plant where my father had been working for the last ten years or so (and from which he would eventually retire, after forty years on the line, with a gold watch and lung cancer); on the port side, the villages and farms of the green Canadian mainland; and directly ahead of us, the choppy, open waters of Lake Erie.

As the large boat glided serenely through time and space and the band struck up "Sentimental Journey" yet again, what went on in the houses on both banks seemed humdrum compared to life on the boat. With its four decks, its ballroom, its music and flags (the Stars and Stripes and Canada's Red Ensign), its lifebelts, its glass-enclosed axes and other white-painted boxes that could contain anything, all the mysterious paraphernalia that comes with ships, I thought it was pretty close to paradise, a perfect world of simultaneous motion and stillness.

Boblo itself was all pretty low-key—no supercoasters or wave pools, no Mickey Mouse to greet you, just a few square acres of playing fields and picnic grounds, with the additional enticement of an old blockhouse left over from the War of 1812 and a small but well-conceived amusement park that lit up the scene as you left the ship.

But for a few hours I was on an island—a real island, with water in every direction—and within sight of one of the Great Lakes. And as I think back on myself on those moments, I realize I was gazing out on the same channel that my pioneer ancestors had sailed up one hundred and fifty years earlier, when Michigan was still a territory. Every one of them would have passed within shouting distance of the very beach at Boblo where I stood waving optimistically to the freighters and fishing boats.

The sights they would have seen along the shore and on the various islands, the deep forest broken only occasionally by an isolated cabin or a native fishing camp, were very different from my experience of the scene. But when they turned and looked back at that wide expanse of blue water gradually disappearing into the horizon, with the wind whipping up whitecaps on the surface and a few clouds drifting across the sky, their view would have been identical to mine (and, for that matter, to my father's on his solo canoe voyage). The lake seems, in retrospect, to unite all our generations.

Obviously, two very different early experiences. But by adulthood Lake Erie had pretty well vanished from our consciousness. As had the overall Great Lakes watershed, the cities of Detroit and Cleveland and in fact the entire Midwest; as soon as we could, we had turned our eyes eastward and lit out, not for the territories, but for New York and Europe and what we confidently expected to be the delights of the bohemian life.

A lot has happened since then; we got married, raised our own family, lived in half a dozen widely scattered places, and are now back more or less where we started, although on the other side of that midwestern, mid-water border. But more to the point, the realities of life in the nineties have led us to take a second look at things we ignored or even scoffed at during the years when we and the rest of the western world, convinced of our glorious, ever-expanding, always brighter future, became infatuated with technology and almost embarrassed by the natural world.

The Great Lakes head our list of candidates for that second look. This enormous chain of inland seas, 246,000 square kilometres in area, containing 20 percent of the world's supply of fresh water, remains, as it has always been, largely unknown. A lot of North Americans would have trouble fitting the right names with the right bodies of water or drawing a rough map of them.

The one attempt at an overview of the lakes to enter the general consciousness was a book called *The Late Great Lakes*, published in the 1980s. A jeremiad in the style of *Silent Spring* or *Death and Life of Great American Cities*, it trenchantly outlined the extent to which man was killing off the lakes and asserted that the process had gone considerably farther in Erie than anywhere else. Like most people, we took that to mean that the lake was poisoned beyond recall, that it had become an enormous pool of pollution inhospitable to any form of life other than sea lamprey and algae, and would forever remain a grim reminder of man's destructiveness.

And yet after a number of recent trips into the area in the course of researching magazine pieces we had gradually become aware that along the northern shore and even at a few places on the American side people still swim off Erie's beautiful beaches without ill effects, that the world's largest freshwater commercial fishing fleet continues to sail out of its ports, that sport angling thrives, and that its remaining wetlands are among the most extensive and important on the continent. Did Lake Erie die and somehow revive, or were reports of its demise greatly exaggerated?

We also began to be intrigued by the lives of the people who lived along the lake. That's partly because among those widely scattered places we'd once inhabited was a "handyman's special" in a remote rural county. Our house, such as it was, backed onto a small river and as years passed we began to feel a link with the other residences along our waterway; in a way the connection was even stronger than the one provided by the gravel road in front. If a tiny body of water like the Delisle River had the power to create its own world, what must be the effect of a geographical entity as large as a Great Lake?

We wanted to know more about the millions of people who live along Erie's shores, some of whom worry about daily survival in dilapidated, drug-devastated slums while others drift through the American Dream in tidy suburbs, studiously oblivious to anyone else's problems, and still others rise at dawn to work their farms and pursue a daily routine not all that different from that of the first pioneers to settle in Ontario.

Where had they come from (and why and when), what place in the ongoing social history of the lakeshore did they occupy, what kind of communities had they developed? Had common patterns evolved from one side of the lake to the other? How alike and how different are the two cultures that share the shoreline? Above all, what influence did this immense body of water, 25,700 square kilometres in area, larger than nine American states, among them Vermont and

New Jersey (and five times greater than Prince Edward Island) exert over its population? What was the world of Lake Erie?

We packed a few clothes, grabbed some notebooks and a bunch of maps, threw them all in the Mazda and took off for a long-delayed closer look at the Great Lake we had only caught glimpses of as kids.

Looking
for
Lake Erie

PART ONE

The Eastern Third

Chapter One

Lake Erie begins (or, if you want to be hydrologically correct about it, ends) at that most celebrated of all natural North American landmarks, that wonder of the world that every Siberian schoolgirl, every Patagonian campesino, every African cattle-herder who ever spent some time in a mission school keeps tucked away somewhere in his or her subconscious. There can't be many earthlings who haven't at some time in their lives seen a picture-postcard or a Viewmaster slide of Niagara Falls, even if they haven't a clue how to locate them on a map or even whether they actually exist.

Like all midwestern families since time began, each of ours made ritual pilgrimages to view the Falls. In both cases this was sometime back in the late forties; gasoline rationing had ended, jobs were plentiful, and Americans were starting to get caught up in the postwar rush to reward themselves for surviving the Depression. Not to mention single-handedly defeating the Axis powers in World War Two and having the foresight to be born in the greatest nation on earth. The exact year is fuzzy, for both of us, but talking about it, we realized our visits could easily have taken place during the same summer, maybe the same month.

Or even, strange to contemplate, the same weekend. Imagine it. Some grotesque jest of the gods could have placed our two families—squabbling children, determinedly cheer-ful, fixedly smiling mothers and harried fathers—side by side in the crowded back row of a tour bus or in a packed diner where the only seats available were next to each other.

Only a few moments would have elapsed before John Macfie, that world-class misreader of social situations, a man simultaneously gregarious and tongue-tied, turned to the pathologically conventional, equally conversationally chal-lenged Sobols and blurted out the suggestion that since we all got along so well we should exchange names and addresses and Julie and Ken could become pen-pals. At which point our two blushing, pre-pubescent selves would have expired on the spot and this book would never have been written. Fortunately we were spared, and another fifteen or so years would pass before our two families were afforded the oppor-tunity to stare at each other in horrified disbelief over the Macfies' coffee table.

Despite the wide disparity in what we brought there, the memories we took away were identical. First was an overpow-ering sense of wetness. Standing at the rail on the *Maid of the Mist* as it gingerly approached the Falls (then stopped and bobbed around disappointingly far away), peering out from between regiments of yellow-slicker-clad adults, what we both recall is vainly trying to wipe the spray out of our faces so we could actually see what was out there. If you wore glass-es as one of us did from the age of six on you could forget the whole thing.

Our second common reaction was a surge of chagrin at the realization that the Canadian Falls were actually superior in every way to our own. No amount of geological exegesis about the fact that the 64-metre-high American Falls are a full ten metres higher than the Canadian, which is why 90 percent of the water chooses the path of least resistance, etc., etc., could explain it away; we knew when we were being cheated.

As Americans we naturally rejected the idea of sharing a major geographic wonder with a foreign country; for that matter, the very existence of other countries, with their strange foods, their pointlessly incomprehensible languages and their stern un-American faces and behaviour, seemed acts of defiance against the natural order of things. (Israel and Scotland were granted exemptions, but only just.) Even the flower gardens in the Canadian riverside park were prettier and better laid out. It was too much for any two-fisted, patriotic midwestern child to take lying down. There didn't seem much we could do about it, of course, but we burned with indignation inside.

On the whole we kept such thoughts to ourselves, vaguely aware of their immature nature. This was not the case with a writer of best-selling aviation books named Stephen Coonts. "It's a heck of a waterfall," he proclaimed enthusiastically in *The Cannibal Queen*, his 1992 account of criss-crossing the continent in an elderly biplane. "Best I've ever seen. This is the Grand Canyon of Waterfalls, absolutely the biggest and most stunning... American hearts swell with pride." But one aspect of their grandeur left him rueful. "It's too darn bad we have to share this waterfall with the Canadians. If only we could get them to sell us a hundred-yard-wide strip of Ontario shoreline for a mile in each direction, it would be all ours."

The obverse of that proposition did not seem to have occurred to him, much less the dangerously progressive notion that nature may not actually belong to human governments. But in this case he's hit the American nail dead on the American head. Deep down, most U.S. citizens would probably favour purchasing the Falls and transporting them whole some miles across the border, if only such an act were physically feasible.

But of course the Falls were there before there was an America, or a Canada. "*Dites-moi*, once more, *s'il vous plaît*, what is this place we're going to?" Hennepin or Jolliet or La Salle or whatever early Frenchman first undertook the long journey to the extreme western end of Lake Ontario must have demanded of his native guides. "Yes, I heard what you said, but what exactly does it mean, the place where two large land masses come together and a lot of water falls down in the middle?"

And being Europeans, the intellectual heirs of Pascal and Aquinas, they no doubt shook their heads and smiled at the childlike literalness of aboriginal people. A lot of water falling down. *Franchement.*

There are conflicting claims as to who saw the Falls first, but Father Hennepin's journal of 1678 provides the initial written description. He called them "a vast and prodigious cadence of water," one of those classic Jesuit locutions that doesn't actually mean very much but sounds so much as if it does that it has been quoted repeatedly ever since.

What he was trying to say was, basically, that there was indeed a lot of water in that place. Even today, after a series of gigantic hydroelectric plants have considerably reduced the flow, the river crashes over the Canadian Falls at the rate of 200,000 cubic feet per second. And though the author of the book in which we came across that figure apologizes for using a mere statistic to convey the magnitude of the onrush, in reality that single number is more evocative than any number of glossy photographs.

It's hard enough to hold the image of a single cubic foot of water steady in your mind. Trying to imagine 200,000 cubic feet of the stuff hurtling by beneath your feet every second is such a feat of concentration that you feel yourself momentarily swept away in the torrent, carried out to infinity even as you try to visualize its limits. *Cela*—as a less educated *coureur de bois* might have put it—*cela c'est beaucoup de l'eau.*

Like the explorers who had preceded us, we decided that our gateway to Lake Erie would be that renowned cliff at the midpoint of the turbulent thirty-mile strait known as the Niagara River. Arriving on a steaming late July day in the summer of 1993, we realized we hadn't taken a good look at the Falls since those childhood visits so many years ago. In fact they had barely entered our consciousness in all that time, except by way of an annoying TV jingle that rhymes "Niagara Falls, Ontario" with "a wonderful place for you to go" and is repeated at least once every ten minutes on all Toronto stations. And strangely enough, Niagara Falls really did turn out to be a wonderful place to go—especially if you happened to be one of those long, low, narrow structures with a great many bedrooms and a large electric sign out front. This is an entire fair-sized city (pop. 76,000) approximately 97 percent of whose buildings are motels. There are so many motels they block your view of other motels. It's like a science fiction movie in which alien hostelries have taken over America and sooner or later everyone will stay in one and become their victim.

There must be newsstands, medical centres, beauty salons, video stores and all the rest of the standard urban infrastructure somewhere, but if they exist we never came across them. (It occurred to us later that the place to look was, of course, inside the motels, but by that time we had moved on.)

But it was the Falls we'd come to see, and once past the motels they were easy enough to find. Follow any street into town and you eventually find yourself funnelled down Clifton Hill; and then when you look up there they are, just—well, falling, then rising again in gigantic clouds of cold white mist.

The American cliffs come into view first, directly ahead. (That's something else that got us mad the first time. You can only get a good view of the American Falls from Canada.) Then the real showpiece, the Canadian Horseshoe Falls, appear slightly to the south.

As we walked toward the viewpoint closest to the falls, we were joined by a group of elderly Japanese tourists, a slow-moving Pakistani family ("Mummy, come on!") and a young New Age monk in worn brown robes trailing his slightly strained-looking middle-class family behind him. Conversation died away as we politely converged at the look-out; even the monk stopped lecturing his companions as, elbow to elbow, we all leaned over the stone abutment, watching the rushing water and listening in silence to the constant, unceasing thunder of nature.

A few gnarled trees sticking out from the edge of the cliff provided a frame for the whole wide, arcing panorama. Seagulls swooped and called to each other above the small islands that dot the upper river and the huge granite boulders at the foot of the enormous waterfall. The little *Maid of the Mist* plied her way through the lower river valley (actually it's *Maids*—there are six of them now). The water continued to pile endlessly forward over the edge of the Falls, holding us fascinated and for a long moment blocking out all the rest of creation. "That's amazing," people murmured in several languages.

Then an anxious-looking thirtyish man in a green shirt with a yellow pterodactyl on the breast pocket elbowed his way in beside us. "Sorry, excuse me, can I get in here?" Without waiting for an answer he leaned out over the railing, raised his gadget-laden Nikon and frantically went through a whole roll of film in less than a minute. *Clickwhirrclickwhirrclickwhirrclickwhirr.* He seemed genuinely fearful that if he didn't get a shot of Niagara Falls that very instant it would vanish, and he would have to slink back to Slippery Rock, Pennsylvania, or Joe Batt's Arm, Newfoundland, or wherever he came from and shamefacedly admit to his friends and relations that he'd almost got it but had waited just that split second too long. "Thanks, sorry, excuse me," he murmured as he finished the roll and hurried away, but with that our communal Zen moment came to an end and we reverted to being individuals once more.

All the young people who work at the Falls are identified by their nicknames and jobs on the front of their green Parks Canada shirts. This practice always leaves you with the peculiar sensation of knowing the bearer of the name-tag intimately without having any idea who he or she really is. As we stepped up to pay in the cafeteria across the street from the Falls, Woody the Groundskeeper was engaging Cindy the

Cashier in an animated conversation. "Hey, Cindy." "Hey, Woody." "How's it going?" "Good. Hot out there?" "Yeah. No air-conditioning." (Both laugh.) "On your break?" "Yeah." "That's good." "Yeah." Feeling like chaperones, we stood mutely, trying to look as if we were passersby who just happened to be loitering around the cash register with trays of food, but they noticed us and reluctantly returned to the workaday world of ever-hungry tourists and grass that needed cutting. "Bye, Cindy." "See you, Woody." She followed him with her eyes as he walked away, waved when he glanced back, then began adding up our bill.

The park along River Road, with its copper-roofed public structures and its neat red and yellow flower beds in which Woody and his colleagues were digging, was redolent of nine-teenth-century gentility, but when you raised your eyes to the hill above, the last half of the twentieth century assaulted you with every tourist enticement in its arsenal. The escarpment was dotted with garish viewing towers in which visitors pay a near fortune to be raised farther and farther away from the sight they came to see, so that ultimately they get to look down on tiny specks of people who, at no expense, are stand-ing close enough to feel the spray. Alongside the towers, workmen were erecting additional high-rise hotels that will allow travellers who can afford the pricey rooms to view the Falls not only from a great height but prone, in the comfort of their own queen-sized beds.

On Clifton Hill, the street that connects the two levels, we strolled through the open-air funhouse that is the downtown of Niagara Falls. "The Street of Fun at the Falls" was lined with brightly coloured, plastic-fronted, thrill-offering, once-in-a-lifetime experiences like Ripley's Believe It or Not! Museum, the Criminals Hall of Fame Miniature World, The Dazzleland Family Fun Centre, the Loveboat Steakhouse, Louis (no relation to Madame) Tussaud's Waxworks and Movieland Wax Museum, The Haunted House, Birdies & Bogey's Miniature Golf and the Guinness World of Records (not the book, just the world).

It was not quite kitsch. Kitsch demands a measure of true-believer tackiness, a who-gives-a-damn-what-anyone-else-thinks vulgarity and bad taste that English Canadians have never quite managed, at least in public. A couple of centuries from now, when a young museum curator out to make a reputation comes up with the bright idea for a show called "Ripley and his Believers, 1950–1990," or "Memoirs of the Midway—Carnival Kitsch in Early Post Modern North America," this is what it will look like.

Slightly discouraging if you were hoping for a *soupçon* of true scuzziness. But while down on River Road we had noticed a large sign advertising a Daredevil Museum on one of the buildings that line the plateau. That sounded more like the real thing, so we gave up our hard-won parking space on the "Street of Fun" and set off into the moonscape of towers and sculptured high-rises to search out the daredevils.

After slipping through a passage between the Oakes Inn and the Horseshoe Falls Motor Hotel, passing by the Sheraton and the just opened two-storey glass-and-cinder-block Japanese-owned OK Gift Shop, we pulled up before the museum entrance. But a glance at the boarded-up doorway and broken windows told us we were too late.

About five years too late, according to the shopkeeper who stood in the entrance of a small and mysterious mall across the street. Mysterious not for its four or five stores, which offered debatable East Indian fast food in addition to the usual I-Saw-Niagara-Falls T-shirts, imitation copper wall plaques, half-price leather goods and water-squirting wristwatches, but because the whole complex had been thrown up near the end of an otherwise deserted dead-end road where no pedestrian could be expected to walk and which drivers would use only for U-turns.

It looked like a set for one of those early sixties European art films in which someone like Marcello Mastroianni grows old knocking on glass doors in hopes that Jeanne Moreau will let him in, while Max von Sydow sips borscht in a corner and two mimes pretend to be driving a bus. Who shopped here?

Why would anyone struggle all the way up to this godforsaken spot to pay the same prices for the same souvenirs on sale at their convenience everywhere else?

They wouldn't. That was the short answer, judging from the glum demeanour of the proprietor. Tall and chubby, in his early thirties, he resembled a large, brown, Bermuda-shorts-wearing balloon from which the air was slowly but irreversibly leaking. For an instant as we'd approached the entrance he had brightened, but as soon as it became apparent that all we wanted was information he quickly sagged back to normal.

We stared together at the scruffy vacant lot across the equally scruffy street. "I don't care what they build," he muttered morosely. "As long as it's not another souvenir store. That's all we need." Following his glance, we noted that an identical store to his had been thrown up just down the street so that in the unlikely event any tourists did ever happen to wander up that way, and in the even more unlikely event they had failed to fulfil their souvenir quota at any of the dozens of similar shops along the way, they would go into the new place. No wonder he was depressed.

When we eventually found the Daredevil Museum, it turned out to have been absorbed into the Imax Theatre complex. This museum is dedicated, as you might have guessed, to the people who, of their own free will, have chosen to descend Niagara Falls in barrels. It seems a simple enough proposition—there can't be many physical challenges more straightforward than climbing into a small, womb-like container and being dashed the equivalent of fifteen storeys down a raging waterfall. In three or four seconds you are either dead, maimed or grinning like a madman. (Except if, like a man named George Strathakis, your barrel gets trapped behind the curtain of falling water and after a few hours you die by suffocation. That sad event took place in 1930.)

A cursory viewing of the old clippings and photographs covering the walls revealed that one of the appealing aspects of shooting the Falls was the fact that, as daredeveil events go, this is one of the most democratic and easily accessible. Anyone with the urge could pick up a used barrel, throw in some bedding and recruit a friend to cart them down to the Niagara River. You didn't have to be rich, or personable, or in particularly good shape. (In spite of the fact that the stunt has been illegal since the fifties, every once in a while someone attempts it; a local death-defier went over again successfully just last year.)

Most important, you didn't have to be male. In 1901 Anna Taylor, a fortyish spinster schoolmarm from Bay City, Michigan, squeezed a straw mattress into a slightly modified pickle barrel, tucked herself cosily in, waved goodbye to her supporters and became the first person ever to go over the Falls. What was the point? Judging from her press clippings, Taylor was a plucky suffragette type who had grown tired of the limited role assigned to her by small-town society and was looking for a way to make a larger mark. She gave no evidence of being the least bit worried about the outcome; if she had been, as a sensible woman she probably would have respected her instincts and looked for something else to try. Anna Taylor just didn't happen to be afraid of a bunch of water.

But for the men who followed her example, a gnawing need to confront and master their worst fears appears to be precisely the reason most of them tried it. Canadian Dave Munday admitted to being both claustrophobic and frightened of being anywhere near water when he climbed into his barrel. When he stuck his head out a few minutes later he was still that way, but now he could tell the world that his fears hadn't prevented him from going over the Falls in a barrel. Another male daredevil, when reporters rushed up to him for an interview after his successful trip, dismissed them with the terse comment that his reasons for going were "very personal."

A lot of these guys were playing with something less than a full deck, of course. One explained, "The Falls, she is the seventh wonder of the world. I am the seventh son of seven. My father, he is a seventh son. I go over the Falls in the seventh month. See?"

Most were also hoping to make a buck out of the deed, though none were especially successful. Anna Taylor ended up trying to sell off splinters of her barrel, along with appropriate documentation, to anyone gullible enough to believe they were getting a piece of the real thing.

The problem for her, and for all her imitators, for that matter, was that none of them ever came up with a convincing scientific justification for this endearingly cement-headed feat. Early twentieth-century car racers, fliers, balloonists, mountain climbers, marathon swimmers *et al* convinced the world they were extending the frontiers of knowledge, technology, exploration or human endurance, even while they were busily flogging tickets. But swallowing the notion that improved barrel technology would be a significant step in ameliorating the lot of mankind required a leap of faith few people could be persuaded to make.

They tried. "Lest we not forget our predecessors who's mishaps have given us knowledge" was boldly and ungrammatically printed on the hull of one handmade contraption as it headed for the Falls. But no one bought it.

Nor did the act of throwing yourself off an enormous cliff of water ever really catch on as an act of physical derring-do, even if you did manage to avoid crushing all your limbs. The balance was off; it called for too much passivity and too little response, more derring than do. No, this just seemed dumb, and it's to the credit of the human race that none of the practitioners of the art was ever able to convert his folly into big-time success.

The tightrope-walkers who frequented the Falls and who share daredevil billing at the museum make a more convincing case for themselves. Their act in any form requires grace and balance, and here they had the perfect setting for the crowds that came to gawk: an international boundary, a dizzying, dangerous height and the roar of the Falls as accompaniment.

Initially we were surprised (and, reverting to our childhood patterns, even indignant) to learn that they actually set up their tightropes not over the Falls but across the river gorge some hundreds of yards further down. But our disappointment was forgotten when we took a close look at the variations that successive walkers dreamed up.

The immortal Blondin, who in 1859 became the first of the Falls' daredevils, over the years pulled off a variety of stunts that included carrying his manager on his back and, on one windless day, stopping in mid-rope to cook his breakfast. But our favourite is Maria Speltertina (also spelled Spetlerini), an Italian *artiste* who not only chose a name so patently phoney you can only applaud in admiration but also proceeded to sashay back and forth over the gorge with peach baskets tied to her feet while blowing kisses to her public. This particular performance took place in 1876, and we're sorry to have missed it.

But we weren't sorry to leave the Daredevil Museum; it struck too close to home. One of us is claustrophobic, and the other gets dizzy looking over the edge of the bed in the morning. Neither being sealed up in a small, dark, airless barrel nor teetering on a wire hundreds of feet above a rushing torrent ranks high on the list of experiences we wish we'd gotten around to trying.

Of course we couldn't leave Niagara Falls without investigating the honeymoon scene. Do newly married couples still go on them, and if they do, is Niagara Falls where they do it? Do Oscar Wilde's words still apply? (Wilde, in one of those celebrated *bon mots* that he first stole from someone else, then polished until it glistened and packed away for future use, called the Falls "the second greatest disappointment of the American bride." Of course, if you view the Falls as a sexual metaphor there probably aren't too many men who could live up to it.)

The Niagara Falls Tourist Bureau is pleased to offer honeymooners an official certificate. But though we explained to the unsmiling clerk behind the counter that when we got married we hadn't been able to afford a proper honeymoon and if they played their cards right this could be it, neither the sentiment nor the logic behind our request impressed her. She was adamant that only newlyweds get certificates. "We can spot them a mile off," she informed us gravely. "They have that inner glow." All we had was heat rash.

She was willing to let us have a demonstration certificate after first carefully writing "Mr & Mrs SAMPLE" in bold magic marker strokes above the "name here" line. (This was presumably to alert the participating attractions about any possible attempts we might make to horn in on such honeymoon discounts as three free laps for the bride at Niagara Go-Karts or complimentary admittance for the lady to the Criminals Hall of Fame.)

The tourism people claim to give out fifteen thousand of these certificates a year, the great majority to tour groups of Japanese newlyweds. Herded into the bureau in gangs of up to a hundred couples, their names are entered in the guest book whereupon they receive their personal certificates. If some are in English, some in French, no one seems to mind, given that rarely can any of the tourists make out a single word of either of Canada's official languages.

Besides, since Niagara Falls is usually their last stop on a mind-numbing seven-day whirlwind dash across the country, beginning in Vancouver, hurtling on to Banff and Lake Louise, then winging east to stare in wild surmise at Toronto and the Falls, by now they have probably lost all sense of where they are or why they came.

The Japanese tour schedule does have something to be said for it; one day in Niagara Falls is just about anyone's limit. The motto emblazoned across Niagara Region Tourist Bureau publications reads "More than Just the Falls." They left something out, however, which is the word "Not." It can go at the beginning or after a dash at the end, but it's got to be there somewhere. Why do they need more, anyway? The Falls are enough.

One last note: the Falls are eroding at the rate of a foot or so a year, which means that in the not-distant future the American part will simply disappear. (In 1969 engineers drained the American side for a closer look but found no solutions.) Take that, Stephen Coonts. But Canadians can't feel smug; they will probably have less than a millennium to gloat before their Falls in turn become little more than a longish rapids. So don't delay, whatever your nationality; make your reservations now.

Chapter Two

The accident of geography that gave Canada the niftier Falls
has also resulted in a reversal of the two nations' normal
entrepreneurial patterns; in contrast to the bustling grab-that-
dollar atmosphere on the Canadian side of the river, the sadsack tourist section of Niagara Falls, New York, was a narrow
stretch of defeated-looking hotels and motels with an obliga-
tory convention centre, a strange, circular, fifties-style information building and museum, numerous flags on numerous
flagpoles and forests of green road signs whose presence
seemed to tacitly admit that most people wanted only to get
out of town as soon as possible. I-190 East this way, I-190
West that way, Robert Moses Parkway North over there,
Robert Moses Parkway South over here, NY 384 straight
ahead then turn, New York State Thruway somewhere vaguely in the distance.

After some confused last-second lane-hopping we managed
to direct the Mazda onto Route 62A, which takes the tourist
first through a working-class, mostly black section where people wait at bus stops and glance expressionlessly toward the
cars streaming by, then through a small suburb of postwar
bungalows. A few moments later the houses, the sidewalks,
the people in the street had vanished into thin air and we
were On The Road in America, the midsummer sun glaring

down on the roof of the car as it rolled past an endless strip of vacant lots, ageing or closed factories and nostalgically named concrete block structures—Memory Lane Motel, DeeDee's Dairy, Relaxed Travel, Friendly Restaurant, Yesterday's Restaurant, Country Cafe, Calico Corner Collectibles, The Duck Pond Gift Store.

"Look, look, look, Build Your Dream Home!" cried a large billboard, as if expecting Mr. and Mrs. Blandings out for a Sunday jaunt. Everybody involved in running these enterprises seemed to want to turn back the clock, if not to the late nineteenth century then at least to the early fifties.

But we were headed even farther back in time, almost to the beginnings of the republic. Barely decipherable in pale-blue lettering next to the words "Tonawanda Creek Road" on our Rand McNally state map was the parenthetical designation "Erie Canal," words that brought back the great days of nation-building and the folk songs kids of our generation learned at camp.

Among the historical differences that distinguish Canada and the United States are their dissimilar collective memories of the pioneer trek west. North of the border you think first of canoes and then steamers heading up the St. Lawrence past "the land God gave to Cain," as Jacques Cartier put it, and finally the railroad carrying new settlers to the prairies and beyond. In the States the corresponding modes of transportation are the canal boat (the Erie Canal connected the Hudson River and therefore New York City and the east coast to the Great Lakes) and later the covered wagon.

So as midwestern kids we sang the canal songs. "Had an old mule, her name was Sal, fifteen miles on the Erie Canal," we belted out before rest period one day, and "Oh, the Er-i-ee was arisin', the gin was agittin' low, and I scarcely think we'll git another drink, til we git to Buffalo-o-o, til we git to Buffalo" after our orange juice the next.

Long before that (on February 19, 1839), one of Julie's great-grandfathers, having purchased 160 acres of good Michigan farming land, sent a letter to his six brothers and sisters in County Cavan. Since their parents had recently died, there was nothing to keep them from emigrating *en masse* to join their brother in the New World. He explained in detail each step of the long voyage they were about to undertake. They had better watch their step every inch of the way, he admonished them sharply:

> ...be careful that you all keep together and be sure to be there at about the time appointed for sailing lest some of you be left behind...give no heed to any [would-be advisers in the ports] for they are one and all a set of shavers and robbers.... [At New York] take passage on the Western Canal for Buffalo and be careful that they do not charge you an over price. The regular price is one cent and a half per mile; the distance is 363 miles. When you get to Buffalo (on Lake Erie) take your passage on the steamboat for Detroit....

The flatboats are long gone, but we were eager to see how much of the canal still existed and whether anyone still used it. Did barges loaded with coal, or computer parts, or whatever, continue to travel its length? Had they preserved the towpaths? Could we stand on its banks and see in our imaginations the generations of westward-heading immigrants, all those great-great-aunts and uncles, as they gazed out from the open deck at the deep woods of their new land?

We'd reached the outskirts of North Tonawanda, but there was no sign of the canal, or of Tonawanda Creek for that matter. Where had the damn thing got to? Finally the road crossed a small stream, then almost immediately another, but no names were posted. Was one of these the remains of the canal? Why wasn't it marked? Didn't these people have any sense of history?

Finally we locked onto some water. Whether it was the canal, the creek or the headwaters of the Colorado River still wasn't clear but it was headed in the right direction, cutting west through a pleasant, older, middle-class suburb. A few brown ducks paddled around on the surface; an occasional power boat was tied up to a dock at the foot of someone's back yard. At the entrance to a small municipal park a sign read not "Yes! This is it—the Erie Canal!" as we had hoped, but "Picnic By Reservation Only." (An unusual concept— "Hello, I'd like to reserve space for four under an oak tree, please. Seven o'clock? That'll be fine. Thank you.")

Just past an ornate erector-set railroad bridge under which three young boys were fishing, an Elks Lodge offered "Bingo Every Wed / 8 PM Fish Fry." Then the road came to an end amid the small office buildings of downtown North Tonawanda. Now what?

Our waterway passed under a bridge, then turned abruptly to the right. Determined to force it to reveal its identity, we continued on foot along a riverside bike path until it joined another stream to form a third, wider channel where a large sign, evidently directed at boaters coming inland, proclaimed "Welcome to New York State Canal System, Mario Cuomo, Governor." Well, that was promising, but the absence of any historical marker, not to mention the word "Erie," was puzzling.

The first of numerous accidental separations that would take place during our travels occurred at this point; one of us, sweating like a pig, risking sunstroke, trudged the entire perimeter of the bike path and back, vainly searching for the other, who turned out to have sought relief from the million-degree heat under a small tree twenty feet from where we had parted. "Where did you go?" raged the first, when he finally staggered back and saw her. "Nowhere," was the reply. "And you can just stop yelling."

Back on Main Street we struck out again on foot. But the tourist information booth was closed, apparently for the summer, and nobody at the Chamber of Commerce admitted to being conversant with anything as far back as history. Trudging back over the small bridge, we stopped to read a plaque cemented onto a small granite boulder plopped down

on a widened space in the middle of the sidewalk: "Donated
to the youth of the Tonawandas Exchange Club, July 4,
1974." Weren't those kids lucky? Their own rock. But perhaps this so-far-fruitless attempt to rediscover American history, not to mention the oppressive thirty-five-degree Celsius
heat, was making us testy.

The bridge across Tonawanda Creek, which was what we
had been crossing and recrossing, connects the downtowns of
Tonawanda and North Tonawanda. Originally there was only
one town but somewhere along the way the Northies got
mad at the Southies and broke away to freedom. Since then
no amount of common sense has been able to reunite the two
duplicate city governments. Today they are known, at least
among themselves, as The Tonawandas.

This was all learned from an intense, angular old gentleman
at the local Historical Society over on Webster Street, where
we eventually ended up. Here, if anywhere, someone should
be able to tell us something about the Erie Canal—for example, how we had managed to miss it. But this being The
Tonawandas, where for every action you could count on a
contradictory reaction, acquiring information was not as simple as just walking in and asking.

It's not that Mr. Dittmar didn't know all about the canal.
He did. He knew about everything. He just didn't want to
discuss the subject. "The Erie Canal was only four feet deep,"
he snorted disdainfully. "It was nothing but a ditch." What
he really wanted to share was the history of Tonawanda—its
politics, its economic fortunes, its industry, its social divisions, its role in the War Between the States.

And so, standing under faded photographs of town worthies
and oil paintings depicting celebrated nineteenth-century
steamers, the three of us began an intricate contrapuntal tug of
words. For every question we posed about the canal, the stub-
born old geezer (just kidding, Mr. Dittmar) had an answer
that feinted toward the water then leaped three-quarters of a
century or so into the historical factors that made Tonawanda
into the town (or towns) that it (or they) is (or are) today.

Mr. D.: "You interested in the ethnics? You should be. Years ago I could stand on the corner and hear six languages spoken, especially German. The Germans know good land. A lot of them were headed for Michigan, but here they stayed."

K.: "So from Lockport to here the Erie Canal was part of Tonawanda Creek, is that right? But there was a dam where the bridge is now on Main Street, so while the Creek continued west, the canal—uh…"

Mr. D.: "The Polish took the iron-working jobs, lived in Polaktown, that's the third Ward of North Tonawanda. Italians worked the railroad, Hungarians for the Buffalo Steel Company."

J.: "…the Canal turned south from the dam and ran parallel to the Niagara River all the way down to Buffalo, where the passengers disembarked? Is that right?"

Mr. D.: "See, they all followed the Great Central Iroquois Trail across New York State. That was the only way west—everything followed that, first the settlers and then the canal and then the New York Central, and then I'll be darned if when they planned the Thruway they didn't do the same thing."

Both of us: "So why didn't we see it? We've crossed that bridge ten times. What happened to the canal?"

That question he was happy to answer. "It's an Interstate."

"What?"

"I-190. That's the Erie Canal. They filled it in and made it into an interstate. First the Niawanda Parkway, then I-190. When you go to Buffalo from here, you're riding right over it."

So long, Sal.

Located at the point where the lake flows into the Niagara River, Buffalo is a reasonably big city (city pop. around 330,000; county nearly 1,000,000) that started out to become one of America's great metropolitan centres and

never got there. You can see traces of grand ambition everywhere. The downtown is built around a beautifully proportioned central circle (perversely called Niagara Square) that
dates from 1804, from which wide thoroughfares radiate
optimistically. Around the square and on the connecting
streets a piquant assortment of splendid early skyscrapers
have arranged themselves, including the most perfect of
Louis Sullivan's Chicago-style designs, the twelve-storey
Guaranty Building on Church Street. Posh department
stores, elegantly appointed hotels, an impressive Gothic
Revival cathedral with a bank of violet-hued Tiffany windows, and up-to-the-1920s-minute municipal and federal
buildings filled in among them. The centrepiece of the whole
civic tableau is the 1931 City Hall, whose ornate, rounded-off
shaft emerges from a massive, block-long gingerbread rectangle to reach twenty-eight storeys into the sky like a gigantic
art deco erection.

When the upper crust built their mansions in outlying dis-
tricts, they often brought in the best talent the nation had to
offer. Buffalo contains masterpieces by all three of the icons
of American architecture; besides Sullivan's skyscraper, there's
an H. H. Richardson hospital and a splendid concentration
of Frank Lloyd Wright private homes (five in all, the largest
urban grouping anywhere), as well as a series of linked
Frederick Olmstead parks.

At the end of the parks, next to a small lake, you find the
Albright-Knox Gallery, one of the most renowned of that
string of mock-classical art galleries that dot the land from
one coast to the other. Before it all stopped dead in its tracks
sometime around the beginning of the Depression, this place
was on its way to becoming an absolutely beautiful city, a
mid-American showpiece that only Chicago could rival.

Today, most of these architectural wonders, like much of
Buffalo, are in the process of falling apart before your very
eyes. Sullivan's Guaranty Building is largely untenanted; from
the still-exceptional free-standing stairway that takes you to
the mezzanine, you look down into empty shops and a

deserted bank. Upstairs it's shabby and unkempt, a ghost of a once-great building. Chunks of masonry from Wright's most important urban residence, the Martin House, are broken off, roof tiles are missing, the walkways are cracked. Peering through the windows into the art deco paradise it once was, you can see warped panels in the walls and broken edges of furniture. Once operated as a museum, a sign on the door now reads "New York State's current fiscal condition has caused the closing of the Darwin D. Martin House to the public until further notice." Hawking copies of that sign, with a blank space left for inserting a different structure or business, would be one of the few new profitable enterprises anyone could imagine in contemporary Buffalo. The entire city, despite an occasional post-modern stab at renewal, looks like a set for a play that never opened.

The heart of it all, City Hall, was typically comatose when we arrived to see what was going on. Before the wide steps that led up from the square, half a dozen embarrassed-looking women trudged back and forth holding signs that read "Keep our Kindergarten Aides." This was probably the most glumly ineffectual demonstration we had ever seen; the marchers looked as if they expected to be ignored, and they were. No one paid them the slightest attention.

Hoping against hope that the place might be air-conditioned, we staggered up the steps and through the heavy glass doors to be met with a blast of fetid, furnace-like hot air that nearly knocked us over. This is a big building, so we split up; one of us was designated to follow the tourist trail into the small and dubiously functioning elevator that an ancient placard claimed took one up to the observation deck; the other would poke around downstairs.

JMS: The dimly lit, vaguely seedy-looking lobby was almost deserted. No pin-striped, manicured business people rushed by waving important papers at each other; aside from an occasional office worker headed for the elevator or someone stopping off to purchase a newspaper at the magazine stand, it was just me and a few loungers.

A hall led off to the right, at the end of which was a large, high-ceilinged room marked by one of those small signs indicating that this space was designated as a public shelter in case of nuclear war. Inside, next to a counter where people were lined up to pay their traffic tickets or utility bills or whatever, a police officer sat under a wall decorated with paper shamrocks left over from St. Patrick's Day and stared into space. Most of the clerks were white and most of the bill-payers black, and there was a strangely detached air about the scene; no one in the long line was chatting with the person in front, or sharing a joke with the clerks. But at least this scene proved the city was functioning at some level; if the citizens of Buffalo were still paying their taxes, the city couldn't be completely moribund.

Back in the central lobby I felt as if I had suddenly returned to childhood. At first in the dim light I had barely noticed that virtually every inch of the interior walls, floors and ceilings was glowing with patriotic scenes, art deco mosaics, animal friezes, swirls and curves and gold-lettered mottoes exhorting the public to behave, or at least to take heart. As a child I had found myself transfixed by Diego Rivera's powerful, brightly coloured scenes of muscular working men and women, which dominated the central courtyard of the Detroit Institute of Arts, and I have never been able to walk past a public mural since without stopping. In spite of the fact that it badly needed a new lighting system and a visit from a good restoration crew, Buffalo's City Hall shouted out the exuberance of the era when capitalism met craftsmanship head-on in public buildings.

Down one hallway a pre-feminist Prometheus labelled "Protection" was fulfilling his directive to keep what appeared to be famine and slavery away from some pink-cheeked cherubs, while a woman labelled "Charity" doled out bread to the old and feeble. Near the bank of elevators a gigantic binational woman holding a Yank in one hand and a Canuck in the other, accompanied by the words "Frontiers Unfettered by any Frowning Fortress," towered over the office workers. On the American side of the mural there was also a society matron holding a jewel box and a man with some model cars tucked under one arm; the equivalent Canadian grouping, more rural in tone, included a serious-looking little boy carrying some schoolbooks, a man with a huge basket of fish on his head and a lumberman strangely loaded down with a live white turkey.

There was more. Across the lobby, facing the front door, we learned "Talents Diversified Find Vent in Myriad Forms." Among the talents, or maybe the forms, were a *Showboat*-type black man bent nearly double under the weight of two sacks of grain, a native holding a sheaf of yellow corn and a white man hoisting a large L-shaped girder.

The moralizing was heavy-handed, even incoherent, and the draughtsmanship didn't come close to matching Rivera's, but still it was fun. It lifted the spirit. If I ever become mayor somewhere, I pledge to hire artists and craftspeople and put them to work on the bare walls of today's public spaces.

KS: The antique elevator rattled slowly up to the twenty-fifth floor. No one else got on, and no one was waiting to go down when the doors finally gasped open. Three additional storeys up a gloomy staircase take the intrepid tourist into a dank, clammy, low-ceilinged chamber. Glass doors open onto the deserted yard-wide outside observation walkway, which is fenced in with plastic panels rising several feet above the head, presumably to discourage the average suicidal citizen from trying to splatter himself on the pavement below.

Through slots between the murky panels, the view was dynamite. The western side looked out on the elevated interstates and beyond them to the riverfront and the beginnings of Lake Erie, a hazy blue expanse shimmering in the summer heat, growing wider and wider as it disappeared into the horizon.

(Later that day we drove down behind the highways to find an active shipping area where cargo was being loaded onto container ships, a few small boat yards and marinas, a maritime museum featuring mothballed U.S. Navy fighting ships and a lot of "we are the greatest and bravest nation on earth and we always have been and we always win every war and we always will" rhetoric, and a stretch of scruffy lakefront that drag racers and junkies probably find handy. We also encountered a few friendly black men fishing off the piers.)

From the other three sides of the balcony you saw the city itself, a clump of tall buildings surrounded by a vast, treetop-high sea of inner slums and outer suburbs, punctuated by occasional smokestacks and medical office towers and a trail of old factories and warehouses along the interstates heading outward toward the city boundaries.

After staring for a while, a new thought suddenly hit me. Here I was, completely alone on a ledge twenty-eight storeys above the ground without the slightest chance of help if your friendly neighbourhood mugger or serial murderer happened to drop by. They wouldn't find my body for days, especially if the discovery depended on my claustrophobic wife working up sufficient nerve to get in the elevator to come search for me. The emptiness was truly disconcerting; cities are supposed to have people in them, and when they don't you are left with a sensation of something terribly wrong.

Ground level didn't alter the picture much. Standing in the middle of Niagara Square on a normal working day, the whole of downtown Buffalo spread out around us, no more than a dozen or so pedestrians could be counted on the sidewalks. Nowhere in sight was there a single ice-cream vendor, hot dog stand or soda pop wagon; no long-haired kid stood behind an open guitar case droning out early Dylan, no one sold T-shirts, there were no alternative jewellery makers or hot watch purveyors spreading out their wares. In short, there was nothing that you might expect to see on the sidewalks in a living, breathing city.

What we're talking about here is clearly more than simple economics. It's race in post-World War Two America. The

Great Depression of the thirties and changing industrial patterns might account for Buffalo's initial decline, but the city's abject inability to integrate its various racial and ethnic communities is what lies behind today's almost total paralysis.

Sitting in an inconspicuous side booth in Garvey's, a venerable downtown chop house and tavern, we couldn't help tuning in on a conservatively suited, reedy-voiced lawyer in his fifties as he swapped racist jokes with the bartender and another stool-sitter. They began with Indians—"What does an Indian do at the beach?" Soon they had moved on to blacks—"Yo, mama. I ain't yo mama, I'm yo..." and then switched to Italians. Belatedly realizing that there were strangers present, they stole quick looks to see if we might be of that last persuasion, then continued with lowered voices, just in case.

Back outside on the sidewalk, two categories accounted for most of the few people you did see; one encompassed poorly dressed non-whites, several of whom were shouting at the passing cars or mumbling unceasingly to themselves. Through their ranks, prosperous-looking men and women in blazers and dark suits, including some middle-class blacks, passed with purposeful strides and unseeing eyes. They had the look of lawyers, lobbyists, city and county officials, civil servants and other assorted municipal types stuck down here against their wills in what passes for the heart of the city. You could sense a strong distaste for the whole urban thing in their stiffly held bodies and straight-ahead stares. At five on the dot, as the working day ended, they poured swiftly out the doors of their office buildings and into the parking garages, heading out toward the suburbs and the ethnic neighbourhoods of the South side as if pursued by banshees. Within half an hour the middle-class tide, insubstantial at best, had washed away, abandoning the city to whoever had the bad luck to have to live there.

One evening we wandered into a funky neighbourhood of theatres, restaurants, welfare hotels and rooming houses, empty warehouses, grotty grunge bars and mysterious, curtained storefronts just west of downtown. Seeking sustenance, we dived into a likely looking place with oak floors and large, colourful, vaguely surrealist paintings on the walls.

The only other customer in the Calumet Arts Bar was a buttoned-down man who looked as if he might be a trainee accountant; he ordered a beer, then furtively wiped the glass with a handkerchief before lifting it to his mouth. A moment later he was out of there, leaving us alone with the lanky, pony-tailed barman. In his mid-thirties, with a deep, deejay type voice and a laid-back manner, he looked like a Buffalo version of the classic ultra-smooth New York or Hollywood bartender, the kind who can deflate an over-friendly patron's pretensions simply by looking the other way. He brought us our drafts, then drifted away down the counter without speaking.

But even super-cool bartenders must grow lonely sometimes, and a moment later he drifted back. "Don't get me started," he warned, when we made a comment about the place, and then, with his next breath, before we'd even had time to wonder whether we were in fact doing what he'd asked us not to do, he launched into a prolonged and heartfelt explanation of how the bar was being mismanaged by the new owners. His name, by the way, was Scott O'Connor.

"This guy from New York bought the building two years ago. The bar is supporting the place, but the restaurant next door, that's his baby, you know? But, man, it's dying. What do they expect? I mean, Jesus Christ, this is a small town. If you provide inferior food and bad service, that's your word of mouth. I've tried to tell him, I've lived in Buffalo all my life, I went to college here, my experience ought to be worth something, but—" He gestured in one ear and out the other.

We asked about Buffalo. "I've lived here thirty-six years. It's not a bad place. Great climate [yes, that's what he said], hiking and skiing not far away, Canada right over the bridge. But it's divided strictly on ethnic lines. Hispanics in the lower West side, the West side across Main solidly black. I taught there one year. I'm not afraid of a lot, like I'm a pretty big guy and I keep myself in good shape, but I'm scared in there. You don't have to be involved in anything, they'll take your life away, anyway.

"We've been cursed for God knows how many years with the last of the Mayor Daley types, a guy named Griffen who runs everything by race. You know, keep everybody in their place, straight racial politics. He put together a coalition of the whites on the East side, the Irish and Polish, Italians, and they kept him in. It doesn't have to be this way, but that's the way it is. Griffen isn't running this time, so there will be a new mayor, maybe something will change. Maybe. But you know, if you're white and you go in the black or Spanish area, they give you the look. You're black, you go on the East side, they give you the look. You see a few interracial couples, usually they're young kids. Everybody gives them the look."

He drew us another round and that seemed to bring him back to his original subject. "You know, this area is okay. It's sort of like a DMZ sandwiched in between downtown and the black and Spanish sections. It's not really dangerous, seedy maybe, but the suburban twenty-five to thirty crowd, which is what you need to keep these places going, they'll come down if you give them a reason. It makes them feel like they're living dangerously. I mean, I tried to tell him that…." His voice trailed away as he reflected on the obduracy of his employer. The bar began to fill up at that point, and he left us to return to his duties.

In his wide-ranging ramble through Buffalo's life and times, Scott had several times touched on the city's Spanish population. So had a couple of other people we had talked to; even Mr. Dittmar in faraway Tonawanda had tacked them onto his catalogue of ethnics. Each of them had accompanied their commentary with an expression of bemused puzzlement, as if unable to quite figure out what a bunch of tropical homepersons were doing in a place where the sidewalks are buried in snow for almost half the year and where the breeze blowing off Lake Erie in midwinter could freeze-dry a chili pepper in seconds. Neither could we, so we went to look for ourselves.

Any doubts dropped away when we got near Virginia Street, a few blocks north of downtown. Suddenly it was all Spanish services, Spanish signs, Spanish names, Spanish graffiti—Colon Grocery, Fogon Restaurant, West Side Latino Records, "*No se amontenen en esta area*," a heart with "Eliseo + Mera" inside. The area looked something like one of those languid provincial centres in Central America, with its low, crumbling apartment buildings and seedy houses, handmade Virgin Mary bathtub grottoes, cavernous churches, usually converted from earlier incarnations, and old posters peeling off walls.

"It was Puerto Ricans first," Lourdes Iglesias told us. "Like me. Puerto Ricans are legal, remember. My mother came up to pick strawberries in the fifties and just stayed. There weren't many then. Today officially there's 22,000 Latinos, but I figure the real number, counting illegals, is between 50,000 and 60,000. The city just ignores us. No political power."

We were sitting in a small upstairs office at the Hispanos Unidos de Buffalo, a solid, red-brick building that began life in 1889 as the Free Methodist Church and now, dressed up with some ornate wrought-iron grillework, served as the main Latino community centre.

The temperature up there was even higher than out in the sun, and the small fan in the corner managed to move the limp air no more than a few inches beyond the tip of its slowly rotating blades. But Lourdes (pronounced Lour-dess), young, upbeat, the centre's social affairs manager, and Director Jose Pizarro, older and more world-weary, seemed accustomed to it. Lourdes is also used to double-takes over her name and laughed when we asked. "Yes, my mother was very devout."

Jose on politics: "There are, like Lourdes says, at least 50,000 of us here, from Central America, Cuba, Puerto Rico, Colombia, Ecuador, Chile, Dominica, all over. And we're growing. So they're courting us more. Of course a lot of our people are illegals—there's also a big bunch waiting to get into Canada—but in close votes we have enough to make a difference. So now we've been gerrymandered. They tried to split our vote, we're in court right now."

Lourdes: "There's a lot of stereotyping. If you're Puerto Rican they expect you to carry a blade."

Jose: "A lot of people moved up here from the City to get away from drugs. But that created a new market, so the dealers followed them. Just your basic entrepreneurship."

Lourdes: "Is there much mixing? No, there isn't much mixing."

Jose, with a trace of bitterness: "The whites who have the money and the jobs don't want to give anything up. They talk about equal opportunity but they don't like to look at how people get jobs, which is mostly through knowing someone, like through their uncle or their father. That's the way it works."

Walking back downstairs into the busy first floor lobby, we got the look from the teenage boys lounging against the wall, the old-timers resting their tired bones on benches, the workers stepping outside for a smoke, even the young mothers. But it wasn't unfriendly, just curious; they don't see too many unofficial Anglos around here.

Or too many strangers in any of the ethnic neighborhoods which make up most of Buffalo. People stay within the boundaries of their ghettos and rarely share a common vision of the wider city. The free flow of ethnic boundaries that you find in Toronto, the nearest large city, is unimaginable here. In spirit it's more like Belfast.

Back at deserted Niagara Square, on our way out, Buffalo looked a city utterly disconnected from its own past. No one seems to have figured out a way to make use of that splendid gift from those earlier generations of a still essentially intact, easily accessible, genuine city centre. They don't know what they're missing. Or maybe they don't care. It's hard to tell.

Chapter Three

South out of Buffalo, Route 5 leads past the factories and housing developments of old lakeside suburbs with names like Lackawanna, Blasdell and Wanakah. We didn't go that way, however. After all, we're midwesterners by birth, hard travelling is in our blood, and after the urban intricacies of the last few days our systems cried out for a shot of head-clearing superhighway. So we treated ourselves to ten high speed miles of New York State Thruway and got off at Angola.

Fate quickly took its revenge for our indulgence. Moments after turning onto the bucolic two-lane road that was supposed to take us directly to Angola-on-the-Lake, a genteel-looking matron with carefully arranged bluish white hair waited until the most dangerous possible moment to slowly angle her late-model Oldsmobile out into traffic just in front of our car. Then, while chatting with her colleague from what must have been a meeting of the Cattaraugus County Chapter of Slow Drivers of America, she proceeded to lead us, and what gradually became a cortège-like procession of vehicles that piled up behind us, on a stately twenty-five-mile-an-hour tour of rural New York State.

At least it allowed plenty of time to read the bumper stickers plastered onto her tailgate, the mildest of which declared

"Abortion Kills Children" next to a graphic illustration of a dead fetus. You see this combination of fanaticism and grandmotherly piety frequently around here. For example, on the front lawn of a Baptist church, the congregation were chatting amiably next to a large billboard that screamed in blood-red letters "Rest in Peace...1,600,000 abortions yearly." Perhaps this attitude shouldn't be surprising given the fact that back in the nineteenth century upstate New York served for a long time as the first California of the New World. Self-declared Messiahs ranging from Joseph Smith and his Church of Latter Day Saints to Handsome Lake, the Seneca prophet who resurrected traditional Iroquois ceremonials, as well as countless lesser-known mystics who were forgotten as soon as their last disciples drifted away, preached their gospels in this new Jerusalem.

Successive waves of immigration from Ireland, Italy and eastern Europe added large numbers of devout working-class Roman Catholics to the area, and the blend of these two very different but equally impassioned spiritual outlooks has left a curious devotional haze in the air, an atmosphere in which over-the-top attitudes are seen as perfectly normal. You don't find a great deal of that old devil rationalism in these parts.

Finally the Golden Girls pulled into a driveway and we turned our attention to the lush countryside rushing past our windows. Grapes are the main crop along the lee of the lake, really the only crop unless you count an occasional field of corn or neatly laid-out vegetable bed; every available open space was covered with geometric rows of vines, marching off in whatever direction the land dictated. The long lines of fruit were almost hypnotic in their beauty, their supporting wires smothered in glossy leaves, all standing at the same even height, running right up to the barns and farmhouses, into every odd corner, over little rills and almost onto the road shoulder. Everything here was some shade of deep, rich green—the trees, the bushes, the grass, not infrequently even the houses and outbuildings. You felt as if on each leaf or painted plank you should be able to find a little stamp saying

I "Product of the Land of Plenty."

The one colour you almost never saw, at least at eye level, was blue. Although Route 5 rarely veered more than a few hundred yards from the enormous expanse of Lake Erie, we had caught only a few glimpses of its waters; between us and the lake stood the homes, estates and communities of the favoured few who had got there first and who intended to make damned sure no one else squeezed in after them.

Signs declaring No Admittance, Private Road, Restricted, Police Patrolled, No Parking Except by Permit, Members Only, Local Use Only, No Stopping, No Trespassing, Keep Out, Protected by this or that security company, appeared frequently. Maybe the fact that Jose Pizarro's words about the exclusivity of white society were still resonating in our minds caused us to react more strongly than we might have normally. It wasn't hard to imagine how unwelcome someone of another race would instinctively feel.

At long last we came across a small public park where a narrow stretch of grass leading to the low cliffs provided an unimpeded view of the lake. In spite of the soft, hot, midsummer day, the surface was almost empty—a couple of sailboats far to the east, probably out of Buffalo, what looked like a freighter in the middle, and that was all. The water was an intense cerulean blue, smooth as ice, stretching out serenely as far as you could see in every direction.

This was the *Lac du Chat* of the early French explorers, named for the fierce local tribe known as the cat nation. (The Brits who superseded them tried to make out the actual Indian name, and eventually came up with Erie.) Today, the only land anywhere on Lake Erie still in the possession of natives, at least according to our map, was a Seneca reservation which ran down to the water along nearby Catteraugus Creek. Unfortunately, in what was quickly becoming normal operating procedure, we couldn't find the place.

Then we happened to notice a pickup truck pulling onto the road from a vegetable field and its passengers waving to a station wagon full of people who were pulling in. Either watching rutabaga grow was a major leisuretime activity in these parts or there was something happening on the other side of the patch. So we followed the trail of the station wagon—very slowly, throwing up massive clouds of dust as we skittered into ruts the size of moon craters and growing more dubious with every sideways lurch.

Suddenly the field ended and the tractor path magically became the main street of a village of summer cottages clustered along the placid waters of Cattaraugus Creek. A moment before the mid-afternoon sun had been burning down in a cloudless sky, but here, under the interlocking canopy of tall, mature trees, everything became cool and dark.

We had stumbled into Brigadoon, or its American equivalent, a perfect prewar summer world frozen in the time of Young Tom Edison and *Saturday Evening Post* covers that obviously came to life one day every generation and today was it. The older ramshackle frame cottages, some raised on stilts, looked weathered and comfortable—a few little more than tarpaper shacks, others larger, with proper porches. Later arrivals had built their dream cottages down the narrow side lanes—not as desirable a location as those that backed onto the river and had their own docks within sight of Lake Erie, but still appealing.

Just before the creek entered the lake, a small channel had been dredged to provide additional water frontage; over this arced an antique metal footbridge that led to an even more private group of cottages. A boarded-up cinder-block restaurant with the remains of advertising posters on its sides, a deserted garage and a shed that might once have been used for boat repairs stood near by. Further along, rusting backhoes and an old crane marked the demise of someone's grand scheme for developing the area. His plans had obviously come to nothing, and the sleepy beauty of the place remained intact, hardly touched even by the presence of several incongruously flashy power boats at anchor.

When we saw a sign on one front porch, "Stop Hassling the Indians," we asked a blond young man in shorts working in his patch of yard whether that meant this was in fact native land. For a moment he looked puzzled, then allowed that he thought maybe the Indians rented to the cottage owners, from one of whom he himself was renting, but he wasn't sure and couldn't think of anyone else who might know. He didn't act unfriendly, just like someone who, as an inhabitant of a parallel dimension to ours, wondered what species we belonged to and how we had got there but was too polite to actually inquire. Everyone else we met reacted in the same manner. A family lugging fishing gear down to their boat glanced over, then averted their eyes, possibly on the assumption that we were an optical illusion that would be gone when they looked that way again. We felt like Gene Kelly and Van Johnson in the movie, when they first arrive in Brigadoon and the villagers stare at them in barely disguised amazement.

Assuming its reality for the moment, what had probably preserved this simple earthly paradise was the fact that the development money had jumped to the other side of the creek, where you could make out a new, trendy, happening summer condo/cottage community. Real-estate-wise, as they would probably put it over there, we were on the wrong side of the river, but soulful-wise, we'd take this every time.

Some miles further west along the lake lay the small industrial city of Dunkirk (pop. 14,000), the only town of any size between Buffalo and the Pennsylvania border. Years ago a thriving commercial port, today its main distinction lies in its zoologically inclined selection of street names. Driving down the main street, you cross Beaver, Beagle, Ermine, Genet, Leming, Armadillo, Jerboa, Ocelot, Serval, Margay, Rabbit, Martin, Otter, Antelope, Gazelle and Zebra (all spellings as found). Just to keep you on your toes they've thrown in ringers such as Ounce, Fizell, Pangolin, Stegelsek, A, B, C, D and Ice Cream Drive. Talk about addresses you'd rather not live at.

There was activity on the municipal pier, so we followed a

small crowd out to its end. Docked there we found a fully rigged sailing ship, what would turn out to be the first of a fleet of full-size replicas of early vessels that we would encounter wandering the lake over the course of the summer. This particular Tall Ship was a *Nina*, one of the more popular models. But not just your ordinary *Nina*. Built in Brazil by genuine Brazilians, this was the very ship that had been constructed to impersonate its namesake in the dreadful and universally denounced film *1492*. Now the Brazilians had sailed it up to the Great Lakes, where they were charging three dollars for the privilege of climbing aboard and peering into the interior.

Intrigued by the dark mahogany planking and the creaking of the timbers, we purchased two tickets and took our places on the deck of the small caravel, picturing in our minds this tiny, virtually open, modified fishing and trading vessel threading its way across an entire ocean. The *Queen Elizabeth*, on which we had once braved that same body of water, had carried lifeboats about equal in size.

Sitting on folding chairs on the pier, an older couple surrounded by grandchildren were carefully baiting their hooks and casting their lines into the water. Even to the eye of a non-expert this didn't seem to be the optimum spot to have chosen; noisy activities were taking place all around, and boats were cruising in and out of the nearby marina. "Is this a good spot to fish?" seemed a natural question. "I don't know," the man replied. "I'm not from around here."

Beyond Dunkirk, the bountiful American countryside really spread out before the traveller—a land of overflowing fields and lovingly tended lawns and gardens where the fences were always in good repair, flowers bloomed in every yard and neat but not secretive hedges marked the properties. The barns and even the roadside stands were clean and sparkling. Every tidy blade of grass, every daisy in every meadow, every chockfull corn crib, every purple grape hanging from every vine seemed to have preened itself for the illustration that would appear on next year's hardware store calendar.

And in the middle of all this beauty, rambling frame houses with wraparound verandas and an infinite variety of gables and shingled half-roofs kept aesthetic pace with nature. Some gleamed with new white paint, but just as often the owners had experimented with fanciful combinations of pastels ranging from turquoise to mauve and trims in varying shades of brown, deep blues and purples, yellows, greens, even red, all of this colour set off with a carpet of thick green lawn. Slender, ornately turned pillars, decorated in cheerful patterns, buttressed the porch roofs, and windows came in a dozen pleasing varieties—Romanesque rounded, shuttered New England, stained-glass panelled, Queen Anne dormer, straightforward Colonial or whatever else had struck the builder's fancy.

This is what the architecture textbooks refer to as "vernacular," which is to say that the houses were built by local carpenters using the local woods and making up their designs more or less as they went along, referring mainly to accumulated past experience as their guide. Through some mysterious artistry that theoreticians have never satisfactorily explained, these nineteenth-century craftsmen created an entire civilization of light, graceful buildings perfectly suited to the landscape and sturdy enough to be in use a hundred years later.

There was only one drawback to the scene, at least for any lover of the genuine countryside. Except for the grape fields, real open spaces barely existed. There was too much and too little at the same time—too little distance between one village and the next, too much local industry, too few farm animals, too many antique dealers and doctors and sports car salesmen from the cities. Crops and gardens were squeezed into unlikely corners, and new houses were in the process of appearing or had just been put up wherever there was a free piece of flat land.

Many of the newcomers seemed to have brought the urban entrepreneurial spirit with them. Produce stands, flea markets, cut-rate satellite dish importers, homemade cider bottlers, hobby shops, factory outlets for dishes and clothing vied for your dollar at every dip in the road. Rickety motels advertised special rates. Craftspeople offered quilts, wool, jewellery, ceramics, wall hangings, antiques, pottery, local water-colours, repro signs, semi-precious minerals, and every-thing else you probably didn't ever want any more of. It was Christmas in July, a kind of permanent PBS auction that left you yearning for a few miles of plain old nature.

Most of the local grapes are destined to be crushed into grape juice at a Welch's plant. The company is a major presence around these parts. It was to Westfield, a small town with a gigantic central square and a county courthouse to match, that Thomas Welch, a dentist who dabbled in non-alcoholic drinks, came in the 1890s. He wanted to "perfect a process to make unfermented grape juice from the Concord grape," as the *Chautauqua County Travel Guide* puts it.

(Westfield was also the home of Grace Bedell, the little girl who first suggested to Abraham Lincoln that he grow a beard. It's probably a significant demonstration of the marginal sta-tus of women in nineteenth-century America that this single, not exactly earth-shaking act catapulted Grace Bedell into the ranks of American heroines. She lasted well into the 1950s as a central figure of exemplary anecdotes in school readers.)

The town may feel it has a small bone, or perhaps a grape, to pick with Dr. Welch. Instead of rewarding Westfield for its inspirational environment, in 1910 the dental-surgeon-turned-juice-magnate chose to erect his main processing plant just across the Pennsylvania border in a town called North East. All Westfield seems to have got out of the deal was a distribution warehouse.

Which today was on strike. "They're cutting thirteen jobs," the shop steward marshalling the troops at the main gate told us. "Out of thirty-two. We know they have to do it, but we're asking them to do it more slowly. We're trying to save all the jobs we can. I mean, if you're looking for a job around here, you'd better look on a farm, because for sure none of the plants are hiring." He paused and thought for a moment. "Me, I retire in two years. I'll be ready. Somebody younger can have my job. If there is one." He wished us well, gave us a comradely wave, then picked up his placard and went back to his fellow picketers.

In among the grape juice ranches an occasional family winery has set up shop. Not that wine is new to this part of the lakeshore; back in 1830 Deacon Elizah Fay of nearby Portland produced six gallons of the red stuff in his cellar still from Isabella and Catowa vines he had been carefully cultivating to maturity. ("Oh, the deacon went down in the cellar to pray, but he got so drunk he stayed all day, I ain't gonna grieve my Lord no more." This old camp standby, which often alternated with Erie Canal ditties, may of course refer to another deacon, but Fay is a strong candidate.)

When neighbours came around asking whether they could swap a few dozen eggs for a bottle of Elizah's *vin ordinaire*, other local farmers saw the deacon was onto a good thing. By the turn of the century the county was producing two million gallons annually and the industry had become an important prop of the local economy. But the big-time wine and liquor interests which had taken over production and distribution throughout the state quickly sponsored regulations that put the little growers out of business; not until the 1970s was legislation passed in Albany that allowed small wineries, limited to 50,000 gallons per year, to market their own products.

We turned in at the sign of the Schloss Doepken Winery. A slight incline took us to a yellow frame farmhouse covered in vines and a large barn behind which, to the south, we could see fields of grapes, and beyond that the tree-covered slope of the old lake ridge, blue and hazy in the heat.

In the large front yard, bordered by a single railway track that passed through the fields alongside the farm and disappeared around a small hill, a picnic table had been placed under one of the large shade trees and a squad of robins were busy pulling worms out of the damp grass. Whoever the

Doepkens (or was it the Schlosses?) were, they had found a beautiful site, one you would never grow tired of looking at.

"Come on in," a muffled voice shouted when we knocked. So we opened the screen door and stepped inside into a tasting area in what had once been the parlour—only to find that the owner of the voice had vanished. After an awkward interval of wondering whether this was our first self-serve winery, a preoccupied man in his forties poked his head in and proclaimed that he was J. Simon Watso, the winemaker. Then he disappeared once more.

(Back home, we mentioned his unusual name to a friend who collects such oddities. He thought it over and decided that somewhere along the way the family must have been victims of a clerical error; a lazy county recorder, or perhaps a parish priest, by accidentally leaving off the final "n," had doomed this line of Watsons to pass through the rest of eternity as the Watsos.)

As we waited, a party of fit-looking senior citizens bustled in. Augie and his wife, whose name we didn't catch, lived near Westfield, while Mel and Ursula were visiting from Kansas City. Augie had been here before and wanted his friends to share the experience. Watso eventually returned and, with a benignly maniacal expression, lined up twelve different bottles of wine on the counter, followed them with rows of little plastic cups (the type they use in hospitals to bring your ration of pills) and more or less dared us to start drinking. In the process he modestly tossed out some tawny/fruity/smoky/tangy/oaky wine jargon, but only enough to demonstrate he could do it if he chose.

As we soon discovered, you can get a lot into those little cups. By the fourth shot one or two of the party were starting to lurch uncontrollably. Even so, our taste-buds hadn't completely lost their cunning. "I don't know much about wine, but this one tastes like horse medicine," Mel confided in a loud whisper.

But if Watso had heard he chose to ignore the remark. "The bud break in '91 was the first week of April," he informed us, and we nodded knowingly. "Then the hot dry summer hit after a mild winter. A perfect year." He looked happy just thinking about it. More nods, as if we had all given this a lot of thoughtful consideration and on the whole found his argument convincing. Then suddenly, out of nowhere, a bottle of his prize-winning Chardonnay from that year appeared before us. "Delightful now," Watso assured us, in a kind of rising shriek, "but it will be magnificent by Christmas!" He was right, at least about the present. It was delicious. We think.

Augie pointed out through a fit of giggles that the real test of wine tasting was whether you could get the little cups to fit together when you were finished, a feat he accomplished after several tries. In the meantime, a retired couple from Cleveland who had joined the party seemed to keep insisting again and again, like a kind of quavery Greek chorus, that we wouldn't recognize the town now.

Watso obviously knew what he was doing. Before we rolled out we bought a couple of bottles of the soon-to-be-magnificent white stuff, which by a curious coincidence was his highest-priced product. Mel picked up a case of cheap red to take back to K.C., perhaps with vague plans to sell it as a dozen of *dernier cru* to the leading restaurants of that Midwest city. We didn't notice what Augie took home, if anything, but of course he can come back any time he likes.

The lake ridge that we noticed in the distance from the Watso farm was more than just another pretty landmark, it was a geological legacy from the days when advances and retreats of successive ice ages created, wiped out and recreated vast lakes and river systems across the middle of the North American continent. The last of the glaciers had dug out the series of five deep depressions we know today as the Great Lakes before it began to recede something over fifteen thousand years ago (and then continued retreating for some ten millennia). The lake ridge was actually the remains of an immense pile of soil and rock this river of solid ice had once pushed in front of it. In New York State, where it begins, the low line of hills parallels the lake a few miles inland; then, after crossing Pennsylvania and moving through Ohio, the ridge swings south, away from the water, as it approaches the Maumee River valley.

A close look at a Great Lake, we were beginning to discover, keeps bringing you up against the inexorable movements of nature. Not all that long ago in the planet's history, two hundred feet or so over our heads primitive fish swam and Pleistocene ripples rippled, and no doubt some day our own age will be given one of those difficult scientific designations by future researchers. Today the entire million-square-kilometre watershed of the Great Lakes drains into the Atlantic Ocean through the St. Lawrence. In fact, since the short channels that connect the various lakes—the St. Marys, the St. Clair, the Detroit and the Niagara Rivers—could more appropriately be called straits, you can think of the whole system as a single river—one vast, rambling body of water that repeatedly widens out, narrows and then widens out again as it gradually descends from the hills of Minnesota and the Laurentian Shield to the Atlantic coast of Canada.

As the water moves eastward, its height above sea level gradually drops, imperceptibly for the most part; only at Sault Ste. Marie, and of course at the daredevil plunge of Niagara Falls, are these reductions especially noticeable. But the water is moving all the while; the proverbial message in a bottle thrown in at Thunder Bay or Duluth could, in theory at least, eventually be netted by a fisherman in the Gulf of St. Lawrence.

Though all five lakes are part of the same system, Lake Erie is in many respects the odd body of water out. Its overall latitude is by far the southernmost. Unlike the others its bed lies well above sea level. And it is extremely shallow. With its deepest point only 64 metres (Superior descends to 406 metres and Huron 229) and its average depth a mere 20 metres, Lake Erie resembles a kind of elongated bathtub.

The lake's frequent shoals and reefs are often a nightmare for navigators, and storms here are unusually dangerous; one of the lake's compact ten or twelve foot waves packs a good deal greater wallop than would one of equal size in a wider or deeper body of water, where it would have room to dissipate. So it's no accident that perhaps half the known shipwrecks of the Great Lakes have occurred here.

On the other hand, the lake's very lack of depth makes it a great place for fish; the treacherous shallows that drive mariners crazy are the kind of breeding grounds any intelligent fish would choose for a place to raise a family. And where any equally perceptive fisherman would choose to drop his line.

Even those of us who live near the Great Lakes have trouble grasping how truly unique a place they hold among the world's inland waters. Not just for the fishing; within their varied micro-climates and landforms—coastal sand dunes, rocky cliffs, barrens, estuaries, marshes, and tiny offshore islands—an incredible variety of plant and animal life has taken root, including many which are indigenous to the watershed. Carolinian species flourish along the sand plains of Lake Erie, while 700 kilometres to the north the far shore of Lake Superior contains colonies of arctic flora and fauna left over from the last glacier. You could spend your whole life studying them.

Chapter Four

KS: When I checked the map to see what else there was in this far corner of New York State, I found to my surprise that we had now come very close to a bothersome personal land-mark. When I was eight or nine years old my family spent a vacation at Bemus Point, the leading summer holiday ren-dezvous on Lake Chautauqua, only five miles or so inland from Lake Erie. I have no recollection of where we stayed, who we went with, what we did, whether we enjoyed our-selves or anything else other than the name. But for some rea-son that only Freud could guess at, my subconscious had fixed on Bemus Point for the setting of a recurring nightmare that disturbed me repeatedly for the next twenty or twenty-five years.

I am riding my bike along a wooden boardwalk by some blue water. In the background stands a large, rambling, white frame hotel, perhaps several of them. At first I breeze along contentedly. Suddenly I realize I am being followed by several indistinct figures, also riding bikes. I pedal furiously to main-tain the distance between us. Then the boardwalk abruptly transforms itself into long, parallel white cylinders that stretch out over an inky darkness and I find myself struggling to maintain my balance. I career along briefly, then the wheels slip sideways, plunging me down through the spaces between the tubes into terrifying blackness.

At this point as a child I usually fell out of bed and woke as I hit the floor. When I got older that changed to starting up abruptly in a cold sweat. A long time has passed since I last had the dream, and although by now it's nothing more than a curious memory, every detail remains perfectly vivid.

Now, after all these years, here I am again. Not many people get the chance to check out their old nightmares. Do the locales that so terrified me actually exist? Or did I dream the whole thing, as it were? I guess we should take a deep breath and go have a look.

The Dionysian revels at Watso's winery had left us ready for a good night's sleep before heading into the twilight zone. But to our consternation we found ourselves returning to a different, shared childhood horror—the ghastly, almost mythic moment when the rest of the family realizes that the father's obsession with adding still a few more miles to the day's travel total has condemned them to drive unceasingly through the endless night of No Vacancy, past countless motels and tourist cabins (Heated Pool!!! Air Cooled!!! Free Ice!!!), each of which would have been just the right place to stop. This means spending the night in a place like "M-O-T-E-$$24," which we discovered lurking at the end of a wide stretch of cracked tarmac on a newly developed strip in Jamestown, a small city at the unfashionable southern end of the lake. This establishment did have several vacancies, including a room that resembled a set for *The Masque of the Red Death* as designed by Liberace's couturier. Everything was violently red, flowered and flocked—the curtains, the wallpaper, the bedspread, the thick shag carpet. Even the air felt flocked; the room had recently been doused in so much chemical spray that after ten minutes or so our fingertips began to lose feeling. But it was this or the street, so we dropped into bed to wheeze the night away.

The next morning, still tingling at the extremities, we made our way over to Lake Chautauqua. This admittedly pretty body of water seemed a mere picturesque puddle after Erie's extended vistas, but wherever a slight indentation in the shoreline permitted, a harbour had been created and around it a settlement had grown up. Bemus Point was the largest of these, a village of restaurants, campgrounds, cottages, souvenir stores and, yes, a large Victorian hotel with a wide veranda where entire families sat rocking the morning away.

We found an outdoor table at the Surf Club and consumed a leisurely breakfast surrounded by families from Ohio and Indiana and western Pennsylvania chatting placidly about profit margins, sales routes, the quickest way south in the winter, how difficult it was to get genuine parts or how much drinking they had done or intended to do soon. "We did a little fishing while we were there, but mostly we drank," a woman next to us explained to a latecomer.

A strange slothfulness pervaded the streets. The main activity seemed to be strolling indolently around town in preparation for plopping down at a restaurant to gorge yourself on heaping plateful of gravy-drowned fries and hot fudge sundaes. A considerable number of the idlers were seriously overweight, a percentage which actually appeared to rise as the age of the holidayers declined. It's an odd sensation to be among a group of people in which the elderly are fitter and trimmer than their children and grandchildren. Clearly, no one intended to attempt anything more strenuous during their stay than lifting a Cajun chicken wing or turning on an Evinrude; hikers, joggers, cyclists, canoeists and other physical culture types could go jump in some other lake. Recreational eating was the sport of choice here.

The vacationers were without exception Caucasian. Despite the fact that the resort draws its clientele largely from the suburban areas of major cities in western New York and Pennsylvania and northern Ohio, nowhere among the throngs did we spot a single black, Hispanic, native, East Asian or Oriental face. Lourdes Iglesias had mentioned that once she and her fiancé had made reservations for a weekend at a white-picket-fence-type Chautauqua inn about which they knew nothing except that it had a New Englandish kind of name. "I think we were the first Spanish people they'd ever seen," she laughed. "Boy, did we feel like getting out of there in a hurry."

KS: Oh, yeah, the dream. Well, it was all there, more or less. The row of white frame hotels opposite the water turned out to be in reality a single establishment painted canary yellow, and the water wasn't quite as close to the main street, but the overall geography of the scene felt recognizable. There wasn't any boardwalk, which threw me for a while, but looking at old photos on the restaurant walls we realized that the contemporary cement sidewalks might well have once been made of planks. That simple memory-prompt brought an instantaneous Gestalt and every landmark of my frantic flight came back to me, even to the very spot where the boardwalk had turned into cylinders. (Should anyone want to put up a plaque, it's by the large, garbage-filled hollow tree stump just beyond the lawn of the Lenhart Hotel.)

So what about it? I'm not sure. I've always known the identity of my pursuers, and I didn't learn anything new about them or myself. It did prove that the past actually existed, which is always reassuring, I suppose. Sorry. It's something of an anti-climax to me, too.

Chapter Five

Erie is really three distinct lakes in one. That's another basic geographical fact we learned as we talked to scientific types along the lake. They were referring to the two north-south underwater ridges that cross the lake: the first reaching from Long Point, Ontario, to Erie, Pennsylvania, the other close to the western end. After a little thought on the subject we began to realize that (coincidentally or not) human society along the two shores also divided itself into three distinct categories that roughly match the geography.

The cultural influence of Toronto, which is oriented toward New York City and Europe, extends far into the eastern third on both sides of the lake; so, to a lesser degree, does that of Buffalo. People commonly travel back and forth across the border for business purposes and for theatre, sports events, art exhibitions and other diversions. In the western basin a string of tourist-oriented islands, a flourishing sport fishery and the Detroit-based power boat culture combine to create a bumptious, midwestern-industrialist-at-play atmosphere unlike anything else on the planet. And between these poles, the middle sections that face each other across the widest portion of the lake represent two different versions of the great North American heartland.

So in the end we gave up the idea of following a circular

route, despite its appeal on the basis of continuity and simplicity, and chose a multi-dimensional regional approach. Translated into normal English, that means that it seemed like more fun, and more instructive, to alternate between the two sides of the lake.

We turned back at the Pennsylvania border, returned to Toronto for a few days of R and R, and then set out again for the Canadian side. Leaving the Queen Elizabeth Way (QEW) at the last exit before the Peace Bridge to Buffalo, we pointed the car toward the heart of Fort Erie, Ontario, and followed a series of signs that guided us ever forward toward the "Town Centre." On each small green square a white arrow pointing upward indicated that we were to proceed straight ahead, until the sequence came to an end with a square that repeated the words but left the rest of the sign blank. After a moment of confusion we realized we must have arrived.

Maybe it was the recession, or all that cross-border shopping you keep hearing about, or the fact that a lot of property on this side is owned by Americans who aren't particularly interested in supporting the local economy, but if downtown is any guide Fort Erie is hanging on by its fingertips. Jarvis Street is a sad-looking affair whose two-storey brick commercial buildings are tenanted largely by cut-rate chain stores, thrift shops and social agencies. It looks more like the main street of a faltering rural county seat than the centre of a city of 23,000 citizens.

(Fort Erie is actually the largest city on the Canadian side of the lake. According to figures provided by our trusty portable atlas, the ratio of Americans to Canadians along Lake Erie is something like forty-five to one; between four and five million on one side, less than 100,000 on the other. Either Buffalo or Cleveland could easily tuck the total Canuck population into one of their larger neighbourhoods.)

Walking down Jarvis Street toward the river, we were startled to come across a very substantial second-hand book-store. The long front window displayed an intriguing selection of titles without a single Jackie Collins or Barbara Cartland novel among them; more surprising still was encountering ourselves on the front door, where next to a placard reading "Stop City Hall" was posted an impassioned diatribe that quoted extensively from a magazine piece we had written a year or so before. The writer had applied our description of an architectural contretemps further west to a local battle. The fact that someone somewhere has actually thought about something you've written is encouraging, and here, at the beginning of our tour of the Canadian shore, it seemed a good omen.

On the other hand, this kind of thing always leaves you slightly nervous. Whose side were we on in this struggle we hadn't even known existed? Were our words being used to support a cause we approved of, or had they been taken out of context to provide ammunition for the forces of darkness and reaction?

A bouncy-looking, the-best-is-yet-to-be grandmother dressed in a striped track suit sat behind the desk eating a tuna-fish sandwich. Helen Matthews told us she was minding the store while her son, Bill, was off with Annie Hall somewhere. (Annie turned out to be Bill's wife and business partner, and that was the name she'd been born with.)

The bookstore was easily explained. Having built up a thriving antiquarian book business in Toronto, the Matthews family, for reasons of economy and proximity to the large American market, had pulled up stakes and moved down here. The three floors were crowded with shelves given over to Canadian history, American history, naval history, local history, poetry, children's books and everything else imaginable. Finding a bonanza like this in major cities these days is hard enough; the presence of a sensationally good bookstore sandwiched between Shear Delight Hair Centre and Erie Jewellers in downtown Fort Erie seemed a mirage.

Of course if they had to depend on walk-in trade, Helen explained, they would be bankrupt in a week. "It's not that the Erieites have anything against us personally," she said with a shrug, "but as one of the more prominent socially women told me, her friends would be horrified if they knew she'd gone out and bought a book second hand."

She paused briefly to ring up the sale of a collection of Tennyson's poems to a woman in Mennonite dress, then took up the conversation again. The anti-city-hall placard turned out to relate to a perennial feature of small-town Ontario life with which we were all too familiar. This was the attempt by one faction, usually a majority on the town council, to tear down some historically significant and even architecturally valuable but hard to heat and generally run-down city hall or library or opera house and erect in its place a hideous modern excrescence out on the edge of town between the arena and the incinerator.

Ranged against these people is generally a complicated coalition of political progressives, local historians, school-teachers, and environmental activists anxious to retain an important example of local craftsmanship for posterity. In awkward alliance with these people at rallies and council meetings is a substrata of citizens so obdurately conservative they are incensed by the idea of any change of any kind at any time, but most especially change that involves municipal tax dollars. All of the antis take the position that the building already in place can be renovated for less money than it would take to put up a new one.

Since these buildings are the defining structures of any Ontario town, nothing raises passions as high as the question of their disposition; the bitterness engendered by some of these city hall fights to the death is probably uniquely Canadian. Americans are more likely to blow up over abstract principles such as school curricula or political ideology. Canadians, or at least those living in small towns, seem to need something physical, like a building, as an intermediary factor before they can really vent their spleen.

Fort Erie's city hall, a squat, squarish, twenties red-brick structure which we had passed on our drive through town, did not fall into the category of world-class architectural wonder, but it had an undeniably pleasant, homey look, nicely set into its surroundings. There seemed no obvious reason for the town council to spend a fortune putting up a new building somewhere else when it could be comfortably renovated to fill current needs.

At least that's how Helen Matthews and the other members of her committee saw it. They raised over four thousand signatures on a petition, a figure representing an impressive 20 percent of the population. The response of the town council was to dig its heels in even deeper, and the ranks closed in. The pro-development local newspaper declined to as much as mention the petition in its columns, and when the chamber of commerce drew up its official list of local businesses the Matthews' bookstore was somehow overlooked despite being one of the few thriving enterprises left in the downtown.

Such petty assaults are normal procedure when city hall disputes arise in small-town Canada. A few years ago we'd made the mistake of becoming involved in a running fight over the township hall in the rural community where we resided at the time, and the scars still throbbed. Not so much from being denounced by outraged politicians or trashed in local newspaper columns—we could give that back and better—but from ramming our heads against the brick wall of honest ignorance.

This involves a Mendelian phenomenon that exists in many places but has evolved to its most perfect form in rural Ontario, where you find a whole subset of human beings who have been born without an aesthetic gene. These are well-meaning citizens, usually locally prominent small business people, who genuinely believe efficiency to be synonymous with beauty, who have never encountered anything more pleasing to the eye than the typical dull brown and beige, poorly ventilated, tiny-windowed fifties-style steel and masonry modernist structures everybody else has long since recoiled from, and who will fight to their last public-spirited breath to get one of those for their community. "Yeah, we've got a couple of those," Helen sighed.

"There's one place you've got to see," she told us before we left. "Erie Beach. It was a big deal in the twenties—Mack Sennett's beauties, diving horses, Olympic athletes, boxing, the works." She was so convincing that we ended up driving to the far end of town for a look.

Niagara Boulevard at some point turned into Lakeshore Drive, and just at the point where the shoreline of the Niagara Peninsula began to curve westward, the ruins of the once lavish amusement park marked the true beginning of Lake Erie.

Today all that is left of "Buffalo's Ideal Resort," as the publicity material labelled it, is a crumbling pier, a portion of its mile-long esplanade and a series of disintegrating, half-submerged walls and foundations. An industrial age megalith composed of four support pillars and a thick, horizontal, jagged piece of concrete, once part of a terrace, stuck up out of the water as if to mark the site for future archaeologists. One stretch of wall was covered with fresh graffiti—"NYPD 1993," "Cherry was here May 24, '92," "Geoff sucks," and finally, some anonymously ecstatic adolescent had scrawled in large painted letters "I'm happier than I've ever been in my life."

Judging from the old promotional material Helen had thrust into our hands, Erie Beach must have ranked as the most exotic of the numerous resorts that sprang up on both sides of the lake. Here, a century ago, passenger steamers from Buffalo deposited thousands of fun-seeking families and fashionable young people to swim in what was billed as the world's largest swimming pool, gamble at the casino, picnic on the greens and dance the night away in the ballroom. They could also watch spectacular and bizarre sporting events such as races between people and animals in the 3,500 seat stadium, thrill to the amusement park rides, play games on the midway, roller-skate on the rink, mount live camels or gawk at rare birds in the largest aviary west of the Bronx Zoo.

Where the main structures and playing fields had once spread over several acres, a grove of oaks and maples, sixty or seventy years old now, covered everything. On the beach a few sunbathers were stretched out and two boys were struggling with windsurfing gear in the heavy waves, while far in the distance the skyscrapers of Buffalo formed a modest, bumpy horizontal line between water and sky. With the huge sky all around you, the breaking waves and the scattered ruins of a past way of life, this was obviously the closest thing to Valhalla for local teenagers, and no doubt the scene of innumerable memorable revels on summer nights.

Buffalo seemed a good distance away, but as we discovered when we continued west out of town Erie Beach is probably one of the few desirable stretches of waterfront on the extreme eastern shore of the lake that has not been bought up by Americans.

"We're on the lake and the river, and we don't even have a public dock," one local resident muttered darkly. "The Buffalo Yacht Club and the rest of them own everything." The Yacht Club dominates the area's one sheltered harbour, and as you travel west most of the best views belong to houses that fly American flags. When they go up for sale these homes aren't even advertised in Canada; they are simply exchanged between rich Buffalonians.

At Point Abino, generally conceded to be one of the prettiest sites in this whole area, a young man who looked ill at ease in his official hat and badge stopped us from passing through a gate. He would have to check with the boss in Buffalo, he explained, before he could let us look around; they were having trouble with illegal swimmers and picnicking intruders. But Buffalo turned us down, and with an apologetic shrug he sent us on our way. Comes the revolution, we know which gates we're storming.

As Buffalo and environs faded from view the American presence became less pronounced, and when we cut over to Highway 3 we found ourselves on a true Canadian rural road, haphazardly developed and casual in its approach to signage. Empty fields and abandoned woodlots were interspersed with tidy farms. Small bungalows and roadside businesses popped up sporadically. Mysterious unmarked gravel roads crossed our path and continued on their way to more unseen cornfields and crossroad settlements. Highway 3 might be the main highway along the lake, but like everything else in the Canadian countryside it wasn't giving away any secrets. We considered ourselves lucky to discover on an isolated sign that our next destination, Port Colborne (pop. 19,000), was not far ahead.

The Welland Canal, which bisects this small city north to south is really Port Colborne's main street. Lake freighters and huge container ships from all over the world chug slowly through the centre of town holding up traffic as they move their enormous bulks through the canal's southernmost extension toward the lake. Opened in 1829, just four years after the Erie Canal was completed, it remains the only route a ship can take to get around Niagara Falls. And except for the installation of modern drawbridge and lock machinery, around Port Colborne it looks pretty much the same as it did in the past—a quiet, man-made river with low limestone walls as banks, set into a narrow, grassy strip that doubles in places as a municipal park.

As we sat on the patio of Finnegan's Restaurant overlooking the guard lock, the approach of a giant lake freighter provided one of the great dramatic sights remaining from the industrial age. First the black prow of the *Capt. Henry Jackman* loomed high above us; then the main deck, the length of a couple of football fields, inched along past our eyes. Finally the seven-storey bridge came into view, each additional storey smaller than the one below, as on a multi-tiered wedding cake, but at the crown, instead of a confectionary couple, stood a crowd of impressive-looking antenae. The ship was so long that it took several minutes to creep by and so wide that it scraped through the old walls with only a few feet clearance on either side.

The day was warm; several off-duty crew members had put on shorts, unfolded their lounge chairs and were sunning themselves on the main deck. A few tourists waiting at the drawbridge had gotten out of their cars and were cheerfully exchanging waves with the sailors. A gang of kids, baseball gloves on their belts, jumped off their bikes and shouted something to a crewman, who laughed and called something back. We fought back a momentary impulse to rush over and jot down what they were saying, perhaps even to inquire whether we could fit in a quick word with Captain Jackman himself. Instead we stayed where we were, comfortably sipping our iced tea and watching the great thing creep past our vantage point toward the freedom of the lake.

Exhilarating as this sudden tangible connection to the outside world might appear to a visitor, the Port Colbornians we met seemed barely aware of the canal's existence. Our obliging teenaged waitress, when asked how long it took a ship to pass through the entire canal, looked as stricken as if we had just informed her we'd found zebra mussels in our clam chowder. "Gosh, I don't know," she said finally. "I'll see if I can find out." But no one else at the restaurant knew either.

Evening confirmed the impression that Port Colborne's identity was mostly bound up in its role as an early-to-bed farm centre and market town. That sailor who had a girl in every port obviously never tried his luck here, at least not after business hours. As the saying goes, you couldn't get arrested in downtown Port Colborne after six o'clock.

But we yearned for diversion. So after depositing our bags in a motel room whose large picture window overlooked a field full of contentedly grazing cows, we showered, pulled on some clean clothes and got back in the car to go looking for signs of night life. After all, among nearly twenty thousand people there must be some who didn't fall asleep within an hour of finishing supper; perhaps a few even occasionally left the house after dark.

It took considerable searching, but finally we came across a lively looking sports bar. "Sumo Wrestling every Wednesday," read the marquee, and, as a late-night talk show host might say, darned if today wasn't Wednesday.

Could this be part of that tradition of bottom-of-the-show-biz-barrel touring performers we had not infrequently run into in backwoods Canada? Over the years we had met a troupe of singing and dancing transvestites who played the sex-starved mining towns of northern Quebec and Ontario, assorted Robert Service reciters, snake trainers, semi-pro wrestlers, grass circuses and a long list of similar hard-work-ing-but-going-nowhere-except-to-the-next-small-town coun-try entertainers. Barnstorming Sumo wrestlers would fit right in.

Hooters (not a promising name) consisted of one very large room with a bar against the back wall, a pool table or two to the right and the entire left side reserved as a dance floor and sometime performance space. Blue Jay posters were stuck on the walls more or less at random, and in the place of honour over the bar hovered a wingspan photo of a grinning Michael Jordan, arms extended as if in benediction over the beery crowd. Rough rural was the dominant fashion statement—sleeveless T-shirts, lots of tattoos, hockey scars and mashed-in noses.

The young women looked as if they could hold their own; several had that touch-my-man-and-I'll-kill-you look that not even the freshness of youth can obscure. "How the fuck you doing?" a girl at the bar greeted a friend. "Fucking OK." "Well, fucking all right."

But the night was warm, the beer was cold, no one was blind drunk yet and in spite of the limited vocabularies the general mood was one of good humour. (On the other hand, you felt, when fights did start, not too many of the people lining the bar with us would be content to remain spectators.)

The Sumo wrestling, when it began, turned out to have nothing to do with touring performers, or for that matter with either Sumo or wrestling. A pair of volunteer combat-ants from the crowd were stuffed into inflated plastic bubble-suits, hoisted upright with some difficulty and then let loose to smash into each other. Two out of three knockdowns won the contest.

The mostly female volunteers ranged all the way from teenagers barely old enough to drink to grandmothers. Bump, bump, plop, bang, squish, squeal—and one of the competitors toppled over. The one still standing then got to take a flying leap and body-slam her prone opponent. She was helped to her feet, another round of bump, bump, squish, crash ensued, and eventually a winner was declared. Then another pair climbed into the sweaty suits and it all began again.

Around us a growing mob of twenty-to-thirty-year-olds called to each other over the din. Men discussed women and regaled each other with golf stories, the hockey season being still a few months away. Beauticians and check-out clerks exchanged gossip and cruised the room. Pool sharks with cigarette packs carefully folded into their T-shirt sleeves twirled their cues and cleaned the table. Serious barflies shouted for refills.

Through the swirling cigarette smoke and the constantly shifting figures of the drinkers, we could just make out the Sumo ring, where now a couple of Pillsbury Doughboy grandmothers were caroming back and forth like billiard balls while their daughters and husbands fell over themselves laughing. Even as we stared in dreamlike fascination the racket rose to a point where it drowned out every trace of their grunts and shrieks, transforming the scene into a kind of deafeningly loud, incomprehensibly symbolic silent film— early Bergman as interpreted by Mack Sennett with a sound track by Megadeth or Guns N' Roses.

Prying ourselves off our seats, we staggered out into the night, where the air was sweet with the scent of some unidentifiable shrub, and made our way back to the motel and its herd of placid, grass-chewing cows.

The next morning we took in Tennessee Street, the single site listed in our Port Colborne tourist brochure. This was a narrow waterfront lane where, in the late nineteenth century, wealthy American southerners had built summer houses and had come each year to escape the oppressive heat of Dixie.

One of these was authoress Varina Anne Davis, Daughter of the Confederacy (so called because her father was Jefferson Davis and she was born during the war). It was easy to picture Varina Anne ensconced in her lakeside bower, demure in her long frilly white dress, a pen in one hand and a mint julep in the other, scribbling away on *The Veiled Doctor, A Romance of Summer Seas*, or her best-known work, *The Grasshopper War*. It was even easier to picture ourselves on an upper balcony of one of the clapboard summer mansions; she might not have produced great literature, but Ms. Davis sure knew the kind of setting every writer we've ever met feels he or she deserves.

On our way out of town we dropped in at a local arts co-operative. The usual ceramics and water-colours took up most of the exhibition space, but around a corner we noticed a dark room with some vague shapes bobbing around in it. When we turned on the light and peered in, the air seemed to come alive with dozens of complicated constructions of painted wire and multicoloured strips of fibre that hung from the ceiling, moving gently in the barely noticeable currents of air. Smaller varicoloured shapes projected from the walls or rested on low tables.

"Joyce makes them," the young clerk told us meaningfully, then left us to our thoughts.

Which were that Joyce, whoever she might be, was a woman possessed by the need for air. Her work was literally full of holes, consisting mostly of spaces outlined by thin wires. We learned later that Joyce Homsberger was around our age, had lived mostly in rural Ontario and had become an artist fairly late in life. Knowing nothing more of her history, but looking over what she called her "space carvings," we immediately jumped to the conclusion that her aesthetic must be a response to the smothering paternalism of the small-town Canadian society of her youth. As an artist, breathing room had become an obsession and the real subject of every sculpture she created. If she ever reads this book she may laugh for a week, of course; on the other hand, if we have come anywhere near the truth, think how clever we can consider ourselves. Anyway, we liked the floating sculptures a lot and bought one to hang in our dining room, where guests almost invariably bump their heads on it sometime during the course of a meal.

Chapter Six

All that lay between us and the small lake village of Port Maitland was the wide mouth of the Grand River. Unfortunately, as we had failed to pack the Mazda's pontoons and no ferry service was provided, it was obvious we were not going to get there the way we'd planned.

Our mistake had been believing the map, which put Port Maitland on the river's east bank. It took some wandering through the deserted lanes and dead ends of what seemed to be an ancient waterside industrial park—past empty sheds, a defunct processing plant of some kind and a length of old canal, where the rusting hulks of several largish boats were tied up—until we found the road to Dunnville, the next town upriver. There we spotted a bridge, made a U-turn, followed the winding river road south and eventually pulled to a halt at the exact spot we had been wistfully gazing at half an hour or so before.

Here, finally, was a true lake settlement. Boat builders, boat repairers, boat suppliers, boat charter offices, fishermen, Fisheries and Harbours inspectors—Port Maitland's entire workforce seemed to have a direct relation to the water. The village, built around a wide natural harbour, consisted essentially of two streets: one ran east-west and dead-ended at the water; the other paralleled the river and ended at a parking

lot next to a long concrete pier that formed a protected channel for boats passing out onto the lake, and also was obviously a favourite fishing spot.

Out on the pier several generations of a Vietnamese family
and a variety of other fisherpeople, ranging from ten-year-
olds to aged retirees who looked as if they could easily
remember the day the boys came home from the Boer War,
were casting off the side under the watchful eyes of a selection of kibitzers. A teenaged couple clutching each other
tightly drifted among the crowd oblivious to anyone but
themselves, and next to the pier children were digging busily
in the sand. The branches of willow trees bordering the parking lot moved gently in the light wind.

We pushed open the screen door of the tiny general-store-
cum-tackle-shop that seemed to make up the village's entire
retail section, hoping to get the name of someone with a boat
who might be willing to take us up the reputedly beautiful
Grand River or out onto the lake. Or both. We were writing
a book about a lake and we hadn't been out on the water yet.

"No, I don't know anyone with a boat, I can't help you
there," the middle-aged woman behind the counter replied
guardedly as she filled two styrofoam cups with coffee. This
appeared highly unlikely given the fact that the store was less
than one hundred feet from the pier and the village obviously
contained more boats than people. But it seemed rude to
push the issue, and in any event, our years of living in the
country had taught us the first rule of rural conversation:
people only talk when they want to.

She was more comfortable conversing about non-nautical
subjects, like the house down the road with the big sign in the
front yard. "Yes, some native people from up in Brantford had
an idea to sell things from there a few years ago, handicrafts
and so on. But I guess it didn't work out." That seemed to be
the end of the conversation, so we left her to wait on her next
customer, a young boy with a fishing rod, and drifted out.

Sitting in the car while we drank our coffee, we took another look at the sign. "Welcome to the lands of the Six Nations of the Grand River," it began, and it continued with a brief account of European betrayal illustrated with a crudely painted map.

Basically what happened is that after the Treaty of Paris in 1783, a six-mile stretch on each side of the river's entire length was granted to the Iroquois Nation in perpetuity as a reward for their loyalty during the American Revolution. At the end of that time, which in the judgment of various white governors and landowners could be measured in decades, the natives were casually asked to move over a bit to make room for newly arriving white settlers who wanted what have come to be known as riverfront lots. This revisionist approach was justified by treating the Iroquois willingness to lease parcels of land to white settlers as a forfeiture of their rights.

Eventually the band was driven into the small area fifty miles upriver known today as the Six Nations Reserve. For some strange reason a few of the natives feel bitter about the way they have been treated.

Although the sky was darkening, we decided to stretch our legs and take a stroll out to the lighthouse at the end of the long pier. If we couldn't find a boat, at least we could get further out into the lake this way. As we made our way along the narrow stretch of concrete the wind abruptly picked up; out on the lake whitecaps appeared out of nowhere and began rising and falling in swift succession, where the last time we'd looked there had been nothing but barely noticeable ripples on the glassy surface. Halfway out, we glanced back and were surprised to note that the rod-and-reelers and their observers had departed, the children had packed up their sand toys and gone home, and the young couple were wrapping their arms around each other somewhere else.

Only one other person shared the concrete with us, a tall, cadaverous, whacked-out-looking man wearing a dark T-shirt, black pants and gumboots. He had been sitting on the edge with a fishing rod in his hand, but as we approached he too picked up his gear and without a word or a glance moved rapidly away.

One of us at this point expressed the strong opinion that maybe these people knew something we didn't, but the other scoffed. ("C'mon, if there was any danger there'd be a sign somewhere, or something....") Fighting our way against the rising wind all the way out to the very end of the pier, we propped our backs against the far side of the lighthouse and stared at the waves crashing against the bulwark and out toward a sky that was now almost the same unwelcoming slate-grey as the water. For the first time we were seeing a hint of the sudden, unexpected fury for which Lake Erie is famous. It was quite a show.

We shouldn't have been surprised. All the Great Lakes are dangerous, but Lake Erie's sudden, violent storms have been notorious among mariners probably ever since the first Stone Age sailor ventured out onto its surface and unexpectedly found himself fighting for his life in a tempest that had blown up out of nowhere.

Charles Dickens was as sick as a dog on a U.S. Navy frigate travelling from Sandusky to Cleveland during his 1842 American tour. "It's all very fine talking about Lake Erie," he complained bitterly. "But it won't do for people who are liable to seasickness. It's almost as bad in that respect as the Atlantic. The waves are very short and horribly constant."

It's a pity he hadn't postponed his trip for two years, when something that really would have challenged his descriptive powers occurred. In October 1844, a week of gale-force south-easterly winds virtually emptied out the eastern basin, leaving the port of Buffalo high and dry. Then the wind grew even stronger as it reversed its direction, sending a lake tidal wave, or seiche, crashing into the city. The wave swamped the low-lying areas, wiping out a labourers' slum called Bealsville and drowning several unsuspecting citizens who a moment earlier had been standing on dry land. A six-hundred-ton steamer was thrown all the way onto Ohio Street, a considerable distance inland.

On November 10, 1940, during another gale, the water level in the Maumee River, at the other end of the lake, dropped ten feet. And in the legendary storm of the century, beginning Saturday, November 8, 1913, when massive weather fronts from the Gulf of Mexico, the American prairies and the Canadian Arctic collided over the Great Lakes, bringing with them winds exceeding eighty miles an hour and dropping two feet of snow in less than twenty-four hours, none of the three or four dozen ships whose captains were foolish enough to ignore the weather warnings escaped undamaged.

Lightship No. 82, stationed off Point Abino almost within sight of where we were now sitting, went down with all hands; all that was ever recovered was a life-preserver that washed up in Buffalo harbour and part of a door with "Goodbye, Nellie, the ship is breaking up fast, Williams," scrawled on it. The freighter *Henry B. Smith* of Cleveland, carrying eleven thousand tons of ore, vanished without even that much to mark its passing. So did the *Regina*, and another large freighter out of Cleveland, the *Charles S. Price*. All told, 235 seamen were known to have been lost, and how many more anonymous passengers is anyone's guess.

The ships that survived were the ones lucky enough to be driven onto the shore. An early Tall Ship, a replica of the *Santa Maria* cruising the lakes before a planned tour of the west coast, had the great good fortune to be blown out of the water onto a mudbank at Erie, where she stuck fast.

Estimates of the total number of ships lost or stranded over the years in the Great Lakes vary wildly. The *American Lakes Series* put out by Bobbs-Merrill in the forties sets the number at something over twenty thousand vessels, beginning right at the beginning with the first sailing ship to ply the lakes. The *Griffon*, a tiny barque built in 1679 by La Salle in the Niagara River a few miles above the Falls, just missed foundering on a reef off Long Point, then went down somewhere further west, most likely in Lake Huron.

At first glance that estimate may sound absurdly inflated,

even if it does take in more than three centuries of sailing. But Lake Erie, with its ever-looming lee shores and reefs, and the Detroit River, which lets into it, were naval superhighways in the nineteenth and early twentieth centuries. (Even today the Detroit River remains the busiest waterway in the world.) One of Julie's ancestors, on an expedition in 1846 to visit relatives in the East, wrote back to her great-grandmother in Michigan that Buffalo harbour was so crowded with ships their steamer had to wait twelve hours before a space cleared for them to dock.

According to the statistics of the Lake Carrier's Association, as late as the 1930s, despite advances in communications, meteorology and shipbuilding, between twenty and thirty commercial carriers were being lost each year. So maybe that figure of twenty-thousand-plus lost vessels is not so unlikely after all. No wonder experienced Lake Erie sailors always seem to be casually sneaking glances at the sky while they go about their business.

(Many of the ships burned before they sank, by the way. The danger of fire, especially in wooden vessels, was every bit as great as running onto a lee shore. And while the risk of fire was naturally greatest during a storm, some of the worst disasters have taken place at dockside. One hundred and thirty-nine passengers died when the *Noronic* caught fire while tied at its berth in Toronto in 1949.)

On our way back to Dunnville we came across an old World War Two RCAF training base. Inside the fence, spread out across the flat fields, were a half dozen or so abandoned hangars and administration buildings with broken windows, their doors hanging by half a hinge and banging against their frames in the wind. A historical marker near the front gate revealed that this home to flying fools and heroes-in-the-making had lasted from the opening of the base in 1939 to the end of the war.

It seemed little more than a ghostly reminder of a long-forgotten era. Except that a car was parked outside one of the staff houses and a dog was tied up outside. Who lived there? Squatters? Smugglers? An aged airman who had quietly returned to live out his remaining years? None of the above, as it happened. When we turned in and drove up to the house, we found ourselves face to face with a puzzled Dutch immigrant couple. They looked like farmers, but what were they farming?

The answer was turkeys. The old air base was now a huge turkey farm owned by a turkey conglomerate and managed by the couple. At any given moment no fewer than 54,000 Thanksgiving Specials were living in the old hangars, exchanging pecks and stuffing themselves with whatever turkeys eat. Over the wind, once you knew what to listen for, you could just make out a constant, low, droning gobble floating across the old runways.

Every September, they told us, a batch of the surviving airmen who received their training there participate in a flyover; they dip their wings to the memory of their old comrades as 54,000 bemused turkeys and the two blue-eyed Dutch farmers look on. There had to be some sort of deeper meaning here, some important truth about the relationship of martial glory, Thanksgiving dinner and The Netherlands, but we couldn't figure out what it was.

So we continued on to Dunnville (pop. 11,500). This is an old town, dating from the days when the digging of canals and the building of railroads had started to make travel less rigorous and settlement was beginning to spread west along both sides of the lake. You could tell it was an old town because it had a Market Street and a still functioning public market. The original village was surveyed back in 1829 by an American adventurer named Salmon Miner who, like many Yankee pioneers during the great westward migration between 1815 and mid-century, had taken a shortcut through southern Ontario on his way to the Michigan territory. Also like many others, he had liked what he found along the way in Canada and gone no further. In the words of the town's tourist brochure, he'd stopped where the "golden waters meandered to a remarkable harbour...the fertile marshlands kissed the banks of the subdued Grand River, [amid] the lush green Carolinian forest."

Despite these promotional raptures, on this particular August afternoon the town's outstanding characteristic seemed to us to be its absolutely straightforward nature. The Canadian Tire outlet and a small A&P could be spotted downtown, but other businesses appeared to prefer a tell-it-like-it-is approach to the potential customer. We could have eaten at Bob's Place or Mary's Restaurant, browsed through the tank-tops at Dee Ann's Ladies Wear (or, for the gentleman, Uncle Bob's Men and Boys Wear), then completed our shopping spree at places like Elroy's Farm Market, Peter's Engine and Rental Centre, Lymburner's Auto Supply, Hauser's Pharmacy or its rival, Nugent's Pharmacy. Other merchants considered even that approach too highfalutin; their establishments were known simply as "Gas" or "Restaurant" or "Eat" or "Jewellery." Here you knew who you were dealing with and what you were getting—Bob, Mary, the other Bob and Dee Ann were not shadowy figures in some absentee multinational conglomerate. We were definitely nearing the outer edge of the Toronto-Buffalo orbit now; compared to Dunnville, Port Colborne had resembled Paris in the twenties.

Next to an old-fashioned riverfront take-out eatery, a sign read "BOAT TOURS." This might be our chance, we thought, to get out on the water. No one was at the dock, but a young man carrying a pair of oars told us that Jim Allen was the man we wanted. He knew every inch of the river. So we called Jim at home, and hung up a few minutes later having somehow rented an entire tour boat for nine o'clock the next morning.

This turned out to be the *Willy-Anne*, a 12-ton, 31-foot, 12-foot beam, blue-and-white converted patrol vessel with a double-sealed hull driven by two 130 hp engines and named for Jim and Mary Allen's two children. (Jim had bought it a few years earlier from the Nanticoke Atomic Energy plant, but they had never told him exactly what it was used to patrol.) The *Willy-Anne* was set up to carry sixteen passengers and two crew, which, since we hadn't yet talked money, caused a moment of anxiety and a quick mental survey of our cash-flow situation. "Just pay the gas," Jim said. "The season's practically over, anyway. We got time."

"Rather do this than sit at home," Mary added. "Not that we don't have a million things to do. I'm a bookkeeper. Jim's got his towing service."

Jim was in his mid-fifties, built like a Russian heavyweight weightlifter, tall, broad, crew-cut, with a substantial stomach over which you could break two-by-fours. He radiated the authority of a master sergeant, which was not surprising since his long and eclectic career had included several years in the military as well as stints as a professional wrestler, a stock car driver and a policeman; he had also played goalie for the local senior hockey team and probably kept pucks out of the net just by glaring at them.

Mary—energetic, good humoured, softer, but equally strong-minded, sporting earrings in the shape of small anchors and a white blouse with anchor trim on the pocket— looked like a good match for Jim, the kind of woman who would be not only the best bowler on the team but also a unanimous choice to keep the score sheet. The four of us were nearly the same age, had been married within a year of each other, had children at about the same time and in general felt like two different sides of the same coin. (Or at least we did.)

"The economy's bad everywhere, but you feel it more in a small town," Jim said when we asked him how Dunnville was doing. "We lost Lundys and IMC. It's a bedroom community now. A lot of Stelco employees live here. But the biggest industry around here is still agriculture."

"Everybody's hurting," Mary added as Jim eased the boat out into the channel. "I see all these young guys with a pick-up truck and a wheelbarrow in the back...everybody's being forced to look for other ways to make a living."

"See those?" Jim said as we passed a series of lush, reed-covered islands at the point where the channel joined the main river. "Those were once all under cultivation. Three feet of bulrushes and then you've got fantastic soil. Bill Rowe farmed them, used to load his machines on a barge and take them from island to island. Now the Natural Resources people own them, came in and bought eighty-five acres to protect the herons. Well, I'll say one thing, we got a hellova lot of herons now. There goes one now, looking for his dinner."

Great blue herons were everywhere, standing in the shallows of the islands, skimming the water with their ungainly, floppy flight, even perched on low branches that overhung the water. Various varieties of ducks and geese bobbed past the boat, barely deigning to get out of our path. "There's more loons lately, too, and the possum and beaver are coming back. I can't say why. Could be the milder climate."

Jim's approach to history was enthusiastic and idiosyncratic. "Before the dam went in the hardwood forest used to come right down to the water," he told us. "The sky would be dark with wood pigeons in their millions flocking in to shelter in the trees." He spoke so intently that you felt he was describing the scene from memory, though in actual fact the dam was built in 1828 and no living man has ever seen a wood pigeon. "One thing I like about local history, in Europe it goes back thousands of years, here only about three hundred. The first settler, his grandsons have been on this boat. You know the great Chicago fire? The lumber to rebuild it came from Port Maitland. Think of that."

Along the banks, mostly on the west side, we could see a scattering of older cottages and docks among the willows and reeds. "Now we're entering the river itself…twelve to fourteen feet of water here." A string of baby Canada geese trundled past. "The mother'll be nearby. These are wetlands, you can't build here any more. You can fix up the boathouses that are already there, but you can't put up a house or anything like that."

"The Grand is fast," Mary broke in. In her hand she clutched some carefully copied-out notes which she uses on tours and was eager to read to us. "Four of its seven Indian names mean 'fast current.' According to Galinée they called it *Tinaatoua,* 'those who live by the swift current.'"

"Look, see?" Jim pointed to the west bank toward an old boathouse on the roof of which was poised a thirty-foot cabin cruiser with what looked like a bikini-clad woman provocatively leaning over the rail. Upon closer inspection we could see she was actually a mannequin. "This guy wanted to live out here on the river so he got around the government regulations about no more cottages by buying that old boathouse and hoisting his yacht up on top of it, and that's where he lives." We all waited for someone else to comment on this, but no one could think of anything to say and soon the house was left behind.

Jim pointed out the site of a burying ground of the Neutral Indians, a nation wiped out by the Iroquois during the wars of expansion in the mid-seventeenth century. Then a moment later the RCAF turkey farm came into view. According to Jim a couple of Harvards had crashed in the marshes across from it. "They're still in there somewhere—no one ever bothered to go in after them." (Presumably the pilots had bailed out earlier.) "And right up that crick is where the first boat registered after Confederation was launched, called the *Maryanne.*"

Another short stretch of river brought us to an active boat yard and marina owned by one of the influential families of the area, the Powells. "They built landing craft there all through the Korean War, now they build ships." Two of the craft docked there caught Jim's attention. One was an ocean-going floating palace called the *Marine Shark,* which two days earlier he had towed in from the lake where it had gone dead in the water. They were taking the thing to Florida, that is once it got going again.

The other was the *NIMBY,* a pugnacious-looking yellow-and-black converted tugboat owned by a woman named

Patty Potter who uses her vessel to take people out on tours of the river, during which she not infrequently points out the local communities' environmental failings. It was clear that Jim had a small bone to pick with this radical environmentalist freethinking feminist stirrer-upper (our words, not his). "You know what NIMBY means, don't you?" he growled. "Not In My Back Yard." As far as we could make out, what most irritated Jim and the other town fathers—he turned out to be the deputy mayor of Dunnville—was the fact that this ecology person was a Powell herself, something of a renegade who had joined the opposition. (Back home we checked with our younger daughter, a professional in the field, who informed us that Patty Potter was a hard-working hero of the cause.)

As the lake came into view the conversation turned to fish. "Bullshit!" Jim exclaimed when we mentioned that we'd heard that Port Dover, a short sail west, was until recently the centre of the world's largest freshwater fishery. "Thirty years ago Port Maitland right here was the biggest. All those boats at Dover used to be here. Then for some reason the damned fish decided to go to another part of the lake. First the whitefish disappeared, then the perch. But they'll be back. Nature recycles in a great big circle."

He enumerated the features of Port Maitland, the best natural harbour on the whole northern shore of the lake, in Jim's opinion. He loved it. Everywhere he turned he had something else to point out.

"This used to be a big rum-running port, during Prohibition. The bottom is still littered with bottles. Divers bring them up all the time, unopened, good as new. Better than new because whisky was made better back then. Not that I've tasted it. I don't drink myself.

"Over there, on the east side. That was once where the largest naval base in North America was, from the seventeenth century right up to the War of 1812. Down there, that's the old feeder canal—that used to be wall-to-wall fishing tubs...that old green building was a four-storey hotel…an old upright steam tug went down in the water over there…that was before my time, that's ancient. Those docks, there used to be a ferry from Port Maitland to Ashtabula that brought coal on railway cars.

"That old plant," he pointed to the derelict factory we had driven around the day before, "that's IMC, that was IMC, I mean. International Mineral and Chemical. That was the industrial area. They're dismantling the whole thing."

"That's one bunch of people who've got work," Mary said. "Environment inspectors. They're watching the place like hawks." RAILWAY CAR "GRAND · RAPIDS"

Two large ~~auto~~ ferries stood rusting at the canal that led to what had once been the IMC docks. Welders were taking them apart for salvage. "They brought them down here three years ago from the Makinac Straits, they were car ferries up there for, I don't know, probably since before the war 1926. They'll have that one apart in a week, then it'll be melted down."

"I've been on that boat," Julie realized suddenly. "We took it across to the Upper Peninsula when I was twelve or thirteen. I remember the crowds pouring off it."

Jim pointed us toward the lake, heading into the channel that ran alongside the lighthouse pier. Yesterday as we had walked out we had seen boats rocking back and forth wildly; today the water was a flat, glassy plane.

"You never know," he said, when we mentioned the change. "Even up the river we're governed by Lake Erie. It can be down a foot at Dunnville from nothing more than the wind. And the lake, I've seen her go from calm like this to ten-foot waves in seven minutes. You see this pier we're going by? Looks like a walk in the park, right? But when the wind gets started it sends waves right over the thing. Back when the lighthouse was manned they had a twelve-foot-high catwalk on the pier so on bad days they could get out there without being swept right off the parapet."

"Is that right?" one of us muttered, remembering the previous day, while the other looked at him pointedly.

Jim didn't notice our reaction; he was too busy talking.

"Oh, yeah. You know those heavy winds we've been having? Right over there—" He indicated a point of land a short distance down the shore to the east. "Last week a fifteen-year-old kid got swept out. Coast Guard was busy so they sent me to fish out the body."

A few moments later we were on Lake Erie itself for the first time. In front of us the lake looked absolutely empty, but Jim called that an illusion. "The lake's full of stuff—freighters, pleasure boats, sport fishermen, Coast Guard, supply boats going out to the gas rigs. And the whole bottom around this part is a spiderweb of natural gas wells and pipes. The freighters have to be careful where they drop anchor."

"Don't forget those darned cigarette boats," Mary added. "You get them coming over from Dunkirk. It's only twenty-eight miles across the lake. They can make it in a half hour—less, sometimes, in one of those things. It's always these sleazy-looking guys with hair all over the place and always with their playgirls."

"Yeah, sometimes they come upriver to our docks and go get a sandwich," Jim nodded. "They always ask me if they can tie up outside of us, they don't want anybody looking into their boats. I saw an Uzi sticking out under the seat of one of them. They're beautiful machines, though, those boats.

"I don't worry about them, I've got enough other things to do. I'm like a volunteer fireman, the Coast Guard calls me for emergencies, like when a sudden storm comes up and some boat can't get back to harbour. And the OPP works with me. All I get is money for gas. The divers volunteer, too. Me and my son-in-law, we love it. Rough water don't bother us. Sometimes we're fourteen miles out at night, it's pouring rain, wind blowing. But we've got these powerful lights and we've got a boat radio, $140 and you can talk to anywhere in the world. Some of those goddam people spend $30,000 for a boat and then they won't put a $140 radio in."

"My job is I get to stay home and worry," put in Mary. "It's always at night. I'd really like him to quit."

"Well, I don't always go. That drug bust, I didn't go. I say let the American boys handle that stuff. Their Coast Guard's got all those toys left over from Vietnam. One time in '91 I accidentally crossed the line—the whole lake is under radar surveillance out of Cleveland—this big cutter comes charging over the horizon. There's a fifty-calibre machine gun on deck pointing at me, two other guys with automatic rifles, a couple minutes later two choppers come by. They looked me over, and finally the guy says 'How you doin'?' and they take off again." He laughed. "The Canadian Coast Guard don't even carry a twenty-two.

"The things people do, it's funnier than the devil sometimes. Mrs. Smith phones me, says her husband's five hours late, out on the water; then Mr. Smith shows up and she starts screaming at him like a son of a bitch, so he says, 'But I got these two little fishes.'" Jim mimicked the man's actions, then laughed.

"I could tell you some horror stories. One guy'd never been in a power boat before. He decides he wants to buy one, so he takes his family out for a test spin. They get trapped on Tecumseh Reef, about a mile and a quarter out. It's so shallow he can get out and stand in the water, it only comes up to his knees. So he tells his wife to walk in to get help while he stays with the kids. Only he doesn't realize you could sail the Queen Mary between where he is and the shore and ten seconds later his wife's swimming for her life."

He shook his head at the general foolhardiness of humanity. "Those people were lucky. A lot of them aren't. I only carry one implement with me." He gestured toward an oblong wire basket, five or six feet in length, hung from the roof of the cabin. "For fishing out floaters."

"Doesn't that bother you?"

"It would bother me," said Mary.

"No, I don't mind. Dead people can't hurt you. A live person might stick a knife in your back."

When we got back to Dunnville we handed him twenty-five dollars for the gas. "I ought to get a free copy of this book, too," he added. And so he will.

Chapter Seven

Every few years, whole portions of Ontario's political geography get restructured and renamed for reasons never made entirely clear to the people who live within their jurisdictional boundaries. The populations of Port Dover, Jarvis, Selkirk and four other small municipalities west of Port Maitland, some as much as twenty-five kilometres apart, woke one day in 1974 to find they had mutated into something referred to on official stationery as "The City of Nanticoke." (This mystical metropolis has more in common with the Kingdom of Prester John or the Lost Continent of Mu than it does with other Ontario towns, since it consists of 653 square kilometres of which over 90 percent is farmland, and if you asked directions to downtown Nanticoke, no one would know where to send you.) If that weren't enough, in another provincially decreed reorganization, the county of Norfolk, of which those towns had always been a part, became reincarnated as the Regional Municipality of Haldimand-Norfolk.

H-N, if we may call it that, has always been an odd sort of place. First, there's the climate. Like any large body of water, Lake Erie stores up heat in the summer and releases it in the winter, but Erie's unique combination of size and shallowness has a particularly pronounced effect; portions of the lakeshore are similar botanically to the coastal plain of North Carolina.

Even on a casual drive along Highway 3 you start to notice that something is different about the landscape: southern-looking vines wrap themselves around tree trunks; the smell of tobacco being cured in kilns, which appear like rows of tall motel units at regular intervals, permeates the atmosphere; even the air is somehow balmier. Perhaps most amazing for a Canadian lake, you can actually take a dip without turning blue in thirty seconds.

The grounds of Backus Woods, located just north of Port Rowan, are full of Carolinian trees like sweet chestnut, tulip, sassafras, butternut, black walnut, southern oak, dogwood, black cherry and witch hazel. Warm-weather ferns, flowers and herbs like tick-trefoil, reddish water horehound and pinweed abound. Canadian birders stalk the conservation area's trails seeking to add to their life lists such unlikely visitors from Dixie as orchard orioles, Louisiana waterthrushes and Acadian flycatchers.

Then there's Long Point, the peninsula that forms H-N's western boundary. At over thirty kilometres in length it forms the longest freshwater sand spit in the world, and the marshes of Long Point make up one of the continent's major wetlands, second in importance only to Chesapeake Bay. Like all wetlands, it plays a crucial role in the planet's health by serving as a giant incubator for thousands of plant and animal species—fish, birds, amphibians, reptiles, insects, small mammals, water plants, marsh grasses and many more. All in all, nature has dug deep into its bag of tricks in Haldimand-Norfolk.

Perhaps it's not coincidental that a wide range of human idiosyncrasy has taken root alongside the natural curiosities. The very first prominent white settler was a celebrated eccentric named Dr. John Troyer who wandered up this way from Pennsylvania in the late 1780s. A member of the mystical Brethren of Christ, Troyer was at once a highly reputable agricultural pioneer, boat builder and herbalist and a man hopelessly susceptible to every superstition and rumour that came down the pike. Mortally afraid of witches, Dr. John took the precaution of bolting a large bear-trap to the floor at the foot of his bed just in case one of the ladies in pointed hats made it through the locked door while he was snoozing under his eiderdown. All to no avail, as he dejectedly explained to the neighbours. They always got in anyway, transformed him into a horse and rode him across the frozen surface of Lake Erie to wild cross-cultural parties in Dunkirk. The final indignity was that once there he was tied to a post and not allowed to participate.

Troyer's life was made more miserable by a fun-loving local widow named Mrs. McMichael, who amused herself by sneaking up behind the good doctor when he ventured into the forest to collect medicinal herbs, then scaring the poor man witless by leaping out from behind a tree pretending to be a witch. She would then run home laughing her head off. Whether she took up this form of recreation before or after Dr. Troyer had identified her as one of the sinful sisterhood is unclear in the folk histories.

Indians were among his other terrors. He would travel miles out of his way to avoid coming in contact with the people he regarded as treacherous red-skinned devils. The fact that no record of native comment exists on the antics of this important figure in the history of the white race in Norfolk County is not only a pity for historians but also a great loss for Canadian comedy. On the other hand, young children on the Six Nations Reserve may even today laugh themselves to sleep with stories of Dr. Troyer, Mrs. McMichael and the witches of Dunkirk, and be just too polite to let the rest of us in on the joke.

During Dr. Troyer's heyday the entire lake was ringed with thick Carolinian vegetation; today the American side, with the exception of a few small state parks, has been drained, fenced, paved, lawned over or ploughed under. And in most of Ontario's lake counties the forests have been almost completely mowed down to ground level by lumber and farm interests. But H-N, as always the odd place out, took another route.

Back in 1970, when this was still plain old Norfolk County, someone convinced the county commissioners to put in a stumpage bylaw forbidding the cutting of any tree under sixteen inches in diameter, a figure later raised to twenty for most trees and even more for certain species. Since like much of Canada this area had remained thinly populated and underdeveloped, a considerable amount of woodlot acreage existed even that far into the twentieth century.

The new regulations not only stopped the timber industry dead in its tracks and resulted in the greening of Norfolk but also changed the way the residents thought about their trees. In the last twenty-five years they have come to take seriously the local oaks and maples and the rest of their leafy brethren around here, seeing them as something to be valued rather than a nuisance or potential raw material to be sold to the highest bidder; not infrequently farmers and other landowners assign woodlots or marshy sections of land to the province in their wills.

Old-timers who could be spending their idle hours on the front porch reliving the good old days or complaining to each other about the government (all levels, any government will do) instead worry over the state of the local forests, sometimes even individual trees. For example, there is a magnificent mature black gum in Backus Woods, which one elderly gentleman proudly described for us as if he had personally raised it from a gumdrop; he seemed positively gleeful in letting us know that another big black gum tree in Chatham, farther down the lake, was in nowhere near as good condition, in fact had just taken a turn for the worse.

Around Long Point Bay, patches of dense forest reach to the very edge of the low cliffs above the water. Every so often narrow roads angle steeply down through the greenery to come out at tiny outports with names like Port Ryerse, Normandale and Turkey Point, most of whose houses are plastered against the foot of the bluffs. These places were made for day-dreaming; it takes no effort at all to close your eyes and imagine a pirate ship slipping at night into one of the quiet coves, resting at anchor while the dastardly crew plot their next day's plundering.

We drove down the deeply shaded road through "uptown" Port Ryerse, then had to shield our eyes from the bright reflection of the lake as we burst out onto the waterfront. When our eyes adjusted we found a row of houses running perhaps five hundred yards along the base of the cliff. Just offshore, on a metal footbridge that looked as if it had been improvised by a couple of handy cottage-owners and that connected two portions of a long breakwater, a single fisherman stood casting out into the lake. He nodded silently as we walked by, and the three of us stood looking out to where the water separated into contrasting bands of greenish brown, aqua, dark turquoise, back to aqua again, then farther out toward the horizon an inky blue.

A friend had offered us the use of his summer house, a converted 1870 Methodist church in Normandale, the next settlement down the coast. "I'm not sure what our population is," the woman behind the counter of the general store told us, "but I know we're a hamlet. That means you have to have a store and a gas station. Actually we lost our gas station a while ago but never mind. It's important to stay a hamlet, otherwise you're nothing, and you lose your identity as a separate place." She sounded as if she never wanted to hear another word on the subject of arcane bureaucratic nomenclature, and we didn't blame her.

The little cove at the foot of the hill had a particularly hidden look, almost Caribbean in feel, and despite the fact that the lake is fresh water the air seemed to have a salty tang to it. Maybe it was seaweed, or even just the smog from the factories to the west. Whatever it was, it smelled good. If Winslow Homer or J. J. Morrice had set their easels down here amid the sand cliffs, turquoise water, lush vegetation, small wooden houses and curving bay surrounding an empty beach, the results wouldn't have looked much different from their watercolours of the Bahamas. All that was missing were palm trees in the foreground.

Our friend Carlos is an architect, so he had of course been unable to resist turning the interior of the old church into a showplace of contemporary design: white walls everywhere, sleeping loft for the kids, ultra-modern kitchen, tastefully appointed sitting rooms on the ground floor, comfortable bedrooms and study downstairs, all of it cleverly fitted into a minimum of space. This international-style sophistication in a place where the rafters used to ring with choruses of "Sweet Hour of Prayer" and "Shall We Gather at the River" was slightly disorienting, but a memorial plate hanging near the kitchen provided a reminder of the old days. A few years ago a former member of the congregation had knocked on the door and when Carlos opened it had thrust the plate into his hand, shamefacedly confessing that she had stolen it as a souvenir when the church closed in 1947, but that after a long struggle her conscience had forced her to bring it back home.

Though this is definitely Christian country, full of Baptist Bible study centres, Christian conference centres and assorted other denominational retreats, in H-N you don't find many examples of the bumper-sticker fire and brimstone of western New York. A lot of Mennonites settled along the lake early on, as did a smaller number of Quakers, and their tranquil spiritual tenacity still makes itself felt. "Apples 4 Sale / Not on Sunday" read one hand-painted sign along the road. Even Christ Centred Camping, which sounded as if it might be aggressively evangelical, turned out to be a campground like any other, with the one distinction that it offered a Fellowship Hall where you could repair for prayer meetings and witnessing after you'd finished your day of mini-golf, tennis and swimming.

One evening we set out for an everybody-welcome corn roast on the lawn of a Port Ryerse Methodist church that we had passed earlier in the day. Maybe there would even be a gospel sing after supper. "Lord, I want to be a Christian in-a my heart, in-a my heart, in-a my heart, Lord, I want to be a Christian in-a my heart," reverberated through the Mazda as we approached the village. But we had misread the sign. This was "Memorial Church" not "Methodist Church," and these neatly attired families, all with upright posture and uniformly pleasant smiles, conversing in subdued tones, were Anglicans; there would be no gospel shouting tonight. But what the hell, we were there, we were starving, and six dollars bought you all the corn, burgers and salad you could eat.

So we passed a slow-moving evening stuffing ourselves with slightly rubbery hamburgers and corn on the cob while listening to polite parishioners ask each other how it was going. The conversations ambled along on a even keel, never quite rising to animation or sinking too far into somnolence, the collective gentility so universal you couldn't make out which one among the middle-aged men and women in well-ironed short-sleeved shirts and knee-length shorts might have been the vicar.

At the table next to us a sweet-faced dowager sat with a teenaged girl whom she introduced to a procession of well-wishers, endlessly, unchangingly, with the words, "And this is my grandson Scott's girlfriend, Tracy." Each newcomer would then say "How are you, Tracy?" and Tracy would reply, "I'm fine, thank you."

At another table sat a heavy-set, wild-haired biker couple rigged out in greasy leathers who, like us, had noticed the sign and figured out that six bucks apiece would entitle them to stuff their faces all night. They were forking it down as if tonight's meal would be their last until Christmas. They ate and ate and ate and ate and ate, all the while keeping up a friendly banter with the unflappable parishioners, and were just beginning to assault a table of homemade pies that provided the best part of the menu when we got up to take a quick look around the grounds.

Inside the nineteenth-century sanctuary, hymn number 265 ("Guide Me O Thou Great Jehovah") was posted for next Sunday's service, and a notice tacked up in the entryway announced plans for the town's approaching bicentennial. Outside, in a shady corner of the churchyard, the worn headstones in a small, crumbling graveyard marked the remains of early settlers like Abraham Sells (who "landed and was buried at Port Ryerse in 1798") and Samuel Ryerse ("United Empire Loyalist, 1752–1812"). One tablet was dedicated to the memory of "Three unknown British soldiers who died at Fort Norfolk, Turkey Point 1812, Buried near this Spot."

A cairn-like memorial in one quiet corner extolled the pioneers who first "braved the loneliness of the unknown wilderness of Upper Canada…[who] cleared the forest, blazed the roads, bridged the fords, drained the swamps, and introduced British institutions, laws and ordered liberty…[and] who sacrificed and endured that their inheritors might enjoy in peace and comfort the fruits of their toil." Judging by the verbs, these men and women were considerably more active than their descendants, but they would probably be gratified at the degree of peace and comfort that Tracy and Scott's grandmother and the other inhabitants of their rude outpost were enjoying on this convivial evening.

The picturesque town of Port Dover (pop. 2,600) is the focus of social and economic life along this part of the coast. Both a summer resort and a busy port, Port Dover is as softly pretty a place as anyone could ask for. Down at the harbour, where Black Creek flows into the lake, an old-fashioned waterfront with several fast-fish eateries, a waterfront hotel, a small park and a generally mellow atmosphere has evolved. Most important, there is also a fine sandy beach where the swimming is safe. Nursing a beer on one of the restaurant patios as the sailboats drift in, the sun sets over the lighthouse and swimmers and sunbathers brush the sand off their legs and turn toward home is not a bad way to spend an hour or two.

Main Street, a few blocks back from the shoreline, offers a park with a band shell, more nautical bars and restaurants, a few souvenir and local artist galleries and all the reassuring hardware and drug stores and farm insurance offices you'd expect to find in a busy small town; beyond these lie streets of imposing Victorian brick houses. There's a theatre, a summer arts festival and probably even a flower show if you happen to be there on the right spring weekend.

⌐ Port Dover has lots of recorded history, too, at least by Canadian standards. Back in the fall of 1669 Fathers Galinée and Dollier, the first Frenchmen to set eyes on this part of Lac du Chat, turned into Black Creek seeking a sheltered place to ride out the approaching winter storms. (After a dispute with La Salle, who wanted to explore further south, the Sulpician missionaries had switched their allegiance to the more northerly inclined Jolliet; the three made plans to meet the following spring at a landmark they'd all vaguely heard about somewhere on the lake. Miraculously they actually did bump into each other at the portage at the foot of Long Point.)

Disembarking in a jewel-like little glen overflowing with fruit and nut trees (an acre or so of which is preserved as a small park), the two young clerics were overcome with the largesse of *Le Bon Dieu* and pronounced the spot:

> **The earthly paradise of Canada...no more beautiful region exists in all Canada. The woods are open, with beautiful meadows crossed by rivers filled with fish and beaver.... At one glance we saw there more than one hundred roebucks in a single herd...and bears fatter and more flavourful than the most savoury pigs of France.**

At the moment, life in paradise is slightly tarnished, at least for the average Port Dover working stiff. After years of prosperity as the home port of the world's largest freshwater fishery, today the area's fishermen can only watch helplessly as their nets pull up only a fraction of the numbers their fathers and grandfathers hauled in.

Partly the decline is a lakewide phenomenon, and—as with fisheries around the world—the reasons are both complex and only partially understood. Some involve natural cycles of expansion and decline within a species, as well as fluctuations in climate, but man, as usual, has elbowed his way to the front of the line.

Over-fishing accounts for the disappearance of certain species, particularly herring and sturgeon, while draining and dam building along inflowing rivers have destroyed the spawning grounds of the once abundant northern pike. Erie's prized lake trout went the way of all fish courtesy of a different kind of man-made ecological catastrophe, annihilated by the dreaded sea lamprey, which was introduced into the lake by way of the Welland Canal.

Zebra mussels also hitchhiked their way into the system, while other foreign species like smelt and carp were purposely put in the water by misguided experimenters; all have ended up disturbing the ecological balance in unforeseen ways. So have technological "improvements" such as nylon netting which, while making life easier for the fishermen, wreaked havoc among the fish stocks. (In the old days when a cotton net slipped off its tether it quickly disintegrated, but once one of the modern nylon catch-alls is lost it drifts around the lake for eternity. Indiscriminately snagging anything that happens to swim by, the free-floating net will eventually sink to the bottom under the weight of its random catch, only to rise again once the entangled fish have rotted away.) And last, but unfortunately not least among the ills imposed by our species, is the century and a half of human waste and industrial and agricultural chemicals that have poured, and continue to pour, into the lake's waters.

That's the bad news. But despite all we've done to the lake, even today Erie's shallow waters continue to serve as an enormous fish nursery and the fishery remains a crucial part of the lake's economy. Yellow perch stocks are still viable and with the implementation of conservation programs and pollution controls trout and salmon are showing occasional signs of a comeback. And certain new species (notably the long, sleek, good-eating fish known as walleye south of the border and pickerel in Canada) have begun to flourish.

So you might expect the Port Dover fishery to have at worst

gradually declined; instead, however, it collapsed in a heap. Informed opinion has fixed the blame on none of the factors mentioned above, but rather on the inexplicable but well-documented tendency of scaly creatures to simply take off for bluer pastures whenever the mood strikes them, in this case to the western end of the lake. (Though the real reason for the migration may eventually turn out to be less a madcap whim on the part of the fish than a perfectly logical flight from some as yet unrecognized pollutant or other adverse condition created by humans.) Now if someone could only figure out a way to entice them back east.

The recession of the past few years has taken its toll on other local industries, among them the nation's largest rose nursery. This vast city of roses spread out along one bank of Black Creek abruptly shut up shop earlier in the year. Inside the ranks of deserted greenhouses the plants were left to die on their own, but as we drove through we saw that many of the flowers had bloomed anyway. They stood in neat rows, held upright by their supporting bars, their flaming scarlet petals contrasting poignantly with crumbling brown stalks and leaves below them. It was like visiting a mass grave covered with flowers, except that this time the blossoms themselves were the deceased.

Hard times had not prevented a full-blown municipal blood-letting, as usual over the viability of an old public building, from erupting in Port Dover. This particular debate had the unexpected feature of being after the fact, since the costly and controversial addition to the town museum had already been completed. The situation was as usual complicated beyond any rational comprehension. It seemed to pit several members of the town's founding families, the original sponsors of the addition, against a newer crowd (defined as anyone whose family had been in the area less than a century) who perceived a series of misdeeds ranging from disregard of building codes, failure to provide parking facilities, presenting false documents to government boards and improper tendering of contracts to more generalized complaints of nepotism, cronyism and poor design. (A modest example was their claim that though the architect had included the provincially required washroom space for people in wheelchairs, he hadn't built in enough room for them to turn around, so that once inside they would have to call for help.) The authorities apparently agreed with much of the criticism; a report from the City of Nanticoke cited numerous building and zoning violations and refused permission for the renovated section to open.

A notice in the local newspaper alerted us to the fact that the old guard did not intend to take this assault on its dignity lying down; they would be holding a mass demonstration at the museum at six-thirty this evening. We arrived early to get a better idea of what the fuss was about and noticed immediately that the museum was located smack in the middle of a modest industrial area. The entrance was only a few feet from a marine repair yard where, even as the crowd gathered, welders' torches were spraying the air with sparks. In addition, the only public parking was on the street between heavy commercial vehicles. These deficiencies had, we recalled, been prominent on the opponents' list of complaints.

The rally was just getting underway. A bearded patriarch by the name of Harry Barrett informally welcomed the crowd, then there was a heavy pause. Clearly none of the perhaps one hundred and fifty neatly dressed, respectable-looking men and women milling around the narrow sidewalk had ever as much as seen a demonstration before, except (perhaps) on television, and no one among them appeared to have any idea what was expected. One zealot was attempting to get up a chant using the slogan printed on a bunch of identical placards, but trying to shout "Resolve the parking issue and protect our heritage!" three times in succession would defeat the most trippingly tongued demonstrator, and he soon subsided. If the Buffalo kindergarten aides' demonstration had been feeble, this one was unconscious.

Behind us a woman's voice observed, "I see the Anglicans are here *en masse.*" We could see what she meant; the gathering felt like a continuation of the corn roast at Memorial Church. But was her comment a pun? We turned toward the speaker, an ordinary-looking woman in her forties wearing a wine-coloured tank-top and green shorts.

"How do you know?"

She wasn't fazed by questions from a stranger. "You can always tell Anglicans," she came back acidly. "They always come early and grab off the back seats." And with that this small-town Dorothy Parker turned grumpily and walked off past the fish factory. We longed to ask her for more commentary on local religious practices, or indeed anything else in Haldimand-Norfolk, but we never saw her again.

Finally another cheerleader in the crowd tried to get something going—"Open our museum (pause) NOW!" he yelled, and again "Open our museum—NOW!"—but it didn't really take off, perhaps because no one knew who they were addressing, and shouting at your next-door neighbour didn't seem polite.

Eventually a few Chamber of Commerce types from nearby hamlets, who had been standing in a slightly forlorn clump to one side, were introduced and given a minute or so to express their thoughts. Each was all for the museum in the same sense they were for Motherhood, God, tourism and the status quo, but they weren't about to commit themselves to anything specific. "Is that it?" someone in the crowd asked after the last one had trailed off into silence. After a few minutes more milling it became obvious the answer could only be yes, so everyone drifted off home looking slightly miffed.

The next day we returned to Port Dover for Biker Day. The summer heat was continuing; the sky was blue and cloudless. It was a great time for a fiesta, and a tingle of anticipation could be sensed all over town. According to a woman behind the counter at the Sub-Conscious sandwich shop, this Gathering of the Bikers is traditionally celebrated on the first Friday the thirteenth of the summer. (That's the official line, anyway. The first Friday the twelfth or Friday the fourteenth or Thursday the thirteenth doesn't have quite the same ring to it, and no one seemed willing to admit that the event, of necessity, fell on one of those days at least half the time.)

The origins of Biker Day (actually Biker Weekend) are lost in the mists of local legend. It may have begun as an unusually imaginative, or some might say foolhardy, promotion dreamt up by the tourist board in their desperate quest for anything that might bring in a few more dollars, or, more likely, the board jumped on the bandwagon after the pattern was already set. In any case, after several unremarkable reunions the idea suddenly took off. In 1992 more than three thousand bikers showed up and this time around at least double that number were expected. One of the organizers had been quoted in the paper predicting that at least $250,000 would flow into the town's depleted coffers, basing his figure on the assumption that each biker would spend at least $50 on food and drinks.

You could almost hear Marlon Brando or Sonny Barger licking their lips as they muttered incredulously, "You mean they *want* us?" Even more amazing, no one in the town appeared nervous, in spite of the fact that by evening the ratio of bikers to citizens was anticipated to be around three to one. Instead of locking their daughters and themselves in the cellar until the blow-out had passed, Port Dover's merchants had placed "Welcome Bikers" signs in windows up and down Main Street. Even boutiques specializing in nineteenth-century chintzerie and Irish lace doilies were extending an optimistic hello.

By late afternoon the centre of town was under occupation. A couple of thousand riders had already arrived and every moment brought more of them roaring into town from the harbour road, the bikes throttling down with great bursts of *VROOOM* as they reached the heights of Main Street. Some arrived in solitary splendour on their hawgs, others came in pairs (including our well-fed companions from the church supper), still others in clots of ten or twelve. And occasionally whole clubs thundered in, wearing insignia from places all across central Canada and the surrounding American states.

As each biker arrived he (and occasionally she) took a ritual lap the length of the business district, crying out greetings to friends over the heavy metal chords blasting out of the bars, revving loudly at every opportunity before circling back and parking at an angle wherever space was available. They lounged near their bikes for a while, taking in the scene and checking out new arrivals, before joining the crowd surging up and down the sidewalks.

Almost all wore black Harley Davidson regalia in an endless variety of designs; many sported full leathers despite the humid heat, and they all preened endlessly. The ever-growing mass clogged the sidewalks, filled the doorways and store-fronts, took up every bench and stairwell, revolved in and out of the bars with new supplies of beer—a swirling Mardi Gras parade of tattoos and toothlessness, flowing locks and bald skulls, heavy silver belts holding in monumental stomachs, polished riding boots, death's-head earrings, nails through earlobes and silver studs.

Casual conversation among the new arrivals ran along the lines of the crowd in Hooters Bar, only more so. "Fucking" this and "fucking" that and "fucking" everything else. "So I got off the fucking bike, walked up the fucking stairs, opened the fucking door…" one of them was telling two friends before he passed out of earshot and we lost our chance to learn what he had fucking done next. A number had brought their children—little tattooed, earringed replicas of them-selves—and were busily shooting the events on their cam-corders for viewing when they got back home.

Within the swarm of bikers we began to realize there were many who didn't quite fit the stereotype. "You don't mind if I sit down, do you? My back is absolutely killing me," a female biker asked Julie, who had found a bench in the shade in front of the hardware store. In her early forties, she looked nothing like the anorexic, black-clad fashion plates riding behind their leather-freak boyfriends. Instead of an H-D T-shirt and skin-tight jeans, she was dressed in baggy shorts and a halter top, and if anything she was slightly plump. "Oh, we've been coming for years," she said when Julie asked how she was enjoying the event. "This is our fifth Friday the thirteenth. It's a good chance to get away from work, you know what I mean? We run a motel over near Ajax."

She shifted, trying out various positions in an attempt to get comfortable. "This'll be the last year for me, my back can't take it any more." Julie told her about a moulded cushion that had done wonders for her back problems, and the two of them compared notes while the parade continued to flow by.

Motel operator was representative of the kind of job most of the bikers held down in civilian life. Few were true outlaw types: judging from snatches of conversation and various workplace identifications on their clothes or gear, they were garage mechanics, construction workers, truck drivers, messengers, rink attendants, electricians, even accountants and high school shop teachers. On the other hand, it was a safe guess that not too many carried library cards in their wallets or were entirely unfamiliar with the art of punching someone's face in.

All evening the hawgs thundered in, until by last light you could stand at the top of Main Street and look down two unbroken rows of Harleys that stretched out for blocks until the street dipped down to the harbour and disappeared, the setting sun glinting off their polished chrome and fancifully painted gas tanks covered with lunging tigers, striking snakes, *memento mori*, surrealist flames and the rest of the Modern Comix repertoire. All together some six or seven thousand bikers showed up and, incredibly, not a single fight and very few arrests were recorded.

For one of us, anyway, the point of the whole flashy Mad Max display lay in the spectacle; the amazing beauty of the rows of gleaming, perfectly tuned machines, set off by the black glamour of their riders. It was like turning a corner and suddenly finding yourself in the middle of a De Mille extravaganza, or watching the wildest dreams of a Vogue art director come to life. You wouldn't want to live there, but it sure is fun to visit.

The other looked at it differently, partly as a chance to observe a curious mix of people, partly as a happy reminder of the romance of the open road, but mostly as a revealing look at the outer reaches of male vanity. Though there was a sprinkling of carefully turned-out women among the crowd, this was a male happening, and the self-absorption in the air was almost palpable; any curious glance at any one biker from twenty feet away would cause an instantaneous radar-like swivel of his head for a quick survey of the number of people looking him over. The preening reflex was almost touching; it evoked in turn a slightly maternal and easily resisted impulse to go up to each one, pat him on the shoulder, and reassure him that he looked great (even when it would have meant shading the truth a bit).

Others in Port Dover had their own reactions. For the merchants, it was simply the chance of cash on the line. For ordinary townspeople and tourists, it must have been an exciting diversion, a dip of the toe into a more dangerous world without really risking anything. And for the bikers themselves it was a class reunion, an extended family get-together, a skull-and-crossbones version of the annual Sunday school picnic or homecoming weekend. Bikers as a class are notoriously given to lugubriousness. But they need a setting for their sentimentality, and in a textbook display of the principle of supply and demand, here was a pretty little town ready and willing to give the boys a home away from home to ride to every summer.

Chapter Eight

"Lakes have a general character, as I say, being pretty much water and land, and points and bays," a grizzled character in James Fenimore Cooper's novel *The Deerslayer* explains philosophically when his backwoods protégé rhapsodizes over his first ever view of a lake. Hurry Harry had it right. Anyone who has spent part of their childhood at a lakeside cottage has registered the repetition of water/land/point/bay/point/land/water and more of the same, without ever quite articulating it, and the entire eastern third of Erie's Canadian shoreline illustrates that pattern perfectly.

The scalloped coastline is given over to a long series of small peninsulas: first Windmill Point and Point Abino, near Fort Erie, followed by Morgan's Point, Mohawk Point, Evans Point, Grant Point, Featherstone Point, Hooper Point, Peacock Point and Turkey Point. Mohawk Point is typical—a single, narrow road lined with well-lived-in older cottages with an occasional A-frame or west-coast-style cedar construction asserting itself in between them, the ubiquitous kids on bikes, boat equipment lying around yards and not much else, a nice way to spend your summers.

And then, at the end of this stretch of the lakeshore, you come to the mother of all sand spits, the longest freshwater sand spit in the world, Long Point.

The coast of the Norfolk Sand Plain has for four thousand years been shaped and reshaped repeatedly by the fierce storms that sweep in from the west, picking up sediment from the soft cliffs, flinging it through the air and then, when the winds die down, depositing it wherever it happens to fall. In the process Long Point was gradually formed, growing longer and thinner with time, and occasionally even turning into an archipelago when the water levels rose high enough.

Until the last three centuries, except for a few days each fall when small bands of Neutral Indians would gather to catch and smoke enough tasty whitefish to last them through the winter, the seagulls had the sand spit to themselves. But ever since the spring of 1670, when Galinée and Dollier waited at the Long Point portage for that rascal Jolliet to show up, a procession of white *arrivistes*—other explorers, mariners, trappers, fishermen, pirates, hermits, poachers, lumberjacks, lighthouse-keepers, muskrat ranchers, brothel-keepers, millionaire sportsmen and, more recently, cottagers, birders, divers and environmentalists—have pitched their tents in the vicinity.

Abigail Becker, "The Angel of Long Point," was one of the settlers; she used to share a cabin with her trapper husband in the shelter of the dunes out near the end of the Point;

> Said Mother Becker
> "Children wake
> A ship's gone down!
> They're needing me.
> Your father's off on
>   shore; the lake
> Is just a raging sea."
>
> Amanda T. Jones,
> "The Ballad of Abigail Becker"
> (44 additional verses)

The poetry may not scan, but old Mother Becker (actually only twenty-three when the events that made her famous took place) deserves the tribute. When a violent storm back in December 1854 drove a schooner onto the outer bar a half mile from shore, Abigail spotted the eight survivors slowly freezing to death as they huddled in its rigging. She rushed down to the beach to build a signal fire to guide them, then fought her way through the ten-foot waves to help drag each of the exhausted seamen in turn to safety. Not bad for a woman who couldn't swim and was weighed down by her voluminous and ice-laden petticoats, and who, when she wasn't plucking stray mariners from the lake, also raised nineteen children and more or less supported her feckless husband.

A dinner was given in Abigail's honour in Buffalo at which she was presented with a purse of five hundred dollars subscribed to by sailors all around the lake. When Queen Victoria also recognized her heroism with a congratulatory letter and a cheque for fifty pounds, the young woman used the money to buy a farm on the mainland, where she lived out the rest of her days. (The main-floor "Herstory" section of the local history museum in Simcoe, a few miles north of Port Dover, features an Abigail Becker display.)

Some years later, during another wild December storm, the point's lighthouse-keeper rushed out to help guide in a lifeboat full of sailors who had managed to get off their shattered ship, only to stare in horror as the boat lurched into shore with nine men frozen solid in their positions at the oars. (This lighthouse eventually disappeared beneath the waves as, over the last century and a half, the tip of Long Point shifted a full two miles eastward. It has been replaced by Transport Canada's efficient automated beacon.)

For the first half of the nineteenth century, life along the protected inner bay of which Long Point makes up the western side had more in common with Port Said than it did with the rest of rural Ontario. Taverns catering to drunken sailors, brothels with women brought in from Buffalo, safe houses for thugs on the run sprang up in profusion. Poachers shot at everything that moved. Wreckers hung false lights to lure ships onto the reefs, then attacked the surviving seamen and looted their ships, right down to the planking. Dissoluteness and violence prevailed up and down the bay; no wonder Abigail Becker got out as soon as the opportunity arose.

Criminals aside, lumbermen, farmers, market hunters, ship-builders and other entrepreneurs had plans for this bit of prime real estate; there seemed no doubt that, one way or another, its pristine wetlands would eventually be drained to make room for commercial development, as was happening in many other areas on the lake. But strangely enough it was the capitalist cavalry themselves who rode to the rescue, in a rare instance of American appropriation of another country's resources turning out to be entirely beneficial. In 1866 a consortium of twelve American millionaires known as the Long Point Company bought out most of the Point to serve as its private hunting preserve. The thugs were sent packing, as were the lumbermen who wanted to clear-cut the area, the farmers who intended to plant there and the rest. After erecting a group of cabins on one isolated peninsula, the newly organized company closed off everything else and, in a brilliant tactical move, hired, at high wages, one of the most notorious local poachers to make sure their property remained exclusive. Even more wisely, they restricted their own presence to two weeks of waterfowl hunting in the autumn.

As a result, on most of Long Point time was stopped pretty much in its tracks a hundred and thirty years ago. In 1980 the company donated nearly six thousand acres, an area in excess of half its holdings, to the Canadian government, but the heirs of the original buyers still own a large section and continue to make use of their hunting privileges.

Unfortunately, the company didn't bother to buy up the neck area where Long Point connects with the mainland. In the twenties, a man named H. H. Hastings acquired those acres and invested his life savings in an enormous muskrat farm. "Hasty" would have been a more appropriate name, as the project collapsed almost immediately, leaving as its main legacy a large population of escaped muskrats. After World War Two a disastrous decision by the provincial government permitted development of an overcrowded summer cottage community on the grounds of the former muskrat plantation, permanently destroying the natural character of that part of the spit.

Recently, Long Point was designated a World Biosphere Reserve by UNESCO, which means that most of it is permanently closed off to the public. Only a few select people are allowed to tread the storied sands, a list that for some reason omits freelance writers. We probably would have been given permission to take a look had we been willing to spend enough time making our case to the various bureaucracies involved, but our preference was to find someone with a boat who might be willing to take us out there with a minimum of formal fuss.

We thought we'd try Dave Stone first. So we headed inland past Port Rowan toward Backus Woods (officially the Backus Heritage Conservation Area) which, in addition to its miles of sylvan hiking trails and riverside campgrounds, contains a pioneer village. Stone, we knew, was in the process of setting up a maritime exhibit in one of the buildings. Having heard stories of this daredevil diver who had explored much of the eastern end of the lake floor, we were expecting a combination of Captain Nemo and an Olympic gold medalist in swimming—a swarthy buccaneer with a grappling hook in his belt and a gold earring.

The slight, weather-beaten, freckled seventy-year-old we met pottering around in his display room looked more like a diving Fred Astaire; he managed to appear remarkably dapper even in an old pair of shorts, T-shirt and sockless sneakers. But his absent-minded professor appearance obviously belied a powerful constitution; only a few days earlier he had been down examining a new find ninety feet below the surface.

During World War Two young Seaman Stone had taken part in the longest chase of a hostile submarine in Canadian naval history. Maybe his role in adding U-774 to the countless others resting on the ocean bottom triggered a compensatory response, because after the war ended and he came sailing home again to Ontario he made his life's work the tracing of shipwrecks in eastern Lake Erie. By now he has fish-tailed his way across the rotting decks and through the holds of hundreds of sunken brigs, barques, schooners, freighters, tugs and barges.

In Erie's Bermuda Triangle whose three points are Port Burwell, Ontario, Conneaut, Ohio, and the eastern terminus of the lake, Dave has personally documented no fewer than 461 wrecks. Some lie in water so shallow you can descend to them merely by holding your breath, while others have fallen off the underwater cliff just south of Long Point and come to rest two hundred feet down in the deepest part of the lake.

Dave sees no mystery about why so many have gone down in this area. Even aside from the sudden tempests, the unexpected sand-bars and the lack of safe harbours on the Canadian side, "There were always captains who would try to get one extra trip in before the season was over, or save money by cutting a crew of five down to three. That's okay on a nice day but in a storm it's another story."

Off Long Point Dave has located disasters dating back to the schooner *Annette*, wrecked just west of the tip in 1799. One hundred and forty-five years later, the freighter *James Reed* was lost on the same reef; during the intervening period the schooners *Asia* (1878), *Francis Palms* (1874), *Young Farmer* (1827) and *Return* (1863), as well as the brig *Virginia* (1853) and the barge *Alzora* (1895), also went down in that vicinity.

That's nothing compared to a stretch a couple of miles square off the isthmus where Long Point begins; according to his definitive map, which he has entitled "The Ghost Fleet of Long Point," twenty-three schooners, a barge and an airplane all took the final plunge there.

These days everyone is talking about the *Atlantic*, a large paddle-wheeler that cruised the lake between Buffalo and Detroit. One night in August 1852, the *Atlantic* collided with another ship a short distance east of where the *Annette* had foundered and sank on the spot, carrying, among others, two hundred and fifty Norwegian immigrants to their deaths. (The lake was calm, and according to all accounts the travellers could have been saved if they hadn't panicked, a not uncommon occurrence. Two years earlier the popular cruise steamer *G. P. Griffiths* had caught fire virtually within wading distance of a Cleveland suburb, but instead of following the captain's instructions the confused passengers, many of whom did not speak English, lost their heads and threw themselves into the water. One hundred and fifty-four bodies, most unidentified, were buried in a mass grave on the shore after they had washed up. Many others were never found.)

When local divers pin-pointed the *Atlantic's* position some time ago they kept the location secret to prevent American teams with expensive equipment from rushing in and stripping it. (Besides many important historical objects, the *Atlantic's* safe was known to have contained a quarter of a million dollars.) But recently professional salvagers from Cleveland managed to locate the wreck, at which point the Canadian government stepped in to confiscate the remains under the provisions of the Heritage Act. A deluge of lawsuits has been clogging the courts ever since, thus carrying the standard local heritage fight into new areas. Some of the *Atlantic's* gear, including a life-preserver in excellent condition, has mysteriously found its way onto the walls of Dave Stone's display, but all he'd say about the controversy was "The Americans don't have a snowball's chance in hell of getting that shipwreck."

Although a modest man, Dave would probably admit that his lifetime crusade has worked out pretty well; he really has single-handedly resurrected an otherwise forgotten aspect of maritime history. One thing bothers him, though: "The young divers today will never get to see what I saw. The zebra mussels cover everything, sometimes a foot thick. It's a pity."

Before leaving we looked in on Mary Baruth-Walsh, the feisty young curator of what is technically known as the

Heritage Conservation Area at Backus Woods. Mary gave us a run-down of the various official bodies she was required to satisfy in the process of directing the site's affairs, a list only slightly less complicated than the organizational chart of the Byzantine Empire. As far as we could make out, it included the Long Point Conservation Authority, of which both the pioneer village and the woods were small subdivisions, plus a dizzying string of boards and committees including the LACAC (Local Architectural Conservation Advisory Committee), the H-NCA (Haldimand-Norfolk Cultural Association) the LPFC (Long Point Foundation for Conservation), the BHVB (Backus Heritage Village Board) and the OMB (Ontario Municipal Board), among others, plus the political structure of the nearby town of Port Rowan.

Like any outsider, she has also run into her share of small-town gossip. "Sometimes you can't believe people don't have anything else to do," she remarked ruefully. "When I first took this job I thought I should live where I worked, you know, have a presence in the town, so I moved into Port Rowan. One day I hung some new rose-coloured curtains on my windows and the whole town was talking about it. Talking about my *curtains!* That was it for me. I moved." She now commutes from the anonymity of London, where no one comments on the colour of your windows.

"Port Rowan is pretty conservative, and there are people who find ways to object to everything we do. Even though we're all of three minutes away from town and they've never even been out here. But we're also very lucky. We get lots of volunteers for our events, and the mayor is really helpful. Also a lot of the older people around here have a real respect for their woods. I really like that."

No one at Backus Woods had paid any attention to our hints about finding a boat and getting out to see the Point; we were no better off in that respect than before. So, leaving Mary B. to her administrative struggles, we drove a couple of miles south to Port Rowan, a town of seven hundred that bills itself "The Gateway to Long Point and the Hub of the Bay."

While Normandale and Port Ryerse had obviously never grown beyond the hamlet category and might fairly be described as timelessly picturesque, Port Rowan had the look of a real town that had shrunk down to village size. Most of the wooden sheds that lined its wide public dock were boarded up, many stores on the main street had closed, and in the window of the local insurance agent a small hand-printed sign read "Golf balls sold here."

Mary had suggested that we get in touch with George Backus. We drove to his house and found a man in his late seventies cutting the grass in the front yard. George graciously turned off the mower, invited us in, introduced us to his wife Ethel, settled us down with a cup of tea and confirmed that he was indeed one of the Backuses of Backus Woods, the current head of the family that had sold the conservation area to the province. The Backuses (or Backhouses, as they were then known), had originally come from New York, where they had been associated in business with an American cousin we might have heard of—a chap named John Jacob Astor. Well, at least we knew where we all stood socially.

But you can hardly act the patrician in a place like Port Rowan. If you passed him in the street, you would take George for one more tall, lean, wiry old duck-hunter. But he knew his local history; in fact, once he got started, he bore a distinct relationship to Tonawanda's Mr. Dittmar. Although less insistent on his own priorities, like that gentleman he knew everything there was to know about the history of his region. George also had a slightly different relationship to his material; when he related tales of the past, he was often talking about his own family, prominent lumbermen for over a century. This was, in every sense, his town.

"Port Rowan had three big fisheries, an apple-drying plant, a brick and tile factory, cattle and drovers. The train used to come through here…there'd be one or two million feet of lumber piled up in the station. We had a little railway run by oxen, two hundred men working at the mill. My father built that mill. You'd hear a whistle going off, another one down here, another over there. Then the trucks took over and later the fisheries closed up. Now our population's way down." We were still looking for a way to get out to Long Point. Could he suggest someone with a boat? "You can't see anything in a boat," George replied dismissively. That was discouraging. A pause, then, "I've got an old Piper two-seater. I can take one of you, anyway." Yes!...Wait a second. He means an airplane? That he's going to fly?

KS: Julie's back was acting up, so by default I got the chance to pretend I wasn't scared to death of the whole idea. Moments later George's pick-up was turning down the slope into the Bluebill Marina, where at the far edge he had dredged a channel through the reeds and built an open hangar. Inside it sat a 1939 Piper J4 that looked just slightly larger than one of the model planes my cousin Russell used to hang in his bedroom. The fuselage even had those curling air-vent nostrils movie buffs may remember seeing on Spitfires in Battle of Britain epics. Except in this case they were plugged with pieces of foam rubber. "I have to keep them stopped up," George explained. "Otherwise birds build nests in the engine."

The whole procedure of getting airborne seemed a throwback to a world long past. We filled the gas tank by hand from five-gallon containers. The pontoons rested on a Rube Goldberg contraption consisting of a four-sided metal frame with automobile tire rims at the corners, which rolled along two long pipes that disappeared into the water. George had set up a cable with its own motor that hooked onto the plane's undercarriage and could draw it up onto dry land after a flight, but he didn't bother with all that when taking it out. He simple released it to roll into the water, after attaching a further pair of cables and handing them to me with instructions to walk along the side and tow the plane to a floating dock some thirty or so feet along the channel. Two thoughts contended in my mind: (1) Isn't this interesting, and (2) Jesus H. Christ! Man has reached the moon, and I've fallen into the clutches of someone who learned how to fly from the Wright Brothers.

Taxiing down the channel was like driving a thirties coupe. But when we reached open water, throttled up and slowly rose into the soft, hazy air, we turned, in my imagination, anyway, into nothing more than a larger species of one of the ducks or gulls cruising the bay. The cockpit was narrow, uncomfortable and not exactly sound-proofed. Although no farther apart than your average Siamese twins, we could only communicate by radio mike. As we lifted off the water I waited unhappily for the paralysing vertigo that usually afflicted me in such situations, but for some reason it never made itself felt; maybe the scene under us was too idyllic to get dizzy over.

We drifted westward along the coast toward the beginning of Long Point. From George's sunroom the neck had appeared to be covered with a dense thicket of poplars, but as we came nearer they thinned out into a single row of trees lining the edge of the water. Beyond them was the remains of the muskrat plantation, now gone back to lily ponds, cattails, scrub and channels of blue-green water meandering here and there.

Swinging south, we passed over the cottages of Long Point village, following the road. It looked larger than I had expected—as many as two thousand people at the height of the season, according to George. This, too, had once been part of the land where the muskrats rambled. The size of the operation must have been staggering; if muskrat outerwear had stayed in fashion after its initial surge of popularity in the twenties, H. H. Hastings would have become a commercial giant to rival the Hudson's Bay Company, instead of the Edsel Ford of furriers.

I turned away for a moment, and when I looked back the flimsy houses, chip stands and children's toy-like plastic power boats had disappeared; we were over the tapestry of green marsh and blue water that is the real start of Long Point. From eight hundred feet it looked as if clusters of gleaming emerald lily pads of all different shapes and sizes had been flung down at random in a turquoise lagoon. Strings of vegetation ran like green DNA ribbons in irregular streaks and curls through the water, disappeared under the surface, then emerged somewhere else. Tiny white seagull dots glided far below us, over water so clear we could see the sandy bottom.

One of the few solid projections of land in the midst of the marshes housed the Long Point Company's original retreat, a helter-skelter huddle of red frame huts raised on stilts. The cabins, accessible only by boat, are still in use for two weeks every fall, the ultimate plutocrat's plaything, an exclusive sanctuary in which to play backwoodsman.

Past the marshes, Long Point became relatively dry land again. From midpoint to the tip the terrain resembled a small badlands or an endlessly undulating, partially submerged golf course with irregular fairways of marsh grass and a thousand sand traps. Channels sliced through everywhere, bending around little knolls and clumps of trees, widening to form small lagoons. At some places mock rivers ran lengthwise inside the sand borders until they suddenly twisted one way or the other to rejoin the lake and almost cut the Point in two. (Later on we met someone who related how before Long Point had been closed off he had once beached his boat on one side and towed it by hand to the other.)

Driftwood and fallen trees were scattered the length of the beach, a couple of old concrete breakwaters emerged from the water, and near the tip stood a small unmanned lighthouse and a cabin where a lighthouse-keeper once used to pass his quiet days. The lake all around Long Point was doing its turquoise-to-deep-blue-to-almost-green-and-back-again trick before our eyes. No wonder the millionaires grabbed it and UNESCO is determined to keep it pristine. This must be one of North America's most glorious natural floating gardens.

The place needs all the help it can get. From the air it was easy to see how storms crashing in from the west could

change Long Point's contours overnight and overwhelm portions of the plant and animal life. (Besides the descendants of
the original muskrats and other marsh denizens, George
claimed Long Point also supports a herd of deer.) There is
simply no protection against the weather. Sometimes even
after shipwrecked sailors had struggled ashore they died of
exposure.

Abigail Becker's first husband didn't even have to venture
out. Unable to adjust to life on the mainland, he returned to
Long Point where he froze to death inside his cabin during a
winter storm. (He didn't rate a poem, but Jeremy Creek, one
of those constantly changing rivulets traversing Long Point,
was named after him. There is also a False Jeremy Creek,
which is either a comment on his character or a warning to
hunters not to mistake this for the real thing when they're out
in their boats.) As we passed over the tip of Long Point I kept
an eye out for the Becker homestead, until I remembered that
not only would the elements have long since eliminated all
traces of the cabin, but the contours of Long Point itself had
shifted so much in the century since his death that, as with
the original lighthouse, the site was now somewhere out in
the lake.

In retrospect I don't know why I was concerned about
going up in a small plane with a senior citizen at the controls.
Clearly George was in better shape than I. Instead of worry-
ing what I would do if he had a heart attack I should probably have been wondering whether he knew what to do if I
had one. They ought to bottle the air in Haldimand-Norfolk
and sell it as a restorative.

As we were saying goodbye to George and Ethel, a car drove
up and an even more elderly but equally energetic-looking
friend stuck his head out. He'd stopped by to plan the next
day's fishing trip; they were to be out on the water by five,
and maybe they would head down to that spot where the
pickerel were biting.

Only a few weeks earlier, the merest mention of events said

to transpire underwater would have been like Greek to us; all we knew of fish as we started this book was that salmon was pink and most of the others laid on the beds of crushed ice at the IGA were vaguely cream-coloured. Now, we were beginning to be able to talk, or at least listen, fish.

We had come to accept the amazing notion that one fish was actually different from another, and that protocol demanded certain species be greeted with a light laugh whenever they were mentioned, others with a sage nod, still others, the white trash of the fish world, with a dismissive shrug. We no longer doubted that the scaly creatures had preferences as to which part of the lake they frequented, that like birds they migrated with the seasons, that some species were particularly sensitive to light and noise, and that as a group they were clannish sorts who insisted on swimming around exclusively with their own kind. We had also learned that whitefish spoiled very soon after being pulled out of the water so you couldn't waste any time with them, that yellow perch hang around during the winter, and that wherever you find schools of baitfish, the walleye are not far behind. This might not seem like much to a fisherman, but you have to start somewhere.

PART TWO

The Middle of the Lake

Chapter Nine

Since on the Canadian side Erie's eastern basin ends with Long Point, this seemed the right moment to turn around again and explore what the southern shore had to offer.

The isolated, pristine tip of Long Point lies just twenty miles across the water from the New York-Pennsylvania border, but in spirit the distance is far greater. If we needed any reminders that the United States and Canada are very different places, a glance at the official billboard as we crossed the imaginary line between the two states was all it took: "WELCOME TO PENNSYLVANIA / AMERICA STARTS HERE." A similar sign in which one province casually boasted precedence over the others would come close to starting a civil war in Canada.

Most states have come up with slogans based on their own particular misreadings of history and geography, so we hardly gave it a second look. Our Quebec-bred son-in-law, however, had been amazed to discover on a recent trip that he was required to pass through Pennsylvania in order to reach Cleveland. "I thought it was supposed to be in the east!" he had demanded of our elder daughter, in a panic that he had taken the wrong ramp at the interstate entrance and had just driven a hundred miles in exactly the wrong direction. He had a point; Pennsylvania *was* supposed to be in the east.

That canny horse-trader and Pennsylvania patriot Benjamin Franklin was the man responsible for this unexpected manifestation on the shores of Lake Erie. Feeling that an outlet on what he referred to as "the Mediterranean of the New World" was necessary if his state was to participate fully in the glorious commercial future of the western territories, Franklin, with his usual combination of grave probity and slick salesmanship, talked the State of New York into letting go of a triangular piece of land that included a fifty-mile stretch of coastline with a beautiful natural harbour for the bargain price of $151,000.

In spite of Franklin's high hopes, the State of Pennsylvania and Lake Erie have never quite seemed to hit it off. Aside from the harbour of the city of Erie, sheltered by a smaller, domesticated counterpart of Long Point known as Presque Isle, the fifty miles of coast is mostly low bluffs and narrow shingle beaches that get little use. Most of the towns are located a few miles inland, in the shadow of the coastal ridge.

Looking at the map again, we also came to the rather awe-inspiring realization that not only were we on the shore of Lake Erie, with its access to the entire body of the Great Lakes, we were also within a short stroll of the outer reaches of the Mississippi watershed. If you were to portage four miles south from a spot on the lake known as Orchard Beach to the northern end of the Howard Eaton Reservoir, slide your canoe into the water and paddle vigorously south, you would eventually come out in the Gulf of Mexico. If only Marquette, La Salle and the rest of their explorer colleagues who went through incredible hardships taking the long way around the forests of northern Ontario and the upper Midwest to discover the Mississippi had known that the Father of Waters had easily accessible offspring just around the corner.

In theory the journey looks simple enough. Just set out down the west branch of the French River until it joins the south branch of the same stream, then continue on to the Allegheny, which combines with the Monongahela to create the Ohio, which flows onward to the Mississippi itself.

The first settlement the intrepid traveller would come to is the village of Little Hope, a few miles downstream from the reservoir. The name has a certain ominous ring about it, especially since if there ever was a Big Hope, or just a Hope by itself, or Hope Mountain or Hope Heights or some other hopeful place nearby that would account for the naming of a smaller version, no trace of it remained on any of our maps. Little Hope stood by itself, suggesting a cry of despair from some frazzled pioneer who, after a long day spent clearing away the last of the tree stumps from his smallholding, had returned home to find his wife and three of the children in bed with the measles and the fire gone out. Or from a would-be voyageur who, giving up after his canoe overturned for the third time in a day, had thrown away the paddles and refused to go one step farther.

As evening approached we set out to have a look for ourselves and perhaps locate someone to ask about the origins of the name. The long-lasting heat wave gave no evidence of letting up, but by now the afternoon heaviness had lifted and the air had become breathable again. Route 89 sauntered picturesquely past Dr. Welch's grape juice processing complex, curved under a series of railroad viaducts and then headed straight south, climbing as it passed through more green, bucolic scenery featuring an occasional well-built barn, then skirting another lush-looking golf course. The road levelled off for a while, then began to climb again as it crossed the ridge and entered the foothills of the Alleghenies. We passed a small billboard directing us to "Henry's Slaughterhouse," and after perhaps ten miles, came to a corner with a defiant red-white-and-blue sign declaring "Little Hope / An American Village" across from what looked to be a defunct body shop.

Putting a country's name on a product or institution to enhance its prestige is common practice everywhere, and has predictably been carried to extremes in America. Even so, the idea of labelling a whole community "American" was a first in our experience: the implication seemed to be that this particular village was more proudly patriotic than any of the neighbouring hamlets, which had failed to declare their allegiance.

Looking around, it was hard to make out what this place—which consisted of a single, narrow, dirt road lined with neat frame houses, a church, another auto parts place and a small basket factory—had that others didn't. Except, of course, for the flags, pennants and nationalistic insignia that were hung from every post and telephone pole and on every house. Every day was the Fourth of July in Little Hope, every moment a demonstration of love of country. It was these decorations themselves that apparently made Little Hope so much more "American" than anywhere else.

(In the small Ontario town near where we used to live there was a "White Rock Motel." The name derived from a large granite boulder that the proprietors had trucked in, deposited in the front yard and then painted white. The same principle seemed to be at work here.)

The village appeared deserted. Either every man, woman and child was away on patriotic manoeuvres, or they had all gone indoors to watch game shows on TV; except for the flags waving in the gentle breeze, nothing sounded, nothing moved. It felt like something a Nebraska congressman would conjure up when asked for his vision of the true America. You could easily imagine, crouched in hiding behind their lawn jockeys, a mob of insanely patriotic born-again, right-wing fanatics just waiting for some unwary liberal's foreign car to glide to a stop so they could charge out and pelt it with tracts denouncing homosexuality and placards reading "Rush Limbaugh in '96."

The off chance that an unarmed citizen might poke his head out and be willing to chat was not enough to hold us in Little Hope. We discussed following the river further and noted on our map that the next village along was called Lowville. There seemed to be a pronounced pattern of gloom developing in this direction, so we turned back toward the lake to see if things were any more upbeat in the town of

North East. (A name of almost metaphysical insubstantiality. When you call information from anywhere beyond the immediate vicinity, for example, you invariably fall into a kind of Abbott and Costello routine with the operator, who must be convinced there is such a place before he or she will consent to punch it up on the computer.)

North East, which is actually north-west of everywhere else, at least in Pennsylvania, was a pleasant town of about 4,500 at the junction of Highway 89 and U.S. Route 20. The latter is one of the web of historic highways ending in zero that were the main coast-to-coast arteries before the interstates took over; it begins near the green grass of Boston Common, cuts through Buffalo, Cleveland and Chicago, wanders around the upper midwestern states and eventually finishes its nearly four-thousand-mile trip at the edge of the Pacific in Newport, Oregon; along the way it occasionally slows down and, complete with stoplights and crossing guards, becomes the main street in scores of cities and towns. North East, Pennsylvania, was one of them.

The swath of early settlement in these parts originated from the New England states, and not surprisingly towns built by the newcomers resemble the ones they left behind. North East, like many others, had a square, virtually a commons, at its centre. The planners hadn't stinted; this green, like the one in Westfield, New York, where the grape juice warehousers were on strike, was capacious enough for a whole second village to be built inside it.

The business district had only managed to grow up around two sides while the other facing streets remained residential. But it was all pretty much architecturally intact. If you took away the automobiles, pick-ups and tractor trailers rumbling past and put carriages and carts in their place, a turn-of-the-century North Easterner would have felt right at home, especially since supplying the world with its daily ration of Welch's Grape Juice had remained North East's main industry.

JMS: Before going on to Erie we spent the night in the Rainbow Motel on the edge of town. While Ken watched the Blue Jays game in our vintage fifties room (furniture a matched maple suite, upholstery and curtains all mint green) with its picture window that looked south onto open fields and still more rows of vines, I picked up a *Reader's Digest* from the pile on the bedside table, stretched out on the (mint-green) coverlet and read through accounts of drug-addicted but eventually rehabilitated ministers, women poisoners, most unforgettable characters and my wonderful father/my wonderful son relationships. It took me back. I come from a family of magazine readers; in addition to the *Digest,* among the magazines my parents subscribed to were the *Farm Journal, Country Gentleman, American Girl, The Saturday Evening Post, Life, Ladies' Home Journal, Woman's Home Companion, Writer's Digest, Popular Mechanics, Blackwood's Magazine* (for aspiring magicians), *The Scotsman* and *Presbyterian Life,* as well as *Wee Wisdom* and *Jack and Jill* for the younger generation. Most of these were now defunct, but the *Digest* carries on in almost Platonic unchangedness. You can always count on it to leave you mildly depressed.

A few miles further along lay Erie, a metropolis of approximately 108,000. In geographical terms, Erie lies midway between Buffalo and Cleveland (and equidistant from Chicago and New York), in psychological terms midway between the hard-edged East and the friendly Midwest, and in sociological terms midway between true cityhood and overgrown small-townness. It's a *faute de mieux* kind of place—429 miles from Philadelphia, 305 miles from Harrisburg, the state capital, and even 127 miles from Pittsburgh, none of which pay it the slightest attention.

Our first intimation that Erie might be a challenging place to visit came early on with the realization that, despite the fact that one of us had spent summers at camps in north-western Pennsylvania and both of us had passed through the area countless times, not only had we ourselves never been to

Erie, we couldn't recall ever meeting anyone who came from there or anyone who had ever mentioned spending any time in the city. Nor had any of our acquaintances been able to come up with a tourist attraction or university or favourite son or famous atrocity or any other association. We all drew a blank, which was in itself a little strange.

That was followed by the reaction of the border checkpoint officer at Buffalo, who rolled his eyes and commented, "Drearrry, Pennsylvania? How long are you going to stay *there?*" But he seemed satisfied with the answer, "Not long," and waved us on with a shrug, as if to say we were adults and our foolhardiness was our own concern.

Then, during a brief side trip to Schloss Doepken to pick up another bottle or two of their prize-winning white, the college-age Watso minding the store guffawed, "Erie? That'll be a cultural experience." And finally, at the motel with the magazines, we watched a reporter on the late news interviewing former citizens who had come back for "We Love Erie Days." When he asked "What do you think of Erie now?" most of them looked as if they felt the reporter had played a dirty trick on them by asking.

"It's definitely not as bad as it used to be," was the most favourable comment we heard, from a woman who now lived in Charlotte, North Carolina.

We knew how Dollier and Galinée must have felt setting off into the unexplored western territories as we pulled out of the motel driveway and headed west again on Route 20 through another crazy-quilt of older frame houses, new condo developments, roadside vegetable stands, baseball fields, billboards advertising great real estate bargains available to anyone with ready cash for a down payment, large modern churches with elongated spires and strange ski-nose roofs, conference centres, corner shopping malls, rows of one-storey office buildings and more vintage motels. According to signs along the shoulder, this section of roadway had been officially labelled "Purple Heart Highway."

Beyond a down-and-out white area at the city's edge, past

May's Tavern, Thorr's TV and Tackle Shop and a Lutheran church that told us next Sunday's sermon would be "Empowered by God" (what was last Sunday's?), we passed the first black faces we had seen since leaving the Buffalo area—a couple of men deep in conversation as they walked along the sidewalk, then a boy shooting baskets in a driveway. And there we were in the heart of Erie, circling Perry Square, where a fountain splashed and a couple of out-of-work Erieites caught a few winks on the public benches under an already blazing morning sun.

We drove by the ornate main library, the United Steelworkers of America headquarters, the historical museum, a hotel and a church or two, a bookstore, a dance school and something called Gannon University, which we had never heard of before and which we thought at first was Gammon University, as in backgammon or gammon of bacon. In contrast to Buffalo there were people on the streets, but they didn't seem to be going anywhere in particular. The whole town had the feel of a place that has been culturally and psychologically handed over to some grey, all pervasive, entirely self-absorbed, Big Brother-like institution—if not the American Medical Association, then something exactly like it.

The AMA came to mind because the sprawling Hamot Medical Centre dominated the city's prime real estate location, the slope overlooking the harbour, and much of what activity we did come across in Erie seemed to have something to do with health services. Not only were most of the newer buildings hospitals, doctor's offices, medical insurance centres and manufacturers or distributors of medical supplies, but many other services also indirectly revolved around health. The man checking in before us at our downtown motel was waiting out his wife's operation. You got the feeling that without the health industry to fill up motel rooms, hand out contracts to local electricians, plumbers, food purveyors and construction companies, supply fares for the taxis, diners for the restaurants, accounts for the ad sellers, and to provide jobs and disposable cash for all those people directly employed in the business, Erie might just as well take a deep breath and slide into the lake.

Looking for someone to chat with, we stopped in at the library, where next to a stack of "Burglar-proof Your House" pamphlets we found an illustrated map depicting the city's high points (second overall in plastics production in the U.S., first fire department in the country, place where the phrase "Indian summer" was coined). But no one was in a conversational mood. The clerks at the bookstore across the street were equally close-mouthed. So, for that matter, was everyone else we tried to talk to—waitresses, storekeepers, motel managers, even the uniformed official who dealt with the public at the Pennsylvania Fish Commission were all keeping their breath to cool their porridge. If there were any outspoken or opinionated people in Erie, they kept themselves well hidden during the time we spent there.

Maybe they all knew in their hearts that they should really be part of western New York, and the dark secret had undermined their geographical confidence, making conversation difficult. We had found New York State full of ready talkers, and in rural Ontario every quiet Canadian we met was eager to express an opinion about almost everything once prompted, but here silence was apparently golden.

Feeling slightly disgruntled, we finally gave up trying to draw out the mum citizens of Erie and followed the advice of the numerous signs urging a visit to the historic brig *Niagara*, moored in the harbour. But even here reticence prevailed; with patience and some careful probing on our part the guides could be coaxed into letting slip a few details of the ship's dimensions and history, but on touchier subjects like politics or the weather, they dodged deftly away.

Still, merely walking up the gangplank onto the deck of this legendary piece of American history provided a historical shiver. This was the very vessel to which Oliver Hazard Perry had transferred when his own ship was sunk under him during the Battle of Lake Erie, and from which he sent the famous (and to generations of American schoolchildren, famously incomprehensible) message of victory, "We have met the enemy and they are ours." The battle actually took place at the other end of the lake, off Put-In-Bay on South Bass Island, near Sandusky; Erie's connection is the fact that Perry's fleet was built right here, in shipyards just a stone's throw from where the ship now rests.

For those who can't quite remember what the fuss was about, the Battle of Lake Erie was perhaps the most crucial encounter of the War of 1812; victory meant that the United States kept control of the lake and that what later became the upper Midwest remained American territory. Or so the history books say. But a good argument can be made for the proposition that in expansionist terms, Perry's victory on Lake Erie was the worst of all possible results for the new country. That's because even if the British had won, bringing the Michigan territory and the vast acreage beyond it into Canada, large numbers of land-hungry Americans would have continued to flood in from the east. Sooner or later a situation much like the one that was developing in Texas would have come about, with a majority of Americans being ruled from a faraway foreign capital. In no time flat, here too the settlers would have found an excuse to set up a breakaway republic, and, like the Republic of Texas, that independent "country" would quickly have been absorbed into the United States, most likely along with large chunks of what is now Ontario and the Canadian prairies.

Thanks to Perry that never happened, and today the 1,200-strong Niagara League provides volunteers to work alongside a small paid crew to staff the gift shop, guide the tourists and keep this monument to past glories shipshape. On the day we saw it everything had been fitted out, shined up and rigged to perfection; every bit of brasswork gleamed, every plank in the deck fitted snugly into its neighbours, the cannon rested in their mounts, the hull creaked pleasantly as it rolled gently from side to side. This was a beautiful, evocative vessel that in the fall was scheduled to participate with other Tall Ships from both countries in a glorious recreation of the battle off Put-In-Bay.

There is a slight problem, however. The original *Niagara* was scuttled, raised, rescuttled, burned and rebuilt so many times over the years that, as far as it is possible to tell, at most only a few inches of planking remain from the vessel that Perry actually commanded. And we have our doubts about that, since we couldn't get anyone to show us which splinters they were. This is a nice piece of contemporary craftsmanship and some sort of tribute to community involvement, but it's not the historic brig *Niagara*, and the falseness of the presentation makes you wonder what message is intended for the school kids whose teachers bring them here to learn about their country's history. Where does history leave off and Disney begin?

These nagging questions meant that our hour on the waterfront, instead of lifting the spirits, had the reverse effect. By mid-afternoon, after a weekend in Erie, we were spoiling for a heated and not especially rational discussion. When it took place, it seemed to revolve around why American cities and this place in particular were the way they were. One of us held out for racism as the central cause, right down to the conversational deficiencies of this rather woebegone small city. The other felt equally strongly that even if the slave ships had never arrived from Africa, the country's worship of bottom-line capitalism would have been detrimental to human society and would have done its best to ruin America's original beauty. The first countered with the undeniable truth that she was wrong, always his second line of argument. In response she threw in the near-religious character of televised spectator sports as a corollary to the winner-takes-all obsession, not mentioning any names but if the shoe fits.... Eventually we agreed not so much to disagree as to get out of town as fast as we could. Erie seems to have that effect on people.

Chapter Ten

We fled Pennsylvania in such a hurry that by the time we'd pulled over to check the map we found we had driven fifteen miles into Ohio. We were just entering Ashtabula, another smallish lake port (pop. 23,000).

Historically, the whole northern third of Ohio is affiliated with the State of Connecticut. Many Ohioans would probably be surprised to learn that the bulk of this northern tier was in fact once the property of that state, deeded to it by Charles II in 1662 and not relinquished until 1800. It was known as the Western Reserve, which in effect meant "reserved for Connecticuters and the rest of you can go somewhere else."

In the nineteenth century the genteel New Englandish lifestyle of the first settlers was gradually swamped by the development of heavy industry along the lake, and today when you cross the Ohio-Pennsylvania border you plunge from the domesticated, slightly crabby atmosphere of the tag ends of eastern states directly into the crowded, boisterous, upbeat, sometimes shabby, often vulgar, always-struggling-but-still-in-there-punching universe of the industrial Midwest. Buffalo and Erie might be having trouble figuring out where their sense of community lies and where they are headed, but Ashtabula looked as if, even in an age of freeways and strip malls, it was holding its own.

From Walnut Boulevard, high on a hill above the harbour, we looked down on a busy scene resembling a picture in one of those children's books meant to illustrate Means of Transportation to five-year-olds. The city more or less funnelled down both sides of a picturesque valley toward Ashtabula Creek. Cars and transport trucks were moving steadily on the highway that ran along the opposite slope, passing a panorama of trees, brick houses, smokestacks and a radio tower; meanwhile, a red pick-up was descending the hill toward the waterfront, where a few railcars bumped along in the direction of the lake.

Behind the train tracks stood a trim red-and-white Coast Guard station, a few steam shovels, one large crane, a grey water tank, several silos, some commercial buildings and two piles of coal the exact shape and nearly the size of the Great Pyramid. A freighter slowly approached the mouth of the creek, where pleasure boats were moored in their berths. But the two *pièces de resistance* were an old-fashioned erector-set-style drawbridge, which the pick-up had now crossed, and a complicated-looking covered conveyor belt that connected the two sides of the river valley. You could stand here all day and not get bored, and probably there were people who did just that.

Above the "Where's Waldo" world of man, a flock of swallows manoeuvred, and higher still a seagull made its way against the wind in front of a large grey cloud that was pulling away to expose some fluffy white shapes and a strip of blue sky. It was turning into a beautiful day.

Words like "anthracite," "bituminous," "slag" and "pig iron," which we had last heard in fourth-grade geography class suddenly reappeared in the everyday conversation of people in Ashtabula. The coal comes in by rail from mines in the Appalachians to the south and goes out by freighter to Canada, where it is used mostly by hydroelectric companies. Iron ore and pig iron make the reverse trip, coming down from the upper lakes for use in local factories. More recently, something our teachers never talked about called rutile ore, a sort of black sand scooped from the beaches of Australia, pours off the ships on its way to paint manufacturers to be used in mixing pigments.

It was like rediscovering a long forgotten world of sinewy-armed steel puddlers and daredevil engineers roaring down the tracks with a dangerous load. "I got pig iron, yeah! I got pig iron!" chanted Leadbelly in his song "Rock Island Line." In our brave new world of megabytes and fibre optics, it came as a shock to realize that much of our lives are still based on the old verities of iron and steel.

Down near the river, antique shops and restaurants now occupy the buildings that once housed shipping offices, fish wholesalers, boarding houses and bars, where raffish sailors drank away time between ships. "This used to be a rough neighbourhood," a waitress in Hulbert's Restaurant told us. "When I was growing up in the seventies I was absolutely not allowed to go anywhere near Bridge Street." Even today, apparently, there are women of a certain age in the town's suburban edges who shiver at the sight of anything nautical. (On the other hand they, or at least their mothers and grand-mothers, may have had good reason for being wary. Around the turn of the century Ashtabula was reputed to be one of the roughest destinations on the Great Lakes. As many as six hundred sailors might be in port on shore leave in a single day; local lore has it that only Singapore's waterfront had more saloons.)

A fair portion of the original waterfront remains physically intact, and if you ignore the sandalwood incense floating out the doors and the cute names on the shop windows, Bridge Street looks pretty much as it must have back when the Lake Erie ports were booming.

So, we discovered as we continued east, did the lakeshore on the other side of Ashtabula. Beyond the harbour Route 531 skirted the lake, sometimes approaching within a few feet of the cliffs where roughly twenty feet below the wind was whipping up the breakers, then swinging slightly inland to make room for sand-strewn lanes crowded with small, white frame cottages that have probably been packed with holidayers from the cities every moment of every summer for the last seventy or eighty years. Interspersed among the cottage groupings was a grab-bag of small grocery outlets, bars, mini-golf, pizza by the beach, sports rental shops, video-game arcades, small-scale amusement parks, batting cages and souvenir shops, along with boat charter offices and other holiday-by-the-seaside services. Like the cottages, these were mostly older, well-weathered structures, little white frame or cinder-block shacks standing by themselves along the road, not quite ephemeral, since many had lasted generations, but looking as if they weren't built to withstand anything more threatening than a summer thunderstorm.

Along with the typical beach community businesses, tattooing was available in several roadside houses, as were palm and tarot-card reading and most other varieties of fortune-telling. Every little while we passed a biker clubhouse, a messy automobile graveyard, a bar advertising "laser karaoke" on Friday nights or a roadhouse with a half-working neon beer sign. A tidy, tastefully pastel-painted waterside condo development sprang into sight now and then ("Open for Viewing Soon!!! Low down payment!!!"). But this was not yuppie country and overall the tone was resolutely blue-collar.

For at least a century, in fact, the eastern lakeshore has been the traditional vacation spot for urban Ohioans without a great deal of excess money. Factory workers, immigrants, door-to-door salesmen, waitresses and the rest of what used to be called the working class, before that designation became embarrassing in upward striving America, rented cottages along the lake summer after summer in tingling anticipation of a week or two free from the hot city pavements.

Among them was a branch of the Sobols who had been fruit growers back in the old country and were now landless in the slums of Cleveland. They assuaged their feelings of loss by spending part of the season at a farm owned by a Mr. Stocking, near Madison, east of Geneva. One day each

August they would invite the entire family, in what seemed like its hundreds but was probably more like its dozens, to swoop down to pick blackberries in the extensive patch behind one of the pastures. By the time the sun set they had usually picked enough to feed all the immigrants in Cleveland, and by the following week they were so sick of them they couldn't face another berry until the next year's extravaganza.

Those excursions came to an end around 1950, as the family moved into the middle class and the older generation began to die off. The younger kids really recalled only two things; the Great Blackberry Pick, of course, and the Canadian Soldiers, which was the name given to mayflies in Ohio. One year, just after the war, millions of the slimy, inch-long bugs blanketed the area so completely that the roads became greased with a solid layer of them, causing large numbers of cars to hydroplane, or more accurately entoplane, right into the ditch along the shoulder.

These periodic infestations must have been a staple of lake life from the time the glacier receded, but this was probably one of the last; by the mid-fifties an explosion of algae gorging themselves on phosphate-based detergents and fertilizers, along with a series of unusual water temperatures, had so thoroughly depleted the lake's oxygen supply that mayflies, which breed on the bottom, had pretty much vanished. Today, now that these products have been banned, there is tentative evidence that the mayfly might be returning, although cottagers are probably not quite as thrilled about this comeback as scientists.

In the narrow front yard of a small house on the north side of the road just past Geneva-on-the-Lake, makeshift shelves laid across some second-hand chairs were crowded with old bottles, chipped statuettes and telephone insulators. We recognized the signs; this was the home of one of those obsessive dealer-collectors, the type of man or woman whose life rushes by in a stream of objects, hundreds in, hundreds out every couple of weeks, piles of dishes, stacks of magazines, shelves of old iron, matched sets of rickety armchairs, dozens of chipped jugs, scores of foxed prints in cracked frames, hundreds of ceramic figures and ashtrays and necklaces and aggies and mining certificates and wall plaques and wide, framed photographs of The Loyal Order of Moose outings. A sign read "Going out of Business," but we didn't take that seriously. They all say that.

We parked in the driveway and banged on the front door until sounds of movement could be heard inside. Finally the door opened and a man stuck his head out to stare at us. Flowing white locks formed a halo around an angular face set with intense blue eyes; he was dressed in a frayed white shirt long past its prime, a pair of shapeless gabardine trousers, and on his head perched a grimy leather hat with a few feathers stuck into the band, decorated with an armorial badge and three equally grimy happy-face buttons. (Comparing notes later, we found we had both experienced a sinking sensation at this point, as if realizing that we had waked the Ancient Mariner and would be required to hear out his entire tale.)

John P. Yarish turned out to be one of those rare-and-getting-rarer originals about whom you could truthfully say "This could only happen here." As he invited us in, he thrust two blue glass beads into Julie's hand. "So no one can say you've lost your marbles," he explained. We followed him into an enclosed porch and up a short flight of stairs into a room crammed with Elvis memorabilia, biker gear, mouldering stuffed birds, kitchen goods, Charlie Brown glasses, tomes on anthropology, cheap guitars and just about anything else that had been manufactured in the twentieth century.

As we poked around, John related his life story in short bursts of information, alternating the bits of personal history with comments on the merchandise and questions about ourselves. Sixty-eight years old, he had gradually, over the hard years of his life, evolved into what the Beats would have recognized as a Holy Bum or the French would call a *clochard céleste*, one of the prophetic heirs of Whitman who had heard the siren call of America singing and was determined to add his voice to the chorus.

He was a great reader, a writer of verse, painter of pictures, scavenger of industrial detritus, in love with the idea of art and literature and printing and culture, and along with that an impassioned adherent of the notion that every man has within himself the potential to be a poet or artist. He truly believed that art can change the world and that America is the most beautiful of man's creations.

"You're from Canada? You should have brought some Canadian insulators, you could have paid for your trip with them. Or Pez, they like those." When the phone started to ring he ignored it, explaining that he often had trouble with local teenagers. You could see why he would be a prime target for kids playing pranks.

Besides, he had just discovered that we were writers. He was a writer, too, he let us know. He used to have his own column in the *Valley News*, a weekly published in Orwell, Ohio, twenty miles south of here. Opening a crowded drawer he pulled out a clipping dated November 21, 1979. Covered bridges had been his subject that day and he'd composed a poem entitled "The Covered Bridge," which began:

> **With its weathered board**
> **And its wooden floor**
> **Man and beast passed through**
> **For a century or more.**

Then, having dealt with the covered bridge in prose and poetry, he had gone on to take out his brushes and paint several small oils of covered bridges. The walls were covered with examples of his work, and he showed us an old flyer announcing a one-man show at Bill Worthy's Grand River Vineyard ("West off Route 528, South of I-90, Featuring landscapes, seascapes, animals, birds, and portraits in watercolour, charcoal, oil and pastel, as well as indian art and winter and summer moccasins, All by John P. Yarish").

From another drawer he produced a small photocopied sheet that represented the proudest moment of his life, a copy of the Congressional Record of June 13, 1975. The middle column read in part:

> Mr. TAFT. Mr. President, As we approach the beginning of our Bicentennial year, I would like to call my colleagues' attention to one of the grassroots Bicentennial movements in Ohio. The treasurer of the Rome, Ohio, Bicentennial Commission has composed a poem as a salute to our Nation on its 200th birthday. I commend Mr. Yarish on this patriotic effort, and I ask unanimous consent that this poem be printed in the RECORD.

There being no objection, the poem was ordered to be printed in the RECORD, as follows:

A Bicentennial Salute
(By John P. Yarish, May 1975)

We were Colonial States...thirteen,
　　two hundred years ago.
Governed by British...tough and mean,
　　we knew they had to go.
A few important men did meet, to map out
　　strategy.
We knew, they would be hard to beat, we
　　wanted to be free....

He pulled out a pen and wrote with a flourish "to Ken and Julie from John," and handed the offprint to us.

John had four children, three daughters and a son, he told us. The son and his boy come to visit occasionally, but, he added in a puzzled tone, when they do they always insist on camping out in the back yard. A quick glance past the curtain separating the shop from his living quarters revealed a parlour that looked as if the Rodney King riots had just passed through. Heaps of cigarette ashes and butts everywhere, clothes left where they had been dropped, unwashed dishes; John was probably an affectionate father and grandfather, but he wasn't a man who could be called house-proud.

He was born in Crucible, Pennsylvania, that perfectly named, hard-as-nails company town south of Pittsburgh on the Monongahela River, populated mainly by labourers of eastern European descent. "What was that song Tennessee Ernie Ford used to sing, the one about 'I owe my soul to the company store'? That was my father. Crucible Steel owned the town, they owned my father. He never got them paid off. For six years, 1932 to '38, he never even saw any cash. Not a dollar. Just signed his double X in the store record.

"I started work at seventeen, eight-to-eight night shift janitor at that same store. 1942. The war saved me. I got drafted in '43, served in the navy, never went back. Went to Cleveland after I got out in '46, spent my life in different places around eastern Ohio.

"How I got into antiques. I got into electric work in the fifties. A little old German lady I was doing some jobs for had this glass cup and saucer and nappy dish sitting out on her kitchen table. 'How much you want for them?' I asked. She said 'If you vant you take.' The wife liked them. So I went back and then next day I saw this ugly vase, asked her what she'd take for that. We agreed to knock $14.65 from the bill—$214.65 it was. A lot of people wanted that vase. One lady goes out to her car and brings me in a book and shows me it was Gallé, worth $375. I said the highest bid by the Fourth of July takes it. That's how I got started in antiques."

He had no use for organized religion. "They're a bunch of [indistinct mutter.]" Asked about the new President, he gave a thumbs-down gesture and a withering look. "There he goes hugging Arafat, giving away all that money when we need it here. So many people out of work in this area, so many on welfare. It all started when they built that nuclear plant. Paid people twenty, forty dollars an hour, then it's over and what are they supposed to do now? I'm selling out, going down south. Nothing's the same as it used to be."

In a local-colour story about him in a 1983 issue of the *Youngstown Vindicator*, the onset of glaucoma is mentioned, and from hints amid the stops and starts of his conversation it seemed likely that he had other health problems as well. Anyway, we were all running down and the time had come to move on. We shook hands and told him truthfully that it had been a pleasure meeting him. If he really was the Ancient Mariner, we had done double duty as the Two in Three.

As we were about to drive away, John rushed out to the car, stooping down to relate a rambling story he had forgotten to tell us about his in-laws, forty chickens, some missing mash and the importance of trusting or maybe not trusting your neighbours. Oh, and we bought an insulator of an unusual dark-turquoise hue for which he said he had to charge seven bucks.

Just this side of the farthest Cleveland suburbs we came to Painesville, a town of fifteen thousand that could take a lesson in urban planning from North East. Painesville has managed the unlikely feat of starting out with a nicely proportioned town square and a designation as county seat and then proceeding to turn their central core into what must rank as one of the least distinguished downtowns in America. Each of the buildings that ringed the square seemed designed to represent the dregs of a different architectural style. One entire block was taken up by a fifties-style windowless department store resembling a massive guardhouse; next to it sat a more recent addition, an inward-facing shopping mall that had gone bankrupt and now housed brokerage firms and medical insurance companies. In other locations around the square you found a colonial city hall with its proportions all wrong and a grim-looking Presbyterian pile from the turn of the century.

But it was the imposing courthouse that caught the eye. American versions of the Ontario city hall battle almost invariably involve the county court building. Two fundamentally different assumptions about the basis of civil order lie behind these contrasting architectural priorities. American-style Jeffersonian democracy was founded on the principle of the supremacy of law; the towering legal structure of the American Constitution is the central repository of that idea, and the courthouse, the structure where The Law is dispensed and administered, its physical correlative.

Canada (excluding Quebec, which is a whole other story involving such additional elements as the Napoleonic Code and the role of the Church) followed the British example, in which power is entrusted less to abstract principles than to the people in office at any given moment. (Until the recent Charter of Rights there was no written document at all dealing with the people's specific rights.) Consequently, Canadian governments put their main efforts into prestigious municipal buildings rather than courthouses.

Curiously, in modern times the two systems have largely reversed themselves, at least in practice. Americans are notoriously contemptuous of the law while at the same time, despite a great deal of self-congratulation about independent thinking, remaining content to let the well-entrenched political élites stay in power almost as long as they wish; incumbents are rarely removed in American elections. Canadians, on the other hand, can be pathologically law-abiding (in Toronto you won't spot anyone but an occasional rebellious teenager crossing the street against the light) but are becoming increasingly impatient with their politicians, whom they turf out at a rate few other industrial democracies come near.

Back in small-town America, the courthouse remains the most prominent building; all over the country you find examples of superb nineteenth- and early twentieth-century craftsmanship in their construction. Occasionally, however, the impulse toward the monumental has run amok and resulted in massive, formulaic heaps that would have warmed the heart of Albert Speer.

The Lake County Courthouse was one of these, an ungainly neoclassical hulk fronted by four pseudo-Doric pillars and topped by an outsized gilded dome on which sat a cupola, which had another gilded dome on it, and finally, like the cherry on the sundae, a gigantic 3-D version of the ubiquitous glaring American eagle. Two monumental sculptures flanked the front steps, the first a triple-life-size representation of what looked to be a consumptive sower of grain with a bad back, his partner a chap in a loincloth who, judging from the gash across his chest, had just undergone quadruple by-pass surgery and looked depressed as hell about his chances of recovery. A stone tablet near them declared: "The right to a free government presupposes the duty of citizens to obey that government." No attribution is given, probably because the words come from the collected works of Kaiser Wilhelm or some other noted democratic statesman of the period when the courthouse was constructed. What happened to "government by the people, for the people and of the people"? Or "governments are instituted among men, deriving their just powers from the consent of the governed"? The Gettysburg Address and the Declaration of Independence didn't seem to have made much of an impression in Painesville.

Several people on the Canadian side had spoken wistfully of the days when passenger boats and ferries made frequent trips back and forth across the lake; one or two had mentioned rumours that a woman in Grand River, Ohio, was thinking about reinstituting service between Cleveland and the north shore.

The thought of day trips across the water seemed an idea whose time had come round again, so when we neared Grand River, a few miles west of Painesville, we found Mary Ann Rutherford's name in the phone book and called. Following her directions we drove through the village, turned right at the end, and right again through a gateway in a cyclone fence. That brought us to Rutherford's Landing and Cruise

Lines, where the only place to park was a few feet from a sign that read "Don't Even Think of Parking Here."

A heavy rain had come down the night before, and the uneven ground in the compound was a patchwork of mud, gravel and puddles. Facing us was a two-storey cinder-block structure with a precarious-looking upper balcony and a sleepy goat tethered in front. A Lincoln Continental, a Thunderbird, a van and a pick-up truck were parked in casual disarray around to one side; a couple of port-a-johns stood near the fence. Rabbits ran around loose (a pair scampered under our car as soon as we stopped) and at least four dozen ducks and geese were holding a conference on one of the boat ramps next to a small bait shop. A row of seats that looked as if they'd come from a 727 were lined up along one side of the shop, facing toward the river.

On the water, an odd assortment of large vessels of various shapes and sizes were tied up next to the bait store. Downstream we could make out a couple of newish imitation-Cape-Cod restaurants and beyond them, on the opposite bank of the Grand River, some warehouses and docks belonging to Morton Salt and Republic Steel. Mary Ann had told us that she lived "above the marina," but amid all this it was hard to tell exactly where "above the marina" was.

Just then a man well past retirement age strolled up to us, introduced himself as Mary Ann's brother, explained that she was on long distance but would come down as soon as she could and pointed to a small building up the hill. "You know who went to school right there?" He gave us a moment or two to guess, but no names came to mind. "Don Shula," he informed us. "Who?" said Julie. "Don Shula. Miami." He continued on his way without waiting for thanks.

A few moments later Mary Ann herself bounded down the stairs of the cinder-block building and introduced herself. The ducks came rushing over as she was descending and she greeted them fondly. "These are my children," she laughed. "I live above the goat." A short, stocky, grandmotherly person with carefully waved short grey hair and a well-weathered eastern European face, wearing slacks and a neat windbreaker, she radiated energy even standing still. "Sometimes I can't believe I'm seventy-two," were her first words after we introduced ourselves.

She led the way up the gangplank of one of the larger vessels and sat us down in the cabin, oblivious to the fact that it was half open to the elements and that the weather had finally broken and a cool, damp wind was blowing. "You're only as old as you feel," she said, finishing the thought she'd begun in the yard.

This was the first in what would be a long string of aphorisms; she had one for every occasion. "You can't take it with you," for example, was followed by a catalogue of some of her more recent acquisitions. Among the things she couldn't take with her at the moment were seven homes, including a full-size reproduction of Frank Lloyd Wright's "Fallingwater" ("I think I've slept there twice since I bought it"), the four vehicles parked near our car, a 45-foot catamaran that she rents out to fishermen, a 100-foot houseboat brought up the Mississippi which she was converting into a floating bed-and-breakfast, a 106-foot paddle steamer available for cruises and the 146-foot ship in whose cabin we were now sitting and shivering, which had begun service as a supply tender for the oil rigs in the Gulf of Mexico.

The ships were christened respectively the *Mary Ann I*, the *Mary Ann III*, the *Mary Ann IV* and the *Mary Ann V*. (*Mary Ann II* had been sold "to an *A*-rab" some time ago and is now at anchor in some warmer waters.) In addition to this and the other two local marinas, she also owns or has owned at various times a business college, beauty salons, an institute of cosmetology, a fishing lodge, liquor stores, a jewellery store and the restaurants visible down the river. In fact, if there is anything within a radius of fifteen miles she doesn't own, it's probably because she just sold it.

In her own unlikely way Mary Ann is something of a capitalist genius. From a background not so different from that of John Yarish just down the road (her parents were Romanian immigrants, she grew up dirt poor on a farm fifteen miles south of Grand River and had little formal education), Mary Ann set out with dedicated single-mindedness to better herself. For a while she was "in politics" in Columbus, but apparently it wasn't long before her true vocation emerged; she was one of those rare people born with an unfailing sense of what to buy and when to sell it. Her first encounter with the business world was hawking seed packets as a girl on the farm for eleven or twelve cents a packet, and she hasn't looked back since.

Instead of abstract securities and fancy paper, however, Mary Ann preferred to stick to tangible assets. ("My Jewish accountant told me, 'Never put your money in anything you can't see.'") She would walk down a street in some smaller city and through some personal radar pick up the faint trace of a failing business that no one else would think of investing in. Then, after buying it for next to nothing, she would set out to learn everything there was to know about that particular field. ("All businesses are alike.")

She rose early, worked seven days a week, harder than anyone else, and stayed alert. ("God gave us two eyes and two ears and one mouth, so we should see and hear twice as much as we talk.") When profits reached their peak she would sell out and put her money somewhere else, even if her banker reacted with horror. As he did the time she decided to sell off Pickle Bill's Restaurant to pay off the *River Queen* (now the *Mary Ann III*) and buy the imitation Wright house. ("He told me, 'Mary Ann, you've got rocks in your head,' and I said, 'Then let 'em rattle.'") Having bought the house, she added her own touch with a porch shaped like the bow of a boat where she can sit and look out over the trees.

She owes no one anything, pays good money for good work and has no use for people who can't seem to get things together. ("I'm the admiral because I pay the captains.") Like many of her generation she sees the world in ethnic terms, but her biases are economic, not racial; she only dislikes people who won't get out and work for their living. You have the feeling that as her employee you would always get a fair shake, but you'd better start running if you cross her and you'd better not be late for work in the morning.

She is her own universe. ("I don't care what anyone says about me as long as they keep their fingers out of my cash register.") Not even an armchair traveller, she begrudges every day spent away from her little patch of waterfront; business trips take her to nearby cities like Toronto, Chicago and Columbus, and of course Cleveland, and once in a while she visits one of her homes in Florida, but she has no interest in anything foreign.

The central emotional fact of her life, to which she refers repeatedly, was her marriage at the age of forty-five to a high school teacher who, after seven years of marriage, developed spinal meningitis and ended up spending the last thirteen years of his life in a wheelchair. With her strong belief in work as salvation, Mary Ann tried to involve him as much as possible in her wheeling and dealing, talking over each deal and asking his opinion. That he had a drinking problem didn't make things any easier. In fact, she bought the marina and the boats mainly as a means of keeping him out of the bars in the afternoon. When he died, she built a park in his memory by the water, not far from her home.

We asked what she intends to do with her money after she's gone. She hasn't decided yet, but one thing she doesn't believe in are charitable organizations. ("None of them helped me out when I needed them.") Probably at some point a Rutherford Clinic or something on that order will begin to take shape, but not for a while; too many new money-making possibilities come up every day.

The rumours we'd heard on the other side turned out to be right. One of her plans involved the possibility of getting her 146-footer shipshape for tourist runs between Cleveland and Port Stanley, Ontario. She has been exploring the idea, but so far the timing hasn't been quite right. So she'll wait patiently, as always. And when and if the various governments concerned manage to sort out the red tape and the opportune moment arrives, the *Mary Ann V*, or perhaps by that time the *Mary Ann VI* or *VII*, will steam out into the lake, and Mary Ann Rutherford will have shown them once again how far a person who's willing to work hard can go in America. ("It will happen.")

Chapter Eleven

Elgin County is flat and green. And isolated. We were now back in rural Ontario, having exited Highway 401 to turn into the restful countryside just west of Long Point.

Mary Ann Rutherford herself might have been stumped for commercial opportunities in this quiet farmland. Buffalo and Toronto were a good two hours' drive to the east, Detroit farther the other way, Cleveland closer as the seagull flies but even more removed in influence. Instead of signs announcing Bible camps and doughnut shops, the roadside shoulder displayed ads for "Quality Swine Cooperatives" or "Tobacco Growers Flue Cured Tobacco Marketing Board" (TGFCTMB).

We cruised past a succession of prosperous-looking farms: family names painted in large letters on the front of the barns, livestock grazing quietly in neatly fenced fields. Fifty years earlier a man named Angus Mowat had taken a similar trip through the area, and in a letter to his son, Farley, expressed an opinion that, despite this being "wealthy farming country," they had "a lot of the worst public libraries in the world." (The elder Mowat appears to have been that rarest of characters, a sharp-tongued librarian.) Angus went on to add indignantly that "we could see why the farmers were wealthy, having bought a bushel of melons that were very nice on top and very rotten below." Farley, who at that moment was dodging German bullets somewhere in central Italy, does not seem to have found time to sympathize.

Along County Road 42, which parallels the lake just slightly inland and reverses itself at Port Bruce to become County Road 24, the ground was cultivated right up to the edge of the bluffs. When the descendants of the country-slickers who slipped one over on Angus Mowat do their ploughing they must catch a glimpse of the lake below as they make their U-turn at the end of each furrow. At intervals a weathered general store appeared, or a row of grey-and-red tobacco-curing sheds, but no towns of any size.

Faded signs announced the names of villages which might or might not still exist. Port Royal and Houghton fell into the "not" category; Clear Creek (general store, church, outside pay phone, garage at the crossroads) was still functioning—two or three houses stood on the paved road and a few more could be seen along the short, sandy lane that led down toward the lake. (To be absolutely accurate these first towns west of Long Point lie just inside Haldimand-Norfolk, but topographically they belong to the cliffside terrain of Elgin County.) We drove to the end of the Clear Creek lane, parked the car and walked to the edge of the bluff to look out over the wide stretch of pale water and grey sky. But there's no harbour here, and the sumach and ferns looked as if they were ready to reclaim the narrow roadway.

As in Chautauqua County, one crop dominated; but instead of long rows of grapevines it was the wide, floppy leaves of tobacco plants that covered almost every arable inch. The harvest will eventually be carted a few miles inland to plants in centres like Tillsonberg and Aylmer, and from there truckloads of the coffin-nails will roll out to the rest of the country. (Until the federal government lowered taxes, they also went to the States to be smuggled back into Canada and sold under the table.)

Although we both gave up smoking years ago, the sweet smell of cured tobacco brought back the days when cigarettes and sophistication were synonymous, when we were all either Alan Ladd cupping our hands intimately to shield a burning match or Veronica Lake leaning over provocatively to get a light. A woman we'd met back in Port Dover mentioned that she had grown up on a tobacco farm near Simcoe: "I know it's not good for you," she'd admitted. "But just don't forget, the government kept encouraging farmers to grow more and more. My father sold out in time, but a lot of people didn't."

Some distance beyond Port Rowan we passed one of those spots where a driving parent always quietly speeds up, in hopes of getting by before the children notice it. One of us tried this, but the other was alert and insisted that we pull into Sand Hill Park and check out the gigantic, 450-foot-high cliff billed as "Ontario's largest sand pile." Luckily the road came in partway along the escarpment so we had only 150 feet or so more or less straight up to struggle before reaching the top of the pile. What seemed like several hours later, after we had regained our breath, we looked down to see below us an almost vertical drop, forty-five storeys of sand, ending in a narrow beach where a few children were playing. Judging by the tracks, a few daredevils, perhaps inspired by Anna Taylor and her intrepid colleagues at Niagara Falls, had actually slid their way down to the lake. We saw no evidence of anyone climbing back up; the preferred return route seemed to be via a dip in the hill a bit farther along.

In the mid-nineteenth century, a seventy-foot-high weather forecasting station stood on this crest; at regular intervals a Canadian positioned on top of it would flash a mirror in the direction of Pennsylvania. If the American sitting on top of his tower on the other side spotted the reflection, he in turn would flash his mirror back toward the Ontario side. A similar structure at the tip of Long Point made a triangle of reflectors. "From this they obtained satisfactory data to provide reliable charts for the sailors." That's what the Sand Hills brochure said, anyway; what this seems to imply is that the degree of difficulty involved in the sighting was then taken into consideration by passing ship captains. Or something.

If the procedure has a primitive sound to it, you have to remember the staggering losses that both countries were suffering around this time; between 1835 and 1875 an average of more than 400 people a year were ending up as what Jim Allen would call "floaters" in Lake Erie, and enormous amounts of valuable cargo and hundreds of vessels were sinking to the bottom with depressing regularity. Anything that could make a stab at spotting a storm about to blow up was better than nothing.

Nor should anyone forget that while such numbers are safely in the past, nature remains as unpredictable and as dangerous as ever. Just as we were finishing the writing of this book, headlines in the Toronto papers screamed out the chilling story of four young boys, aged nine to twelve, who had gone on a neighbourhood outing from Paris, Ontario, to the giant sand hill. They had been building a castle at the base of the cliff, almost directly underneath the spot where we had stood gazing out at the water, when a ten-ton chunk of sand, loosened by the heavy rain of the preceding two days, broke off and crashed down on them. Within minutes they had asphyxiated; it took rescuers more than half an hour to dig out their bodies.

The multiculturalism that characterizes urban Canada has yet to make heavy inroads into the Ontario countryside; in Elgin County, the people tend to be almost exclusively of northern European descent. In general they look and act like fifth-generation midwestern farmers—slow-moving, friendly and polite, large-boned, with weather-beaten, tanned faces and pale blue eyes and clothes slightly behind the current fashions. If you didn't look or listen too closely, you might think you were in Michigan or Minnesota.

Except for the ubiquitous West Indians on bicycles. When a colourfully dressed Islander with flowing dreadlocks glided along the sidewalk past our car back on Port Rowan's main street, we'd assumed he was a tourist or someone from Toronto visiting a friend in the country. But now, on many side roads and at village intersections, we continued to encounter more men with their hair in dreads, wearing brightly patterned shirts. Some were alone, some in small groups; some were walking or hitch-hiking along the side of the road, but more often they were pedalling along on beat-up bicycles.

The fact that they were migrant workers took a while to sink in. We had once spent some time following Cesar Chavez around Arizona for a magazine piece as he tried to organize the Chicano fruit-pickers. To us, *those* were migrant workers; we hadn't expected to come across their counterparts north of the border. (We should have remembered our conversation with Lourdes Iglesias about her family history, but by now Buffalo was long forgotten.) Anyway, that's of course what they were; as one hitch-hiker explained, they arrive in May to plant the tobacco crop and often stay around until the late fall to harvest it. The bikes they were riding were supplied by their bosses.

At an isolated beach, we ran into a young man from Trinidad gazing out at the lake. This spot reminded him of home, he told us wistfully, and he came here often on his bike. This was his sixth year; his family needed the money, so he kept returning to this strange country where well-meaning but slightly silly people like us always begin a conversation by joking about how cold it gets in winter. Afterward, we noticed he had written his name and home town in the sandy cliff. It must be a lonely life.

But at least one of the imported workers had found a way around the isolation. By chance we heard something about the man we'd noticed back in Port Rowan. Like the others he had arrived to work the fields, but he had met and married a village girl and now qualified as a local himself, providing a welcome dash of colour in the pallid precincts of Port Rowan.

In Elgin County the concept of localness began to take on a

newer, richer meaning. You got the feeling that you could say anything about people twenty kilometres down the coast and not be challenged, or ask a question about what went on two villages over and get nothing but a blank stare. ("We heard everyone in Port X has two heads. Is that right?" After a pause, with polite precision, "I wouldn't know about that. Here in Port Y we only have one head each. But, you know, other people have their own ways.")

At Dave and Jean Mason's bed-and-breakfast in Port Burwell we sat drinking iced tea in the sunroom overlooking the lake, listening as Dave pointed out some tiny wisps of smoke on the horizon which rose from the factories of Ashtabula, fifty-one miles across the lake. "Some day I'd like to see Ashtabula," he murmured. At that moment the American side felt as far away as the farthest peak in Ultima Thule.

Not that Dave and Jean were overall-wearing, down-home types. He was the curator of the local museum, had been a high school art teacher in London, and the house was filled with his Riopelle-like oils; Jean had travelled in Europe after graduating from high school in a time when the great majority of her classmates thought only of getting married and starting a family and a day trip to Toronto was considered risky for any well-brought-up young woman. But even these two had settled into the Twenty Kilometre Syndrome once they had hunkered down in Elgin County.

Back in 1941, when Dave's father built the summer cottage that was now their year-round home, he'd surprised everyone by picking out a site more than seventy-five metres back from the lake. Between his piece of land and the water had stood a full block of houses and the old coastal road between Port Burwell and Port Rowan. But as it turned out, Mr. Mason was a man with foresight; in the ensuing half century all the other houses and the highway had fallen into the lake, leaving his son and daughter-in-law with a marvellous, unimpeded vista overlooking Port Burwell harbour and the widest part of Lake Erie.

That's because those prevailing south and south-west winds drive the waves against the exposed banks, destroying them with the efficiency of a mortar attack. Much of the sand and clay on which the earlier houses sat is now part of the giant sand hill or Long Point, as nature gives with one hand and takes away with the other (and costs various provincial and federal agencies a small fortune as they try to come up with ways to deal with the problem). Luckily for the Masons, in recent years a protective breakwater has been added west of their property; that, plus reinforcing the banks with concrete slabs and groining, means they have a reasonable chance of their home remaining on dry land. Although there is always the possibility that on some particularly stormy night they may reluctantly begin that long-postponed journey to the Ohio side.

(On the other hand, the International Joint Commission's 1993 Levels Reference Study casually mentions that "a strong body of scientific opinion" supports the theory that global warming will drastically effect the water levels in the Great Lakes over the next century. According to the most advanced computer models, the lower lakes could drop by as much as 1.5 metres, which, if it happens, would mean that the Masons would be able to walk halfway to Ohio. The IJC hedges its bets by pointing out that simulations are not precise predictions, but in coming years the definition of waterfront property may undergo considerable change. So think twice before you invest in that charming condo with access to the lake.)

Port Burwell (pop. 700), all dozen or so square blocks of it along Big Otter Creek, is Prozac in human form. Calm reigns. Though as recently as 1986 fish tubs were being built and launched from the harbour, the village's real glory days as a major shipbuilding town are over a century in the past. (Once they specialized in schooners as much as 135 feet in length.) The last boat of any consequence, a coal ferry called the *Ashtabula*, steamed out of Port Burwell one day in 1958, made it safely across the lake to its home port and then sank;

they haven't bothered to dredge the harbour since that time. Courtesy of the new breakwater, which catches sand blowing in from the west, the town does boast an ever-expanding stretch of beach where local people and the tourists who happen to wander by can laze their summer afternoons away.

The pretty little village, with its 1836 Colonial Gothic Anglican church and scattering of Queen Anne houses, is in desperate financial shape, and every once in a while a developer from the city comes around with big plans and promises. The most recent was a London company hoping to entice the province to put its prototype casino at Port Burwell. Dave Mason cleared off the coffee table and spread out a copy of the elaborate prospectus, prepared in part with the town's money, for our inspection. The proposed waterfront complex included an ultra-modern marina, hotel, condos, restaurants and theatres alongside the casino, all in sparkling white— something like Sydney Harbour or a seaside Taj Mahal. The suggestion that the provincial government might have chosen to locate its first gambling establishment in a minuscule village in farming country hours away from any major population centre seemed to us rather far-fetched, but the Port Burwell city fathers didn't see it that way. To no one's surprise but theirs, the casino went to Windsor, and the presentation left Port Burwell $140,000 in debt ($200 for every man, woman and child within the municipal limits).

While it awaits a more realistic proposal, the village is doing the best it can with what it's got. The next morning we dropped in at their weekend outdoor market, climbed to the top of their hexagonal lighthouse ("Canada's oldest wooden lighthouse"), nicely restored by Mennonite craftsmen, and then stopped by Dave's museum to find him hard at work among the nautical displays and videos. His wistfulness about Ashtabula was explained by a quick look through the exhibits, which dealt largely with the days when cargo ships steamed back and forth across the lake between this small port and the Ohio city. This is a place that you hope does find its way back to financial viability; it seems a shame to let it go the way of the ghost towns we had passed along County Road 42.

Al Mayhew, a cheerful, slightly goofy, ex-hippie type from Michigan, was unloading supplies from his pick-up when we drove up. People had told us that if we went to Port Bruce we had to take a look at his house, a mud-brown fieldstone castle whose design had been adapted from an illustration resembling a combination of a lighthouse and a castellated chess rook found on the front of Turret Cigarette boxes (a brand that disappeared after World War Two). The house was constructed in 1929 by a niece of the great inventor Thomas Edison, or maybe it was a sister-in-law (Al isn't sure which), whose father's family came from around here, and in the early days there was even a moat. The motivation behind this strange desire to recreate a life-sized commercial logo and then live in it is a secret she took with her to her grave.

All of this out-of-the-way hamlet in which Al and his family live seems something of a fairy-tale town. The first sign of civilization along the shore after Port Burwell, the whole community is contained within a circular road that comes down the cliff above the lake, passes along the fine (and as usual in these places, almost empty) beach and loops back to climb the hill again.

The grounds of what was once the town hotel, next-door to Castle Mayhew, now hosts a small trailer park. Even with this extra crowd to swell its numbers, however, the village's permanent population rarely rises above two hundred. Residents live a dreamy life under the sand bluffs, hidden by thick foliage from the rest of the world. Catfish Creek provides a channel through which they can sail their boats out onto the lake, and the herons barely bother to look up as they cruise by. There's no school, no downtown, no stores, nothing but Bert's Burgers. Bert has set out a few tables shaded with beach umbrellas, some spiky potted plants, and plays reggae on a ghetto-blaster; this is another locale where without much effort you can pretend that you've just dropped anchor in a West Indian harbour.

The hand-painted sign in front of the house reads "The Captain and the Goddess," but Al is actually a glass-blower who works the craft shows, and his wife Chris a librarian in nearby Aylmer. He showed us around his workroom, pulling open drawers to reveal boxes filled with tiny glass animals, then holding up an example of his current best-seller, a glass globe the size of a tennis ball in which he sets a long wick. The globe can be filled with oil and fitted into the neck of the bottle of your choice, creating a kind of do-it-yourself lantern. "I sold one to a nun who came back with some of her sisters, I guess you'd call them, and bought a bunch more. She said they liked to sit and watch them glowing." We bought a couple to stare at ourselves. They only cost five dollars.

Three times a year Al crosses the lake in his sailboat to replenish his stock of raw materials, which are cheaper in Ashtabula. His life is not stressful. Except for the perpetual struggle with the farmers who govern the township to which Port Bruce belongs and who have no use for people who would rather be sailing, the villagers might forget about the outside world for weeks at a time. After the great storm of 1984, when the lake-dwellers applied for financial assistance, one township official proclaimed, "Anybody who's dumb enough to live down there deserves to be blown away." At this same meeting another township resident rose to express his opinion, which was that "I'm the only man here who's met the Queen with a cauliflower ear." Al finds both of these statements typical of the thought processes of the inlanders.

But the laid-back Port Brucers don't let it bother them excessively. What do those others know of the joys of easy living on the shore of a great inland sea, of fishing off the old pier, watching the winter storms roll in and the red sunsets streak the sky over the water, of picnicking on the warm sand or under the cliffs in the shade of tall trees, and all the rest of what day-to-day life on the lake has to offer? Not much.

It must be admitted that only a peculiar brand of person could come to terms with the isolation on a year-round basis. But it leaves you with a good feeling to spend a little time where people like the Mayhews have found what they want.

Before drifting lazily on to Port Stanley, the metropolis of the mid-lake region, you pass a birding landmark known throughout the region as Hawk Cliff. We were too early the first time through. ("I never even start thinking about hawks until late September," the serious, polite, high school girl in the Port Stanley tourist office put it on that visit.)

So around the end of September we returned to Hawk Cliff, on a day when, according to the bird information line (run by people, not birds), the weather was supposed to be perfect. An overcast sky would require the hawks to fly low and the wind was from the west. As many as twenty thousand raptors have been known to pass by in one day, so with luck they might darken the sky over our heads.

Sure enough, as we neared the eroded cliff at the end of the side road we spotted at least fifty of them. Birders, that is, not hawks. Dressed in a colourful array of shiny Gortex jackets, old windbreakers, elaborately patterned handmade sweaters and knitted caps, they were roosting along the road, squinting through expensive-looking telescopes set up on tripods next to their vans or holding up binoculars that looked as if they could pick up a hummingbird's hum at ten miles. Several younger couples had brought along their kids, who were running in and out of the cars and climbing out to the edge of the bluff.

Unfortunately, though only moments earlier numerous pairs of peregrines had been soaring overhead, the wind had suddenly shifted and the falcons had packed it in, leaving the heavens to an occasional seagull. That's what the birders claimed, anyway. We left them staring fretfully through their elaborate lenses, waiting for conditions to change again.

A few miles west of Hawk Cliff, the shore road bursts out of the ever present tobacco fields and curves down into the most picturesque of all the lake towns on the Canadian side. Port Stanley (pop. 1,800) is framed by low, tree-covered hills as it spreads out around the mouth of Kettle Creek, which, as it winds and doubles back through town, forms a kind of bowl in which the downtown and waterfront have been neatly tucked.

Everywhere we'd been on Lake Erie people had assured us that back in the heyday of lake resorts, before back-yard swimming pools and barbecues kept people at home and charter flights allowed them to travel further away, their town was the vacation spot where things really used to happen— where the most famous musicians played in the most lavish dance hall near the scariest roller-coaster by the longest beach off which the biggest fish were caught.

But Port Stanley has a legitimate claim to having been the hot spot of this part of the lake. As early as 1833 a ferry service brought adventuresome tourists from Buffalo, and by the early years of this century its excellent beaches were attracting visitors from all directions. The town had a casino and a popular nightclub known as the Stork Club which featured a young Elgin County band-leader by the name of Guy Lombardo. Even today it retains some of the feel of those days; if Mary Ann Rutherford's cruise ship ever casts off ("It will happen"), this little town is scheduled to be its Canadian destination.

The hearts of countless storm-tossed sailors must have leapt when they came in sight of its welcoming breakwater; the harbour looks as if nature had gone out in search of the best naval architect on the Great Lakes to help design it. As it empties into Erie, the mouth of Kettle Creek is relatively narrow, but just a bit inland one side widens out to provide a kind of protected inner cove. The west side of the creek, as straight as an arrow, serves as the municipal pier where freighters can pick up and unload cargo. Wide-bodied fish tubs drop off their catch at fish plants there, and further upstream pleasure boats tie up in the marinas.

The town has a pleasingly self-reliant feel about it. Not that it's quite booming, but the bed-and-breakfasts are all booked, the fishery is holding its own, Consumers Gas continues to drill away out in the lake and, in addition to the full complement of tourist attractions (good beach, local museum, unpretentious restaurants that serve fresh fish), a reconstituted short line railroad chugs in and out of port all summer. There's also a pretty little working drawbridge on the main street right in the middle of town, which immediately prejudiced us in Port Stanley's favour.

But getting the balance right between tourism and normal life is always tricky. When we stopped in for a chat with Jean Vedova over at the Kettle Creek Inn, almost her first words were "We've got to make sure we don't turn into another Niagara-on-the-Lake."

Anxious to prove that Port Stanley is a real place, with its own stories to tell, she handed us a local history by Frank and Nancy Prothero, entitled *Port Stanley: Musings and Memories.* Beyond the standard old photos, schoolday reminiscences and other typical entries, the book gives the reader a sense of another, darker reality, a kind of wary, watchful unease with the massive body of water on which the town depends. Successive chapters are entitled "The Olga Disaster," "The Coffer Dam Disaster," "The Flood of 1929" and so on down a long list of local catastrophes.

Two stories in particular stayed with us. On May 17, 1925, a man walking along the shore near Cleveland found a bottle with a piece of paper inside. Taking it out, he found a quickly scribbled communication:

> Sinking south of Erieau. [A town to the west of Port Stanley.]
> No hope of saving boat. Listing badly. We are all taking to the water with belts on.
>
> Bert Butcher

The boat was the *Norinda*, the cargo was a load of contraband beer on its way to Ohio, and the belts didn't save them; the bodies of Captain Butcher and his crew were fished out some days later.

Captain Walter Grashaw of the *James B. Colgate* was luckier. His freighter steamed out of Buffalo carrying a load of anthracite for Fort William, Ontario (now Thunder Bay, on Lake Superior), on October 20, 1916, a day known around the lake since that time as Black Friday. By nightfall the ship was caught in another one of those devastating storms; winds were estimated to have reached 120 kilometres an hour. The *Colgate* was one of many ships that broke up during the night; all but three of the twenty-seven-man crew drowned immediately, but the captain and two others managed to scramble into a nine-foot life raft. During the next day and a half the two crew members lost their grips and slipped into the water, but after thirty-four hours a car ferry out of Port Stanley rescued the dazed, half-frozen captain.

We ate lunch at the Lakeview Inn facing out toward the town's main street—from left to right, Slade's Hardware, the Port Stanley Library, the Port Stanley Festival Theatre, several flagpoles, a memorial cairn to commercial mariners who have lost their lives on the lake, a row of cedars screening a small park and behind that the water of the harbour, then the drawbridge's yellow brick gatehouse. We were the only diners who bothered about the view; the other tables were filled with people talking fish.

JMS: After lunch, I left Ken to read the local paper and went outside to stretch my legs, but at the bridge I noticed the door to the gatehouse stood open. I really wanted to have a look inside the small, square structure and maybe ask how one of these things worked. So I knocked, and when a voice responded, "Come on up," I climbed the stairs to a small room lined with windows. There I was greeted by a short, sturdy man in his early sixties named Leroy Waite. "How'd you know my name?" he challenged. When I reminded him it was posted on the door downstairs, he laughed and then said yes, he'd be happy to answer any questions. I felt as if I'd passed some sort of test.

Happy was an understatement; I'd never met anyone who so obviously enjoyed his work. Dressed in shorts, T-shirt and baseball cap, he stood in the middle of the small space that was his work world and plunged into a detailed description of his daily routine. By the time we came up for air some twenty minutes later, I had learned more about drawbridges than I'd ever imagined I wanted to know.

"Do I like my job? Oh, yes, I like my job. I took an early retirement from Clarke Equipment, that's heavy machinery, then I got into this. That's what I really like, maintenance. Most maintenance I can do myself."

He pointed out the compact sink/fridge/two-burner stove unit that took up one wall. ("We cook all sorts of things here.") In one corner sat a small wooden table with a radio on it and one chair. Facing north toward the street was a control board with rows of flashing lights, red, green and yellow. He explained how the bridge worked, including the safety catch that prevents it from rising when a car has passed the gate, and then pointed to a smaller tower across the creek on the other side of the bridge with two small lights in one window. "That's an extra precaution. I can look over there and they let me know whether the traffic light on the other side is working properly and whether it's red or green.

"I've got a P.A. too. Sometimes there's tourists walking on the bridge when I start the warning procedures, gates lowering, bells ringing, lights flashing, they just freeze up, stand there trying to figure out what's happening. So I have to shout at them. Then they run like anything." To make sure I understood the procedure, he casually opened the bridge, stopping traffic in both directions and probably leaving the drivers and pedestrians scratching their heads as they waited, since no boats were going through. "See? That's how it works."

"You've got to look at this." He pointed to a small television console hanging from the ceiling, turned it on and we were looking at a close-up of one section of the bridge. "That's for the blind spot." Then he opened a cupboard door and pulled a switch, and now we were staring at "Days of Our Lives" on the same screen. "That's because sometimes the last boat comes through around six and I'm here until ten. It's something to do." A folding chaise longue was stashed economically into a small space behind the stair railing. "I brought that from home. If there's a boat coming through at four in the morning and no one else until six, I can catch some sleep. We used to try it sitting up in the chair but this is better.

"This bridge is what they call a connecting link; the water on one side is provincial, on the other side, the outer harbour, it's federal. The bridge is provincial, though. Our work day is six a.m. to ten p.m. I've got two part-time men to help; we work eight-hour shifts. The bridge goes up on the half hour. The village decided that a few years ago, there were so many going through. There's hundreds of small boats, sports fishing with a hook and line, I do that myself, that come through from upriver. But the fish tubs can go through anytime. When they're coming back in the evening, they let me know what time they plan to leave the next morning, usually around five-thirty but it could be as early as four."

Three Canada geese flew low over the creek as we watched through the window, and Leroy fitted them into his exposition without skipping a beat. "There's a hundred and fifty of those that stay here over the winter. The machinery's mostly down underneath. There's a fifty-ton counterweight right below us. Two of them. All summer I'm keeping a list, then as soon as the river freezes over we can begin repair work. That's not much time to fix everything on the list. The bridge closes November 15, then I'm here by myself. Then the boats go out again around the first of March, except in a mild winter like '92–'93 we had some out the first week in January."

At this point I remembered that Ken didn't know where I was and looked out the window to see him searching the downtown with a slightly worried look on his face. After much waving I got his attention and he came over to be introduced to Leroy, who was in the process of relating a story about the worst accident they'd ever had at the draw-bridge. "One night, there was this guy partying above the bridge. It was last call, ten p.m., black as your hat out. Four boats lined up to come in, this guy sees the bridge open, runs to his boat, casts off, tries to beat the bridge coming down but you can't beat this bridge. The operator [one of Leroy's assis-tants] never saw him. Snapped his mast right off, other stuff. He was some mad. RCMP, Coast Guard, the whole works."

Before leaving we asked Leroy about another Tall Ship we had spotted tied up across the river, an obviously homemade imitation of a Spanish galleon called the *Golden Lion*. "Steve Martin built that in his back yard, you can see the house from here, and then brought it down to the water." This must be the vessel we'd heard about that had started out for Spain to participate in Columbus's five-hundredth anniver-sary party in 1992 but had got only as far as the West Indies before turning back, either because the crew mutinied or the weather was bad or the captain changed his mind or they got a late start; no one seemed to agree which it was. Leroy prob-ably had an opinion, but he declined to let us in on it. We thought briefly about looking around for El Capitan Martin and trying to ferret out the truth, but in the end we just added it to our life list of Tall Ships and went on our way.

Chapter Twelve

All along the northern shore of Lake Erie we kept coming across reminders of the mysterious native nation known as the Neutral Indians. Jim Allen had pointed out one of their graveyards as we floated down the Grand River, the education centre at Backus Woods contained a diorama of one of their fishing camps, and we'd heard that the farmer whose property included the giant sand hill, in the days before it became a campground, used to turn up occasional arrowheads and fragments of artifacts.

Apart from the fact that the Neutrals were an Iroquoian-speaking group who inhabited the area west of the Niagara Peninsula, about the only information we'd been able to glean from the textbooks was that they were thought to have developed a highly sophisticated political and military structure, that they tattooed themselves extensively with animal images, and that to the Hurons, their neighbours to the north, they were *Attiwasdaronk*, "people whose speech is strange." (We don't know how they referred to the Huron, but it probably wasn't any more complimentary.)

The European name for them derives from a misunderstanding on the part of Samuel de Champlain. When he encountered them, sometime around 1615, he somehow got the impression that they had carefully stayed out of the wars of expansion between the Iroquois and the Huron, and he called them "*la nation neutre.*" Since the Neutrals were a major power, it's more likely that the others were avoiding them, but in any case, they were already occupied militarily with various hereditary enemies to the west. Only after the Europeans had brought the smallpox bacilli to Ontario and the devastating epidemic of 1638-40 had decimated the Neutral nation did they become fair game for conquest; a decade later a coalition of Mohawk and Seneca armies completed their annihilation, and after 1651 the Neutrals disappear from the historical record.

Nothing we had come across compared in atmosphere to the Southwold Earthworks, a provincial archaeological site near the village of Iona, a few miles north-west of Port Stanley. That's mainly because the site, once you find it, is so secluded that it has remained pretty much untouched since being abandoned sometime in the sixteenth century.

No bulldozers or backhoes have been at work here, there are no caretakers' huts or any other structures, and at the entryway no smiling student stands ready to collect an admission fee and force a brochure into your hand. We parked on the shoulder of a quiet county road next to a small official marker, then followed a wide, grassy laneway bordered on one side by a field of corn and on the other by a dense woodlot where just a few steps off the path and into the trees would take you into cool darkness.

When the lane took a sharp jog to the right, the road and all other reminders of late-twentieth-century life vanished and only the tall corn, the trees and the warm wind remained. Some kind of locust was making a whirring noise that blended with the slight rustling of the cornstalks. When the path turned again and we emerged into the wide, sunlit clearing where the oval-shaped palisaded fort had stood, we experienced something of the elation the Neutrals must have felt at the sudden sight of their home after a long trip through the forest. As many as eight hundred people once inhabited this settlement; that's more than live within the town limits of present-day Port Burwell or Port Rowan and four times the permanent population of Port Bruce.

One of the great discoveries of modern archaeology has been the realization that holes last forever; once man has tampered in any way with a piece of ground, whether to dig a few postholes or to excavate the foundations of an entire city block, the dirt can never be replaced in a way that returns it to its original pre-dug state. As a result, here at Southwold researchers have been able to mark the original outer circle of palisades and the outlines of the dwellings, despite the fact that their tall poles themselves are long gone. Judging from the number of longhouse foundations, the small village, which extends no more than 150 metres at its widest point, must have been jam-packed, virtually a tiny rustic inner city.

Unfortunately the little we know about the Neutrals, aside from these occasional physical traces, comes from a few throwaway remarks by members of other nations and the odd reference in journals of the earliest explorers and priests. Which is slightly spooky and highly frustrating when you think about it; this wasn't an ancient civilization, lost in the confusions of antiquity, or a half-mythical people like the Khazars or the Anasazi; these contemporaries of Elizabethan England were visited by European explorers and preached to by Catholic missionaries. We can almost reach back and touch them, but at the last moment they evade our grasp. Not even the Jesuit Relations have much to tell us about this particular native civilization.

Survivors of the Iroquois holocaust are assumed to have joined the remnants of other exterminated peoples such as the Tobacco, Petun and Erie, who fled to north-western Ohio and collectively became known as Wyandot. But it seems a pity for this once powerful nation, which at its height is thought to have numbered more than forty thousand, to have so completely disappeared that we still don't even know its real name.

From Iona we meandered back toward the lake along a series of concession roads, not bothering about exactly where the car was taking us but just keeping the sun on one side as we rolled vaguely westward, turning right here on a road that cut off at a diagonal, then left again there when the next road veered north. In this purely haphazard way, we happened on the small white church in a ghost town called Tyrconnell, in whose graveyard Colonel Thomas Talbot is buried.

Lake Erie's shores have been home to what seems an unusually high proportion of pugnacious individualists over the years, but if the entire gang of them got together to vote for the person most likely to succeed as class egomaniac, the Colonel would probably win by unanimous acclaim. For as he confided to his mentor and commanding officer, General Simcoe, while they were struggling over a difficult portage at Long Point, "None are more manly than I." Next to the bombastic Colonel, Dr. Troyer was a conventional thinker and Mary Ann Rutherford is a coy country lass.

Descended from the Anglo-Irish aristocracy, Talbot entered the British Army in 1782 at the age of eleven and rose to become one of two young aides-de-camp of the Marquis of Buckingham. His colleague was an equally ambitious youngster named Arthur Wellesley, better known to posterity as the Duke of Wellington, and though the careers of the two well-born chums took radically differing paths, their philosophical outlooks remained virtually identical. Both started life as stone-cold reactionaries and never deviated from that attitude. In some ways Talbot went even further than Wellington; the Duke was merely commander in chief of the British and allied armies and later prime minister; for several decades Talbot reigned as the *de facto* monarch of western Ontario.

In 1790 he was sent to the Quebec garrison and a year later assigned to the staff of General Simcoe, military commander of Upper Canada (Ontario), in whose company he travelled as far west as Detroit. Tensions caused by the French Revolution took the ambitious young soldier back to Europe for six years, but his travels in Ontario had made a strong impression on him and had given him some extravagant

ideas. ("Here I will roost and will soon make the forests trem-
ble under the wings of the flocks I will invite by my war-
blings around me," he had informed Simcoe before heading
home.) In 1800 he resigned his commission to return to the
New World and to begin putting together a kind of private
fiefdom in the wilds along the north shore of Lake Erie.

After receiving a resignation grant from the Crown of five
thousand acres around the mouth of Kettle Creek, Talbot
used his family connections to go over the heads of what he
considered the rabble who governed the territory from York
(Toronto). As a result he received permission to subdivide his
holdings into a kind of Talbot's Sunnydale Gardens and even
wangled a guarantee that for every newcomer he convinced to
settle there he would receive an additional two hundred acres
of his own choosing. Eventually his personal estate grew to
some sixty thousand acres, and he erected what in pioneer
Ontario passed for a mansion just down the coast from Port
Stanley.

Talbot wasn't a slacker. According to Anna Jameson, a gen-
tlewoman friend to whom as an old man he related his life
story, "For sixteen years he scarce saw a human being...he
himself assumed the blanket-coat and axe, slept on the bare
earth, cooked three meals a day for twenty woodsmen,
cleaned his own boots, washed his own linen, milked his
cows, churned the butter, and baked the bread...he has
passed his life in worse than solitude." While we don't have to
accept at face value this version of his herculean efforts, life in
the wilderness could not have been any picnic, and it's undeniable that the Colonel accomplished what he set out to do.

Applicants for land arrived at his door in Port Talbot in a
constant stream; if they passed muster he would assign them
a lot and make sure they knew what was required of them,
which included a yearly fee, upkeep of the road Talbot insisted
they build in front of their property and remaining in residence themselves. (The right to transfer one's property to relatives or sell it to outsiders was not high on the Colonel's list
of basic human freedoms.) Irish and Scots immigrants, always

provided they were sufficiently respectful, usually met with his approval, while Yankees, with their pernicious democratic notions and annoying business acumen, often did not. If his choices proved derelict in any of their duties he simply erased their names from his map and gave the property to someone else. For his friends, the sky was the limit; his surveyor, Mahlon Burwell, got all the land around the mouth of Big Otter Creek, where, following his employer's lead, he founded a community named after himself.

Some of those rejected, who had, after all, abandoned their homes and often travelled thousands of miles to get there, refused to accept Talbot's cavalier dismissals with the good grace he expected. When Duncan Patterson's request for a decent piece of land was peremptorily turned down, for example, the infuriated highlander sought and received a reversal by the simple expedient of throwing the Colonel to the ground and commencing to throttle him. Another hot-tempered Scot, the wife of an early settler, achieved the concessions she felt her family deserved by threatening him with a carving fork. After several such incidents Talbot built what he called a "sliding wall" to shelter behind when approached by an applicant whose looks alarmed him. He would then call out from behind his barricade "What do you want?" and set the dogs on the newcomer if not satisfied with the answer.

Despite this somewhat arbitrary philosophy of land development, by the year 1836 an estimated thirty thousand settlers had put down roots in the wide expanse of forest between Long Point and Amherstburg at the western end of the lake. A good road had been built, towns founded, post offices and schools set up. And every year on May 21, the anniversary of Talbot's arrival, a banquet was held in his honour in the burgeoning community that had been named after him. It was called St. Thomas.

But it all turned sour in the end. Not even as determined an authoritarian as Talbot could keep the democratic instincts of the ever-increasing mass of settlers in check. Vigorous support for the status quo during William Lyon MacKenzie's

1837 rebellion against the Family Compact, in the form of public protestations of loyalty to British ways and the sponsoring of goon squads to beat up opposition groups, were his last hurrah. (One of these attacks had far-reaching consequences. When Talbot's thugs set upon the rebel faction in Port Burwell, their leader, a man named John Edison, was forced to flee to the United States. He eventually settled in northern Ohio, where his son, Thomas Alva, was born a few years later.)

After 1837 Talbot became increasingly irrelevant. "I would not, if anyone was to offer me the universe, go through again the horrors I have undergone in forming this settlement," he told Anna Jameson.

The would-be potentate died a lonely and bitter old bachelor in 1853, but aspects of his legacy continue to permeate the lakeshore counties—psychologically, in the pigheaded conservatism still often characteristic of the area, and physically, in the plans he laid out and the many communities he founded. The very road we had been riding on during much of our travels, the highway from St. Thomas to Leamington, follows his original trail, and the only aspect that would surprise the megalomaniacal Colonel if he could see it today would be that it is known as Highway 3 instead of Talbot's Road.

Our next stop was Port Glasgow, a tiny settlement so small many maps leave it out, where the inhabitants undoubtedly include a fair number of descendants of those Scottish immigrants who made it past the Colonel's scrutiny. At the grandly named Port Glasgow Yacht Club, a modest one-storey frame structure along a man-made inlet at the end of a dirt road just off the highway, we stopped to chat with three old salts in baseball caps who looked as if they had been sitting there staring out at the lake, if not ever since the time of Thomas Talbot, then from an era not long afterward.

As it happened one of the three had just cut short a fishing trip. "It may look smooth from here," he told us, "but out there..." He trailed off, then looked up at an ominous sky and added slightly defensively, "There's a storm brewing." We believed him; just in front of us, the waves were crashing against the breakwater, and overall the lake was beginning to have a distinct swell to it.

"There's lots of fish out there, but you have to know where they are," the returnee went on. In the short time he'd been out he'd caught four large pickerel. "Pickerel are good eating fish. One of these will feed a lot of people." But how do you know how to find them, we asked, expecting a complicated dissertation on the art of fish-seeking. "Easy," he replied. "You follow that guy over there." He pointed to a large charter boat with an impressive array of electronics that was rocking back and forth at anchor just a few feet away. "He's got all the equipment."

"This is the best fishing in the country, right here," one of his friends broke in. "You go up north, you pay all that money, stay at a lodge, what do you get?" He answered his own question, "Nothing but minnows. A little fish this big." He held his hands up, a few inches apart.

The third man agreed. "Down at Port Bruce the fishing's no good. Port Stanley to Erieau's the best place. See how clear that water is out there? The fish all come down here." We had never been fishing up north, or in Port Bruce or anywhere else for that matter, but these three looked like men who knew what they were talking about, even making allowance for local bias.

Back on Highway 3 a few fat raindrops started hitting the windshield and the water over to our left had turned blackish blue. Ahead the land was flat, flat, flat, green and golden-brown, with tiny dark rows of trees, houses and barns, wood-lots and telephone poles marking the far horizon. The whole landscape, now being inundated by the pouring rain, seemed a lesson in perspective, like one of those sketches you see in *How to Draw for Beginners* books.

Past Erieau the rain stopped as quickly as it had started and the sky began clearing. A streak of pale orange appeared straight ahead, then a few small, white cotton-candy puffs arrived from nowhere, all of it topped by ragged grey clouds pulling back to reveal a lighter upper sky. As we neared Leamington, a series of rolling gullies dipped down to the lake from the road. There were few houses and very little traffic; once a Pontiac with a Michigan licence passed us, then several minutes later a pick-up approached from the other direction. But essentially we found ourselves more alone than at any other point along the lake. It was just us and the water and the sky.

We had gone as far as we were going on this foray. It was time to turn around and pick up at the point we had left off on the American side, where a very different set of surroundings awaited us. It was hard to accept that the isolated hamlets we'd been passing all day could exist within the same hemisphere, let alone be situated just a score or so nautical kilometres from struggling, crime-ridden, industrial Cleveland. But the largest city on the lake was our next destination. A cigarette boat could have whisked us there in less than thirty minutes; the drive would take several hours.

Chapter Thirteen

At the end of the Depression Kenneth Patchen, who grew up in northern Ohio, wrote a short lyric called "Cleveland, Oh?" that runs in part:

> ...
> Nothing was as good as being dead.
> The old men never tired of saying it:
> *Nothing was quite as good as being dead.*

> ...
> God was far away and the boats never came by anymore.
> Nothing was very good or even
> At all evil in any ultimate sense.

Obviously even great poets have trouble coming to terms with the city of Cleveland. Maybe it's because, unlike most of its neighbours around the Great Lakes region, the city has never had a convenient hook on which to hang a quick sketch. Pittsburgh was the Steel City, Detroit the Motor City, Chicago Hog Butcher to the World and all that. Toledo makes glass, Buffalo had the Erie Canal and still has Niagara Falls, even little Akron, thirty miles south of Cleveland, was at one time known as the rubber capital.

But when the most populous city on Lake Erie enters any conversation the only association that comes to the mind of the average North American is likely to be ridicule. A venerable truism of stand-up comedy says that every community has another smaller locale nearby to which it feels superior, a place whose mere name automatically evokes a laugh. Ever since the sixties comedy show "Laugh-in" took to calling it the "mistake on the lake," Cleveland has been the Hackensack of all America (or if you live in the Midwest, the Peoria), the city where the river caught on fire, the home of haplessness, boredom's centre of gravity, a great place to be from, or whatever.

Today the joke seems finally to have run its course, and in its stead we kept encountering Clevelanders like the couple back at Watso's winery. After repeating the "no kidding, you wouldn't recognize the place now" mantra they would go on to list such civic improvements as the gentrification of the Flats, the new baseball stadium, the new basketball arena, the ever-expanding Cleveland Clinic and a new university, Cleveland State. Well, maybe. But don't forget that one of us is from Cleveland, and it will take more than Chamber of Commerce slogans to convince him that the city has really changed.

For one thing, Cleveland still lacks a defining industry. For another, the city continues to be almost totally estranged from its only important natural asset. Most cities on a lake or ocean or river or even a creek have grown up along the water and know enough to maintain public access to it. Dockside gathering places help give a city its atmosphere; down by the water, citizens can catch the breeze, find a bit of space to soothe their souls, walk along an esplanade or sit on a bench to watch the changing sky, "ooh" and "ahh" at plush pleasure boats and freighters with exotic, foreign names and generally make a connection to a wider world. Chicago built its downtown along Lake Michigan; Toronto put the Canadian National Exhibition along one part of its Lake Ontario shoreline and turned the rest into parks, cultural centres, hotels and apartments. A bridge connects Detroit to one of its islands and an excursion boat sails to another. Even Erie, Pennsylvania, for all our grumbling about the place, puts its public piers to good use and keeps its focus on the waterfront.

But in Cleveland, it's not just that the boats hardly ever come by any more; today, Lake Erie and its largest city are essentially strangers. If you actually managed to find a place to hire a boat and sailed the length of the city's waterfront, you wouldn't see many strollers to wave to, or find many places to set anchor, or for that matter have very much to look at. Just freeways, a network of train tracks, a small airport, assorted utility plants, a solitary and rather forbidding-looking stadium flanked by a huge parking lot, an occasional well-fenced marina and, to the east and west of downtown, long, lonely stretches of poorly tended parkland that few people venture into even in daylight and where, after dark, even drug dealers enter only in groups. At twenty miles, Cleveland's shoreline is almost as long as Chicago's; the contrasting uses the two cities have made of their waterfronts demonstrate the depths and the heights of American urban planning.

Of course Cleveland didn't start out as the mistake on the lake. In the first decades after the opening of the Erie Canal, as thousands of people poured into this burgeoning new settlement, the shoreline blossomed with flower-filled parks, beaches and picnic grounds. Judging from old photos, you could stroll directly from your centrally located office to the water and spend your lunch hour relaxing amid waterfront gardens and meadows, or sitting under a willow tree by the banks of the Cuyahoga, which serpentined its way right through the centre of town, dipping your toes in the cool water.

And then, around 1860, the Industrial Revolution arrived with a vengeance. Perfectly situated to receive iron ore from the upper lakes and coal from Pennsylvania, Cleveland quickly became a major centre of heavy industry. Monstrous blast furnaces rose from the once bucolic fields, and around the same time local boy John D. Rockefeller hit his first gushers in nearby Pennsylvania and set up Standard Oil, making Cleveland the nation's first centre of oil refining. Good for Cleveland, you might say. Boom times ahead.

But unfortunately for the city, Rockefeller and the other captains of industry who ran Cleveland insisted on building their soot-spewing factories and mills along the low banks of the Cuyahoga (the Flats) as it wound into Lake Erie, a mere two-minute walk from the city centre. This was an urban planning insanity equivalent to putting Ford's River Rouge plant a block from Cadillac Square in Detroit, or shifting the steel works of Gary, Indiana, to the Loop in Chicago.

The downtown waterfront quickly developed into the industrial wasteland it more or less remains today, almost a century and a half later. And in the long run, with its natural amenities poisoned and paved over, Cleveland could never make its centre attractive enough to give people a reason to spend much time downtown. It's certainly not a coincidence that when the industrial barons got around to donating art museums and concert halls and universities to the city they set them in tidy little floral bowers miles away from both the downtown and the lake, in what were then the eastern outskirts of town.

Even as Cleveland was bursting into prosperity in the 1890s, expanding to become America's fifth largest city by 1920 (pop. 800,000), a new series of planning decisions was finishing off the downtown. First the city built two competing and unrelated central squares within sight of each other. The original, known as Public Square, contained hotels, theatres, office buildings and the Terminal Tower, a fifty-two-storey skyscraper whose erection in 1928 marked the high point and the beginning of the end of Cleveland's prosperity. Then kitty-corner to this cluster of buildings, but closer to the lakeshore, they put up an arrangement of grandiose neoclassical structures—county administration building, courthouse, city hall, a public auditorium—around a sterile rectangle known as The Mall. Removed from any natural street life, this is Cleveland's own early version of Brasilia.

Around the same time, the city trucked in a thousand yards or so of landfill between The Mall and the water; when the chain-link fences, elevated highway, the stadium and its parking lot and a small airport were all laid down, the lake was effectively cut off from any relation to downtown activity. Not only could you not get there from here, you could hardly tell where *there* was. In one dazzling swoop, the city planners had managed to complete the elimination of Lake Erie from Cleveland's consciousness and create a downtown so unfocused that even today you can't quite figure out where its centre is supposed to be.

⁀ The popular bathing beaches to the east and west of downtown—with their dance halls, piers, picnic grounds and amusement parks—lasted a little longer, but they, too, were doomed. The cause was partly pollution (early in the century municipal engineers built their main sewage disposal plants right in the middle of the most popular beaches—our parents' generation was right about this) and partly increasing racial antagonism in the north. When after World War Two the prospect of factory jobs brought an influx of southern black families into the neighbourhoods adjacent to the eastern beaches, the municipal government pretty much lost interest in keeping them in good repair.

By then the seeds of decline that had been had been sown by a century of poor planning were coming to fruition. Few cities were as little prepared to deal with the growing obsolescence of their industrial base or changing population patterns. Once the middle-class flight to the suburbs had begun (Cleveland's population dropped 35 percent, to around half a million, in a generation), the city seemed to lose what little identity it had.

One small source of pride did remain; as every local school child from 1900 on could have told you, Cleveland had the highest percentage of foreign-born citizens of any metropolis in the United States. Not quite the same as being the rubber capital or City of the Big Shoulders, but something reasonably tangible to put in the promotional brochures.

What this meant in practice, however, was not cheerful foreign restaurants and festivals with dancers in national dress, but an ethnic segregation as rigid as that of modern-day Bosnia. The Italians seldom left Little Italy and the Italian suburbs, the African-Americans stayed in their place on the East Side, the Jews in the Heights, the hillbillies on the West Side, the Hungarians, Ukrainians and Poles on the South Side, the Slovenes on St. Clair, the Mexicans on West 25th Street (all Spanish speakers were known as Mexicans back then). People crossed the lines for business purposes, but socially and politically you stuck with your own kind. In the last thirty or forty years those lines have blurred to some extent—even Cleveland could hardly fail to be affected by the social changes begun in the sixties—but this is still essentially a city divided by race and country of origin.

So perhaps it was fitting that the first person with whom we exchanged words upon stopping for a meal somewhere in the endless mini-mall of the farther eastern suburbs was a recent immigrant. This was in a Mayfield Heights restaurant called Bob Evans, which turned out to be a franchise of one of the myriad of fast-food chains that have sprung up all across the country in the wake of McDonald's and Burger King.

A tall, thin, tired-looking woman in her forties, our waitress was obviously devoting every ounce of her energy to adapting several millennia of Chinese culture to the bizarre demands of her new homeland. With a glazed smile and worried-looking eyes, every few moments she would swoop down and, with the requisite Bob Evans friendliness, demand "How you guy do today?" Then before we could summon up an appropriately upbeat reply she would mumble, "Thass good," and vanish. This air of enforced conviviality in a place where grandmothers and immigrants in uniform were working like dogs at low-paying service jobs made us feel increasingly like the best friends of the proprietor of a slave labour camp.

As these places go, the decor was pleasant enough. Bob's gimmick is a kind of down-home, checkered-tablecloth folksiness, with a special bow toward senior citizens (they get a discount, and fried mush was featured on the menu) and a pleasing willingness to expand its staff beyond perky teenagers. And our meals, when they arrived, looked promising; the mashed potatoes had a golden sheen, the catfish fillets seemed crisp and hot. All illusion, of course; it didn't even taste like food, at least to our delicate palates. Although everyone else was avidly gobbling it down.

Continuing east along Mayfield Road we reached the pleasant, older suburb of Cleveland Heights, with its classic, small-townish tree-lined streets, mock Colonial shopping centres and satisfied-looking citizens, then turned right into the postwar ranch house neighbourhood known as Forest Hills. There is an actual hill here, on whose slopes a century ago Rockefeller built his ornate, hotel-like summer home (long since burned down), and even the leafy traces of a forest.

Heading down through a tapestry of ball diamonds, lagoons and open fields, we got a glimpse of why America remains the Promised Land in the world's imagination. Peace and quiet, space to move around in, big trees, large, comfortable houses on wide lots, they're all here. The notion that any penniless, uneducated peasant family from some remote dictatorship, if they manage to save enough money to get here and work hard enough after they arrive, might one day see their children settled in a community something like this must still be one of the great animating forces in the universe.

Everything changes as you descend into East Cleveland. Since early in the century this inner suburb has been a working-class ethnic enclave, a kind of halfway house between the city slums and the greener, more distant suburbs. But for the first time it's not just a new ethnic group but a new race that has moved in to occupy these streets. And the homeland their parents and grandparents left behind is not Ireland or Italy or Poland but another part of their own country. In other words, everyone here is black.

Turning onto Euclid Avenue, which becomes Cleveland's main street when it crosses the city limits some distance farther west, we drove for a good forty blocks without seeing a white face—even, to our perhaps naive surprise (having not spent much time in any American city in recent years), on the billboards perched on top of the old buildings, where young mocha-coloured men and women with tidy coifs and Anglo features were cheerfully smoking Newports and Marlboro Lights. The neighbourhood of Superfly Barber Shop, Ali's Food Market, Everlasting Baptist Church, Versatile Records, Boone and Jack's Laundromat, The African Room, Cicero's Club, Evening Star Missionary Baptist Church and the rest was a planet unto itself.

As we drove closer to downtown some of the residential cross streets began to look as if only old-timers would be able to remember when trash was last collected. At one corner a knot of young men with hard, empty faces had gathered. Resigned-looking individuals sat on stoops or lay sprawled out with their backs against a wall, or drifted in and out of makeshift bars and storefronts with metal grilles in front of the windows. (Even the seediest-looking businesses had put out money for these, probably the only kind of insurance they could afford.)

On the whole, however, even at its worst this is not the same type of bombed-out slum as Calcutta or the South Bronx. There's too much space, for one thing. And in many blocks the modest houses were in good repair, and the gas stations, barber shops, soul food restaurants and small grocery stores were humming with the same kind of workaday small business activity that Norman Rockwell used to love to paint.

But the central, overwhelming fact of this quarter is that only one race lives here, and that it is possible, in this last decade of the twentieth century, in this country where the vast majority of the people are of European origin, for an African-American child born on Cleveland's East Side to live out his or her life without ever holding a conversation on equal terms with a white person. He or she will encounter white teachers, cops, social workers and others in authority, may order fast food from white counter workers and purchase goods from white sales clerks, but could easily never have a white friend or even a white co-worker, should they be lucky enough to find a job.

This *de facto* segregation cuts both ways, of course, and everybody loses out. To most of white Cleveland—despite the lip service paid to racial harmony, the posters of black athletes in suburban teenage bedrooms and the record sales of black artists—this whole large section of their city has little psychological reality. Even on the nightly news, reports from the inner city are structured like those from the "war-torn former Yugoslavia": quick sound bites from the front lines, usually involving violence, occasionally leavened by patronizing stories about local residents devoting free time to improving the neighbourhood or about innocent children who have been caught up in tragedy. The fact that some of the reporters braving the war zone are black doesn't much matter; black or white, they all look, talk and act like foreign correspondents.

As we neared the city centre, straight ahead of us the art deco roof line of the Terminal Tower shimmered in the morning sun. A businessman who works downtown had told us a complicated story about this building and its relationship to the inner-city blocks we were driving through. As a key element in their plan to revitalize Cleveland's downtown core, the city government and a consortium of developers had poured millions of dollars into renovating the ground levels of the skyscraper, turning it into a gleaming, multi-levelled complex of exclusive shops. An essential part of the process included hiring a no-nonsense security squad to make sure loiterers didn't hang over the brass rails of the balconies, clutter up the polished passageways or generally inconvenience the crowds of monied trend-setters expected to flock in. Or, to put it more plainly, to make sure poor non-whites, especially the teenagers, didn't get in the way of the suburban dollars.

This meant, of course, ignoring as potential customers the over three hundred thousand blacks and Hispanics who live closer to downtown than anyone else, the people who get their hair cut at Superfly's Barber Shop or who sing in the choir at the Everlasting Baptist Church on Sunday mornings.

Even though many don't have much left over by the time the
rent and groceries and medical expenses are paid for, collectively they would still have more buying power than the tiny
minority of suburban dwellers who might be expected to go
against the prevailing trend and actually make the long trip
downtown. But you can't sell 'em if you can't see 'em, and
guess what? After an initial surge of curiosity the non-white
city people stayed home and the white suburbanites went
back to their malls; the stores, by all accounts, were soon
starving.

We parked the car in a downtown lot (for the minuscule
sum of two dollars an hour, which wouldn't get you a skate-
board space within ten miles of most city centres and made
clear just how far Cleveland had yet to travel on the road to
resuscitation). But cutting across Public Square to take a peek
at the Tower, an ornate piece of walk-in sculpture known as
the Soldiers and Sailors Monument caught our attention.
This over-the-top but rather endearing 1894 memorial
depicts Civil War scenes with titles like "The Advance
Guard" and "At Short Range." Inside a small room, with a
sign at the entrance reading "Gentlemen Please Remove Your
Hats" and an overpowering smell of urine, the dingy walls
were covered with the names of enlistees from Cuyahoga
County and a long quotation by Henry Ward Beecher that
demonstrated a touching faith in the country's future:

> How bright are the honours which await those who
> with sacred fortitude and patriotic patience have
> endured all things that they might save their native land
> from divisions and from the power of corruption.

In the centre stood a square of bronze friezes, among them a
tribute to a cluster of Florence Nightingales on the home
front dedicated to the "Patriotic women of Northern Ohio,
whose activities were similar to those of the Red Cross." On
another side a grateful slave knelt to hand Abraham Lincoln a
musket while a gang of distinguished-looking generals looked

on, a slightly *outré* allegory that might have been sponsored by the National Rifle Association; Lincoln is revered for many accomplishments, but taking pot-shots at the enemy is not one of them.

A few more steps across the square took us a hundred years forward into the plush lobby of the Terminal Tower. Many of the trendy national clothing chains were represented, as well as bookstores, jewellers, luggage shops, modish arts and crafts, every conceivable kind of beauty salon and other pampering service and the rest of the typical upscale mall environment. A smattering of shoppers were strolling past the potted plants or munching salads at the make-believe outdoor cafés, but the whole scene had a slightly strained feel to it, as if hidden cameras were watching your every move and rating your bank balance. A faint feeling of muted fury filtered along the gilded walls, although whether it emanated from the frustrated shop owners, the few lonely bargain-hunters or the gawkers who couldn't afford any of this stuff no matter how much it was reduced was impossible to tell. One thing seems clear: if there is ever a riot in Cleveland, you wouldn't want to be walking around here with a card that read "Manager" on your jacket.

By this time, a few years after the great renovation, some of the stores seemed to have recognized where their potential market lies. The closest thing to a crowd that we encountered was in a record shop that had largely converted to music that appealed to black teenagers. But most of the salespeople were still vainly waiting for those mythological shoppers to saunter in with their bags of gold.

That evening we stopped by the house of some old friends who live in Shaker Heights, a stretch of suburban nirvana that, in the fifties, ranked as the wealthiest community per capita in the United States. We had never imagined Shaker Heights to be a prime candidate for racial integration, but today, courtesy of Chapter 8 Assisted Housing, its more modest blocks are now almost solidly black, and many black professionals have bought homes in the expensive sections.

Our friends were a mixed couple, and the conversation turned quickly and inevitably to race. You can't seem to get away from it in Cleveland. About half of the students in the Shaker Heights school system are non-white, they told us. A few are children of the professionals, but the great majority, many of whom are on welfare, come from that poorer section. That includes an indeterminate but substantial block of kids parachuted into the system by inner-city parents desperate to get their children out of the abysmal and dangerous Cleveland schools. (Where the high school dropout rate exceeds 80 percent, and even hanging in to grade twelve is no guarantee of receiving an education; in 1993, well over half of Cleveland high school seniors were unable to pass a ninth grade level national proficiency test, which meant that approximately one in fourteen of the students who had entered high school in 1989 were eligible to receive their diplomas.)

So for good reason many youngsters are sent to live with a relative or friend to give them a Shaker Heights address. But for a lot of them it's too late; they are already miles behind their new schoolmates academically by the time they reach the high-powered, competitive suburban classrooms.

And they're unprepared culturally; they have different vocabularies, different social skills (the black kids, with their limited experience of the world, generally act younger for their ages), different tastes in music, even different antisocial habits (whites drink, blacks fight, both do drugs, but different ones). The football and basketball teams are mostly black, the soccer and tennis teams mostly white.

Thrust into the land of plenty, where their schoolmates receive large allowances and drive their own cars, the low-income kids understandably cluster together for cultural protection, while the white kids lead their privileged lives as if their poorer classmates hardly existed. There are teachers who work hard to bridge the gaps, and inevitably cross-racial friendships and romances bloom, but the gap between the two groups seems to be increasing, rather than disappearing, as people of goodwill had once hoped. When planning for a common event like a dance, the faxes start flying between various social clubs as they negotiate a balance between the latest offshoot of rap and hip hop and more white-oriented rock. In these debates the whites usually end up compromising; not because they are more open-minded or flexible but because they are less concerned with high school issues than with being accepted by the right university and getting a running start toward a desirable career.

When we asked why a school system renowned for possessing every educational advantage money could buy, from elaborate gyms, labs, libraries and rehearsal rooms to the best teachers and counsellors, wasn't doing better at bringing the black kids into the educational mainstream, our friends both smiled knowingly. Then one of them replied, "Simple. The old assumptions haven't budged an inch." Every year from grade school on, they told us with a certain tightening around the mouth, their older son would finish near the top of his honours (white) class, and every year when he moved to a new grade the bureaucracy of whatever school he was in would automatically place him in the lower level (black) classes. Each time, his father had to take time off work to visit the school and pressure the recalcitrant administration to return his son to the class where his record indicated he belonged. As he progressed through high school, the boy was often the only black male, sometimes the only black student, in his college-track classes.

KS: "Good morning, I'm Russell Baron, I'm running for municipal judge here in Cleveland Heights, how are you? This is my cousin Kenny, he's visiting from Canada."

I haven't been called Kenny in so long that for a second I'm not quite sure who he is referring to, but I shake hands with the prospective voter anyway. When we dropped in on

Russell and Lois early that morning we'd found them in the midst of an election campaign. Their kitchen table was piled high with leaflets and the phone rang constantly. At first, Lois told us, their oldest son, Stephen, was acting as campaign manager. But he is HIV-positive and had an onslaught of illness in the middle of it, so she took over while he recovered.

On this particular crisp, autumn Saturday, Russell is canvassing one of the serene, heavily treed streets lined with substantial old houses that constitute the earliest and still the most desirable neighbourhood in the suburb (which is just next door to Shaker Heights). A street, in fact, very much like the one where years ago he and Lois bought a run-down old house for next to nothing, which they gradually converted into what a bad punster might call "baronial" splendour.

"I just try to make my presence known. If nobody's home I'll leave a flyer, just to let them know I was here. Sometimes I feel like an absolute ass. Most people have no idea what a municipal judge does." I admitted I was one of the majority. "Well, he—or she, the retiring judge is a woman—holds preliminary hearings to decide whether a case will go to trial if the defence asks. And he deals with housing violations and other municipal bylaws. In a way, the most important thing is to give people who have never been to court and are nervous about it a feeling of security. They want to feel that they'll be treated fairly. Fair but firm, that's my only platform."

One person does know all about it. A shifty-eyed, tattooed man in his early thirties, he has clearly spent his share of time standing in front of judges at many different levels. Instead of hostility, however, this potential voter opts for obsequiousness. Grasping the candidate's hand warmly and assuring him that he has nothing but good feelings about previous incumbents, he promises Russell his careful consideration, expresses gratitude at having this chance to meet him personally and wishes him the best of luck.

Russell truly loves Cleveland Heights. He's spent his whole adult life here, and his younger son, also a lawyer, has just bought the house on Oak Road where Russell spent his teenage years and where his parents lived for nearly a half century. One of his campaign stories ("I try to tell people about myself, to come up with little pieces of information that say something about me; it's not like running for a political office, you can't make promises about what you'll do if you win") involves his father's decision to leave the city and move up here. "My father came home in 1945," this story goes, "walked into the kitchen and announced 'I've bought a house in Cleveland Heights.' 'Where's that?' my mother answered. 'Uhhh—well, sort of, up there, somewhere—never mind, just get packed,' was the reply, and that's how we came to this unknown outpost up the hill."

The implication was that Uncle Ben had just come home from the war. In actual fact he'd just come home from another day of selling shirts and socks at his haberdashery. On the other hand, the military connotation was fair enough, since Ben was a veteran of World War One, where according to him his short stature—he was barely five-foot two—meant his head was invariably the last one to emerge from the trenches. He came through every battle unscathed while the enemy was taking careful aim at the six-footers. (Strangely, even though Nettie was even shorter than her husband, their son grew as tall as the farm boys Ben claimed he used to take cover behind.)

Most of the householders are polite and non-committal. Some recognize Russell from his mailings, others are old friends, still others stare apprehensively through their screen doors, as if they suspect we are a new kind of casually dressed Jehovah's Witness. (With his full, although neatly trimmed black beard, Russell looks something like one of those ecstatic goatherds flying over Vitebsk in paintings by Chagall.) Only one woman says she's already decided, and her glare makes it clear that she won't be putting her X next to Russell Baron's name. "Did you sense a certain hostility there?" he laughs as we head back down the sidewalk.

With eight other candidates in the field, the campaign has been long and strenuous, and Russell has a nagging cold. Even though he is amazingly fit and youthful looking, sixty-three is a ripe old age to be walking the streets looking for votes. But he'd like to finish off his career this way; the six-year term would be just right. Over the years he's put what he could back into the community; he's been chairman of the school board, served on innumerable committees, done a lot of civil rights work, and he'd make an excellent judge. If only he could conquer a lamentable streak of sentimentality, he would be perfect.

The notion that people do things differently in other countries always comes as a slight surprise to even the most sophisticated of midwesterners, and Russell was interested to learn that elected judges are a purely American phenomenon. For a while we kicked around the virtues and disadvantages of public accountability versus the potential for the election turning into a popularity contest or being manipulated by candidates with money or backing from particular ethnic blocks. But one trick I will concede to the American way. Occasionally seeing where and how the people who appear in your court actually live should be required of every judge, regardless of how he or she got on the bench.

No one was home at the last three houses, so at each one Russell wrote "Sorry I missed you" on a flyer and stuck it in the door. He actually meant it; he likes meeting people. If he had his way he would shake hands with every citizen in Cleveland Heights, join them in celebrating their luck at living in such a great place and then (if he had time and Lois would let him, which he doesn't and she wouldn't) invite them all over for lunch. In many ways he's attained the American ideal; he's managed to combine private comfort with public service and not compromise his principles too much in either area.

Despite his innate optimism, Russell can only shake his head when you raise issues like racial antagonism. He's wrestled with them for years, on the school board, in his practice, and after all the efforts of people like him the situation looks worse now than ever. But he'll keep plugging away as long as he can contribute something. He's too old to change his ways now, and besides, you never know what new twists the future will take.

JMS: While Russell took Ken on his rounds I tagged along with his campaign manager on a combination campaign and shopping junket. Lois puts in a hard week as a hospital administrator and, like most working women, scrambles for time to get everything done. "I started out so polite and lady-like on this job, now I yell and swear," Lois told me. "Everything would run smoothly except for the damned candidate," she laughed, adding, "I don't even have time to wash out my pantyhose."

Inside the supermarket, I got to help Lois hand out blue "BARON for JUDGE" stickers while trying to buy food at the same time. But simultaneous electioneering and shopping was a tricky feat, especially in the midst of a crowd of serious food people who were piling their carts higher and higher with every conceivable delicacy. A good deal of deep thought seemed to go into their choices; conferences at the delicatessen counter were handled with the intensity of labour negotiations. ("No, I don't want paper between my cheese slices." "Don't you find that you really need it to keep them from drying out?" "No, it works better for us without the paper." "Is that for all cheeses or just Emmenthal?")

At the end of one aisle a harried-looking woman was extolling the virtues of hot dogs packaged already inside their buns and slicing them into bite-sized treats; at the next someone poured out samples of freshly pressed apple cider; while down a third row a supervisor named Bill was cutting up sun-dried tomatoes and boneless chicken and pushing them around on an electric skillet.

A sharp-featured man in his sixties bending over a freezer stood up to shake hands. "Is this your bodyguard, Lois? Can she shoot?" he asked jovially. Discovering I was from Toronto he lost no time in informing me of the deficiencies of socialized medicine. "Hear you're having a lot of problems with your doctors up there. I have friends in Seattle who say the

Canadians come down in droves to get their health care." I was about to demur, but Lois was already moving us along to the next aisle and the next conversation.

Eventually, after what seemed like hours later but was probably only twenty minutes, we made our way to the car with our loaded cart. The majority of shoppers had been friendly and you could tell they liked Russell Baron personally, but most were distinctly non-committal about where they were going to put their marks on election night, as if a vote was an intensely private thing. Which of course it is. (Russell lost the election, by the way, by six votes out of 12,000 cast.)

After wishing Russell and Lois good luck we made our way back downtown to take a look at the Flats; its conversion to trendy playpen for the young and affluent had been touted by everyone we talked to as something we wouldn't want to miss. By coincidence one of us had recently brought home from the library a novel by Andrew Vachss called *Shella*, in which the narrator pays a flying visit to Cleveland after many years:

> I took a plane into Cleveland, told the cab driver to take me to an address I remembered.
> …They called it The Flats, this section.
>   When I got out of the cab, it had all changed. Last time I was there, it was a rough neighbourhood. Waterfront bars, strip joints, whores on the street, places where you could rent a room, nobody asked your name. Now it was all fancy restaurants, little shops where you could buy expensive stuff, looked all new.

Unlike him, we were not cold-blooded professional killers looking for a place to hide out, but we shared his lack of enthusiasm for the new era. Not that there's anything wrong with the idea of a bit of gussying up along the river, especially in a city that has more or less misplaced its lakefront. For a moment, in fact, it looked like a great idea, a way of saving the old factories and emporiums. But for this kind of renewal to work you need more than upscale boutiques and decorator restaurants and bars, patronized during the week mainly by people on expense accounts and on weekends by college kids boozing up.

What's missing is the urban cross-hatching that makes a section like this come alive—connecting links (as Leroy Waite would refer to them) like working theatres, professional schools, cheap lofts, ateliers, bakeries, a market, print shops, recording studios, maybe even residences of some kind, and above all, pathways on which to saunter around taking in the sights. Anything that brings people in to do more than just spend money.

What Cleveland has done with the Flats today is recapitulate the mistakes it made the first time around; they've handed the whole thing over exclusively to commercial enterprises. But then that's Cleveland.

Chapter Fourteen

Not all the old warehouse terminals in the Flats have been converted to restaurants and shops; five million bushels of wheat still arrive each year at Cereal Food Processors down on Merwin Street to be turned into flour, great loads of salt are brought up from mines deep under the lake for processing over at the AKZO plant and barges continue to push partway up the river with full holds.

The area has also retained one completely unaltered link with the past—its bridges. Everywhere you look, one of them interrupts your line of vision, and any route you follow through its narrow streets is likely to cross one eventually. There are complex-looking early railroad bridges that jack-knife up to let boats go through, swing to one side or are raised with cables, or politely lift themselves up out of the way. There's the two-tier Veterans Memorial Bridge (originally the Detroit/Superior) which used to carry streetcars on its lower level, and the impressive 8,000-foot truss cantilever Main Avenue Bridge, which soars over the mouth of the Cuyahoga. Built mostly in the halcyon days between 1900 and 1930, collectively these structures provide a graphic demonstration of the genius and beauty of American industrial engineering. It's not the bridge-builders' fault that nobody could figure out what came next.

We crossed to the west side on the impressive span that used to be known as the Lorain-Carnegie Bridge but is now the Hope Memorial. Whether there actually was a Mr. Hope to whose memory the bridge was dedicated, or the name is just another of those maladroit uses of the English language so common on public structures in northern Ohio, we can't say.

In any event, once across we picked up Lorain Avenue, the West Side's main street. In the past trolleys rattled down the centre of the avenue, and where the asphalt was worn away you got glimpses of the original tracks. But today, the street has a leftover feel, as if everybody who doesn't belong anywhere else is making do here in this neighbourhood of aging housing projects, vocational high schools, missions, second-hand shops, used car lots and liquor stores. There isn't even the street life of the East Side, just occasional stragglers on the sidewalks or solitary drinkers sitting on stoops.

Until 1854 this bank of the river was a separate entity called Ohio City, and it has always been something of a poor relation to the rest of Cleveland. No one except the people who happened to live there seemed to even notice when they built I-90 right through its heart and effectively sliced the West Side in half. Most visitors simply speed through it on the freeway, but we had taken this rather desolate local route to have a look at the block between 88th and 89th streets in which Uncle Ben's haberdashery had been located (the same Uncle Ben who took his family to live in Cleveland Heights in 1945). And where long Saturdays spent working behind the counter serving the hard-up hillbillies and immigrants who patronized Ben J. Baron Men's Wear opened the eyes of the family's younger generation to a world beyond their comfortable and self-absorbed suburbs.

Memories of the old store will have to remain just that. Around W. 84th Street, just at the point when the display windows should have been coming into view, the six lanes of I-90 veered to the right and ran straight over the blocks where the high eighties had been. Ben's, Tony's Restaurant across the street, the supermarket, the liquor store—they're all part of the pavement now.

But we had another nostalgia card up our sleeves. Instead of turning north toward the lake and leaving Cleveland by way of the western suburbs, we headed inland. Ten miles south and perhaps twenty-five miles west of downtown lies the town of Oberlin, the site of Oberlin College, from which we had acquired our B.A.s back in 1959.

Neither of us is particularly sentimental about our time there, and except for retaining a handful of close relationships from those days, our only direct connection with the College over the last thirty-five years has been an occasional glance at the alumni magazine. But as we were beginning our travels for this book, a form letter arrived with the news that, unless funds were found to renovate it, Peters Hall would have to be razed. Normally such entreaties go directly into the wastebasket, but this latest plea rang a small bell.

In the fall semester of our senior year we had both signed up for a class sonorously titled "Introspection and Observation: Philosophical Aspects of Psychoanalysis" which met in a small upstairs classroom in that building. After the first five minutes of the first lecture it had become apparent that few of us had any hope of figuring out what the course was supposed to be about. Except for one brainy girl by the name of Anne Phinney, who baffled both the other students and the professor by actually seeming to find some intellectual coherence in the concepts being presented, our minds began to wander very early on. In our cases it was toward each other, and we spent most of that semester first finding out who that other person was, then saying "Hi" as we passed each other on the stairs, progressing to stopping between classes to chat in the lobby, and finally waiting for one another on the walk outside.

A turreted, late-nineteenth-century limestone clunker full of strange corners, stairways with abrupt turns and deep doorways, Peters Hall was a perfect place to start a relationship; since it served as the main teaching building, all its

rooms were in constant use, and everyone was so busy struggling through the thick clots of students rushing from one
class to another that they had little time to notice who was
over in a secluded corner talking earnestly to whom.

So since we were more or less in the neighbourhood we
decided to *recherche* our *temps perdus* with a quick visit to the
place where we had met. Peters Hall was still standing, directly across the street from another one of those oversized town
squares so popular in this part of the country. But when we
pushed through the heavy wooden doors, we discovered that
the old building had been converted into offices and the dark
little classroom on the second floor was now a counselling
centre.

Looking down onto the ground-floor lobby from the
upstairs balcony, we tried to conjure up the crowds of chat-
tering, carefree girls in white sleeveless blouses and calf-length
skirts with tightly cinched waistlines, and the skinny boys in
chinos, horn-rimmed glasses and geek haircuts (and place
ourselves among the group). But nothing came, no Proustian
reconstruction of the past, no swooning rush of sentiment.
The most memorable thing about Peters Hall had been meeting each other, and we didn't need the actual environs to
remind us of that. As far as preserving the building, we had
no strong feelings one way or the other. Maybe if it had been
crowded with students instead of administrators we might
have been slightly inclined toward sentimentality.

Only the stack of college newspapers resting near a recessed
doorway evoked a response. Early on in our student days we
had both been reporters for the *Oberlin Review*, but one of us
worked for the Tuesday edition, the other for the Friday, and
so once again, as at Niagara Falls, our paths had crossed but
we weren't on them. In any event, one of us was soon fired
for insufficient seriousness ("I have never heard of anything
so unprofessional!" fumed the editor as she cut him loose)
while the other grew restless with covering student politics
and interviewing visiting tenors in town for a concert, and
eventually drifted away.

The truth was, there wasn't much place for people like us amid the straight-arrow, goal-oriented doctors, economists and organists-to-be who made up the bulk of the student body. Plotting out a career did not come naturally to us, much less sticking to a plan once devised; we just wanted to escape to Greenwich Village and start living.

Anyway, we'd seen what we'd come to see, and headed north toward the lake. But back on Route 6 we stopped in at Old Woman Creek National Estuarine Reserve just west of Vermilion and found we were not quite done with this part of our past. After a hike along the wide estuary and through the bordering patch of lush forest, we spent a few minutes in the reserve's visitor centre where on a detailed wall map of the area, we noticed an area designated "Oberlin Beach."

This was a stretch of lakeshore where college faculty members had cottages and where once, nearly forty years ago, one of us had passed a few hours with a professor and his family, shivering in the not-all-that-warm May air and trying to avoid the dead fish which littered most of the beach. To the naive young coed's surprise it turned out to be less a family outing than a disguised first move in a campaign of seduction which came to an inglorious and abrupt conclusion with the prof chasing the intended seductee around his office until she managed to locate the door and bolt to safety. Such, such were the joys.

Chapter Fifteen

We sat in McGarveys, a cavernous seafood restaurant that for fifty years or more has occupied one bank of Vermilion Creek just before it enters the lake. As we dawdled over our salads and stared out at the steady stream of cabin cruisers drifting past the large windows toward the upstream docks, it became clear that we had reached the outer limits of the true power boat culture. We had seen such craft scattered about in many places along the lake, but around Vermilion they had begun to gather in massive flotillas.

This was the first confirmation of a statistic that had astonished us when we came across it. According to a comparison of state figures, more power boats are registered in the state of Michigan (essentially the Detroit area) than anywhere else in the United States—more than in California or Florida with their thousand-mile coastlines, more than in Hawaii's various islands in total. Add in the heavily populated hundred miles of western Ohio shoreline where people live under Detroit's cultural influence, plus the Windsor-Leamington corridor in Ontario, and it becomes clear that in the stretch from the western basin of Lake Erie up the Detroit River to Lake St. Clair you have by far the highest concentration of power boats in the world.

"Oh, yeah, a lot of them are for fishing, of course, but

basically what they are is floating cottages. That's what people use them for," one garrulous boat broker had told us as we stood in a showroom surrounding by gleaming cabin cruisers. "I mean, there's not very much good lakefront land around here, it's too marshy, so they spend fifty, sixty, seventy grand, more if they've got it, on a boat, and that's their family cottage." It's a good sales line, but we wondered how many children are really that eager to spend whole vacations or even weekends trapped in a small cabin in the middle of a lake with their parents, even if they get to steer once in a while.

We were just starting to dig into our perch specials when every head in the restaurant suddenly swivelled to watch a "Miami Vice"-style cigarette boat that had just entered the creek. At the helm of the zillion-dollar maritime monster, riding high in the water above the onlookers and staring smugly ahead, stood a shrunken, older man dressed in the nautical equivalent of a full Cleveland—captain's cap, white belt, pastels and all.

(For those unfamiliar with the expression, a typical full Cleveland consists of a lime green polo shirt, pale yellow trousers belted up as close under the armpits as possible, socks matching one of those colours, tan or white shoes [two-tone optional] and a baseball cap. Think of Bob Hope, who as it happens actually grew up in Cleveland.)

This is big car country, and the same impulse of conspicuous consumption that leads men who've made it big to cruise the roads in Cadillacs and Continentals is responsible for these floating marine equivalents. Boats are even better than cars, in fact. Since no licence or training course is required and virtually no regulations limit the horsepower or size of your craft, the sky's the limit. They're the perfect self-salute. We didn't catch the name on that cigarette boat's stern, but it should have been the "I Can Afford This and You Can't" out of Detroit, Michigan.

Settled by New Englanders, Vermilion (pop. 11,000) is one of those old towns whose shuttered houses and picket fences date back to the first half of the nineteenth century; the sign at the city limits reads "Welcome to Harbour Town, 1837," and on the front window of an office in one of the older buildings a brokerage firm proudly declares "Edward D. Jones, Member New York Stock Exchange, serving conservative investors since 1871." It's also the home of the Great Lakes Historical Society's Inland Sea Maritime Museum, housed in an old mansion overlooking the harbour.

Perhaps we should not have been surprised to find that the lakes themselves are merely bit players in the museum's displays; boats and boatmen are what matter here. Paraphernalia from famous steamships, models of sailing vessels, yacht club flags and much ado about the progress of commerce on the lakes fills the well-designed exhibit rooms. This is history, midwestern industrialist style. There's a small bow to the havoc wrecked by storms over the years, and one wall display covers the whole of the lakes' ongoing natural history, but ecological issues, the fisheries, the historical fact of a native presence around the lakes, the disastrous record of industry in polluting the waters—none of it rates a mention. And a visitor learns virtually nothing about the role played by that other country bordering the lakes, whatever it's called.

From Vermilion, Route 6 took us past Mitawanga Park, Ruggles Beach and Ceylon, communities so much like each other we couldn't distinguish among them as we were passing through, and on to Huron. This is the next town of any size (pop. 7,000) and we made an effort to check out its downtown. As you come into Huron you encounter a large sign giving directions from Route 6 to the business district, which, if you follow them carefully, leads through a neo-Colonial industrial park and some nondescript residential streets, then returns you to the exact spot where you started without passing any hint of a commercial area except for a lone bake shop. Just to make sure we hadn't taken a wrong turn we completed the whole circle again, with the same results. The episode reminded us of the blank space on Fort Erie's "Town Centre" sign.

Something else our fruitless wander through Huron brought home was the utter confusion of the road system in northern Ohio. Roads obviously matter a lot in this part of the country, because there are so many of them, but connections apparently don't. No matter where you are around here, you can't get directly to where you want to go next. Neither the most heavily travelled interstate nor the most obscure dirt roads ever reach a logical destination before petering out in the middle of nowhere, veering sharply toward something else or merging into other roads that may or may not be continuing the same way. The quickest route from downtown Sandusky to downtown Ashtabula, for example, two lake ports 120 miles apart, involves seven different freeways (Ohio 2, I-90, the Ohio Turnpike, I-480, I-271, I-90 again, I-84) as well as a couple of local roads.

Just before we reached Sandusky along Route 2, a series of billboards alerted us that we were nearing the turn-off to Cedar Point. For generations of residents of Ohio, northern Indiana and southern Michigan, these have been magic words. This was the resort that really could claim to have the most thrilling roller-coaster, the longest beach with the whitest sand, the biggest hotel on all of Lake Erie.

We turned off and followed the highway toward the point, curious to see if the original inn was still standing. All the other once-celebrated resorts on the lake, with their elaborate piers, dance pavilions, casinos and hotels, had been demolished by developers, vandalized, burned to the ground or simply left to disintegrate after they had failed financially. Erie Beach, Crystal Beach, the sumptuous combination dance hall and bathhouse at Gordon Park in Cleveland and the rest were nothing more than distant memories. But there was still something to see at Cedar Point, at least according to the billboards.

The six-mile peninsula runs north-west toward another, larger extension of land to form Sandusky Bay, one of those beautiful, perfectly formed configurations of water and marsh grasses and tiny offshore islands that must have struck early inhabitants as a kind of natural paradise. (Although for millennia very few people actually wandered by. At the time of the first European contact, Ohio was virtually devoid of human settlement. Not until the 1660s did the Miamis move into the area from the west, just in time to meet the Neutrals and other Ontario nations fleeing the Iroquois.)

Early in the nineteenth century, white settlers spread west along the lake (both Toledo and Sandusky were founded in 1817), and by mid-century the wide sand beaches of Cedar Point were already a popular spot for holiday outings. In the 1870s a local entrepreneur put up an early amusement park complete with picnic grounds. All that was missing was a place to stay the night, and in 1905 the Cleveland architectural firm of Knox and Elliot completed work on the Breakers Hotel, the largest and most sumptuous watering-hole on the lake. (Eventually it grew to 880 rooms.)

The Breakers defied easy categorization; you might almost think the architects had accidentally mixed together two sets of blueprints, one for an elaborate Second-Empire-style resort hotel and the other for one of those sprawling, geometrical prisons built around the same date—the Saratoga Springs Hotel meets Sing Sing.

Northern Ohio was booming, and the new resort proved successful from opening day; society matrons, honeymooning couples and middle-class families who had scrimped and saved to allow themselves a week at the shore flocked to *thés dansants* and to the ornately appointed restaurants. Even the evangelical movement that was sweeping the country at the time found the place to its taste; throngs of Pastor Russell's International Bible Students registered to be dipped backward into Erie's warm waters in mass baptisms. One year some ten thousand souls completed their spiritual conversions there.

During the roaring twenties the whole Sandusky Bay coastline, with its dozens of small inlets, was an easy entry point for Canadian liquor, and much of it was consumed right at Cedar Point. In the crowded ballroom, madcap young things with newly bobbed hair, college boys on a binge, sugar daddies and their dollies did the shimmy and the Charleston to

Jean Goldkette, Lew Pollack and other top bands, while up-and-coming industrialists mingled with gangsters from Detroit and their colleagues from Cleveland and points east and west, smoked cigars, talked deals and watched the action out of the corner of their eyes. This was as glamorous as it got around the great lakes.

Like many of the other lake resorts, Cedar Point went bank-rupt in the thirties. But for some reason the hotel itself, although increasingly decrepit, remained both upright and open. The high-rollers were long gone, but in the fifties a new generation, mostly of teenagers, flocked to the crum-bling hulk. A dollar a night paid for a shabby room into which as many bodies as the walls would hold could be crammed (Ken among them); nobody cared how late they stayed up or how much booze was consumed. They got falling-down drunk and threw up in the bushes, played sand football, cruised the beach trying to pick up girls, waded out into the lake at two a.m. and made strange noises that echoed spookily across the water as they acted out scenes from *Creature from the Black Lagoon* (a film that exerted a pro-found influence on teenagers of that generation). It was the closest thing to freedom Ohio had to offer.

Pulling into the parking lot, we found the rambling old hotel still standing and, amazingly enough, pretty much in its orig-inal form. According to the general manager, who we tracked down as he was supervising repairs to one of the main lob-bies, the Breakers has been put on the National Registry of Historic Places and is gradually being restored to something of its former resplendence. Though the ballroom is gone and there's been a bit of excess tarting up with the additions of a pool and other inessentials, the place still exudes the romantic atmosphere of a classic lake resort. Even the fact that it now caters mainly to families with young children hasn't altered its golden glow.

Beyond Cedar Point, Sandusky (pop. 30,000) was another pretty, unpretentious, smallish city with lots of pleasing, well-preserved buildings. In other words, it's much like Ashtabula, except that it grew up around a bay instead of a creek, its streets are flat where Ashtabula's are hilly, and in addition to the freighters loading coal in the harbour, ferries depart regularly for Canada and the nearby islands. Judging by the occasional empty building, the city has its share of the usual urban problems, but it doesn't look seedy.

In the old days Sandusky was known as Fishtown, with an aroma to match, but commercial fishing ended when the state put restrictions on gill nets. "The Canadians still use them, of course," a woman at the Chamber of Commerce commented bitterly. This was our first encounter with international fish politics, and looking for someone less partisan to explain the situation, we stopped by the Ohio Division of Wildlife (fish, game and law enforcement) just down the street from the ferry terminal. Talking to a state bureaucrat turned out to be a very different experience from chatting with people like the three old codgers in Port Glasgow; here, fish are no joking matter, and never the subject of tall tales.

Doug Johnson, a tall young man wearing a blue shirt and jeans shook hands, pointed to some chairs and got right to the point. "This is the way it works; the Province of Ontario and the four American states co-operate in setting quotas—they're not legal quotas, but goals. And our law enforcement agents train together and co-operate. I'll say one thing, they police that Canadian fishery very well. They've got regular port inspectors. Here it's spot checks.

"Anyway, 52 percent of the lake is American, so we get 52 percent of the fish. But on this side our mandate is sports fishing, which means basically fishing rods. The walleye catch can go as high as five million fish in a good year, then there's small mouth bass, and the state is stocking rainbow trout and steelhead trout. So gill nets, which are what commercial fishermen use, are banned. The Canadians are more interested in the commercial fishery, so they use their quota allowance for that. And they allow gill nets.

"There's still a little bit of commercial fishing on this side using trap nets and seiners...yellow perch, a bit of catfish, white perch, white bass, carp. One processing plant here in Sandusky, one in Port Clinton, that's it. Our yellow perch aren't in great shape. Why? Zebra mussels, pollution, competition for food supply with white perch, poor hatches due to a cold, windy April, there are lots of theories."

Underneath his straightforward, fact-oriented manner we detected a slight hint that Johnson was not completely happy with the Canadian insistence on retaining a commercial fishery. On the other hand, Americans often appear annoyed on principle about the way other countries carry on, particularly other countries that insist on pursuing their incomprehensible customs within sight of American soil, so maybe we were reading too much into a brief conversation.

As usual, we were looking for someone with a boat willing to take us somewhere, this time to a small piece of land in Sandusky Bay called Johnson's Island (no relation to Doug). And again, as usual, we had not been having any luck, despite the fact that we were surrounded by craft of various shapes and sizes. "Did you know there's a bridge?" Johnson responded after a thoughtful pause, in which he was probably reflecting on the ignorance of foreigners. "From the north shore?"

It wasn't precisely a bridge, as we discovered after we had crossed the bay and wound our way along a back road to the point; it was more of a causeway, with a mechanical gate into which we had to slip four quarters before it would allow us access. At first glance the island's shoreline, lined with summer cottages, looked like any other holiday spot on Lake Erie, and the whine of power saws at work in the distance indicated that new cabins were under construction. But we knew that, quite different scenes had once been played out here.

"Is there anything I can do for you personally?" Abraham Lincoln asked his old acquaintance Alexander Stephens, vice-president of the Confederacy, at the conclusion of their

Hampton Roads meeting not long before the south surrendered. "Nothing, unless you can send me my nephew who has been for twenty months a prisoner on Johnson's Island," Stephens replied. "I will be glad to do it," said Lincoln. "Let me have his name." (From Carl Sandburg's biography of the fourteenth president.)

We don't know what that name was, or indeed if Lincoln had time to keep his word in the few weeks remaining to him. But we hope so, because a large proportion of the approximately ten thousand captured Confederate officers who waited out the war at one time or another in the Johnson's Island prison camp never made it home. Even on this warm, early fall day, the offshore breeze was crisp and the heavy shade of the tall trees made it hard to keep from shivering; for young men bred in the pine woods of Tennessee and the Georgia swamps, this must have been a miserable place to spend the winter months.

Without proper medical care or clothing, hopelessly unprepared for the icy Lake Erie winters (one night in 1864 the temperature dropped to minus 26 degrees Fahrenheit), they died like flies, some of exposure, some by drowning while trying to escape, most from pneumonia or other infections. Toward the end of the war food was in short supply and there were raiding parties on the rats that infested the place. In addition, the barracks had been hurriedly built with green timber, and as the planking weathered, gaps appeared in the thin walls.

The men tried to keep their minds off the cold. Someone got a debating society going, another organized baseball games, the Rebel Thespians worked up some improvised plays. A former teacher offered French and German lessons, and there were always poker games with worthless Confederate money. Others passed the time plotting their escapes, though with a twenty-foot-high fence and a ditch that was dug down to the rock substratum, and beyond that either open water or ice that was likely to give way, they didn't have much hope. Once in a great while escapees did manage to reach Canada, where Southern sympathizers were waiting to help them, but most froze to death or were recaptured before they got very far.

As the bodies piled up they were buried in makeshift graves marked by wooden crosses, but the site was abandoned after the war, and by the time the citizens of Sandusky became interested in the history of Johnson's Island the buildings had been torn down and most of the crosses had disintegrated or become unreadable. During the 1890s new headstones, made of Georgia marble and inscribed with whatever information could be found, were erected over a few of the graves, and in the early part of this century the Ohio Daughters of the Confederacy raised funds to create a proper cemetery.

Today, seven neat rows of identical white headstones run in a north-south direction toward the water, ending at a conventional, heroic, bronze statue of a Confederate soldier holding a musket in his right hand and shading his eyes with the other as he stares forward, as if keeping a watch out for damn Yankees. An iron cross nearby reads "*Deo Vindici* 1861-1865." The trees that keep the site in perpetual shade, frame a cool, dark and evocative final resting place for these men who died the most anonymous of deaths, hundreds of miles from their homes and families.

We pushed open the low iron gate and walked between the rows, reading the markers as we passed. The 206 graves represent only a fraction of the men whose bones rest here. Two give their occupants' ages: G.W. Gillespie, Capt., 63 N.C. Cav., age 26 and W.T. Norwood, Lieut., 6th S.C. Inf., age 30. The rest provide only names and ranks, and sometimes less than that:

J.B. Wood, Lieut., 10th S.C. Cav.
J.M. Hill, Capt., Dobbins, Ark., Cav.
S.H. Bankey, Lieut., Ala. CSA
John J. Nickell, Surgeon, 2nd Ky.
J.B. Hardy, Capt., 15 Ark. Inf.
Peter Cole, Private, 60th Va. Inf.

J. D. Cassaway
J. W. Mullins, Lieut., 1st Miss. Cav.
B. Anderson, Private, Mo. State Cav.
B.C. Harp., Lieut., 25th Tenn., Inf.
R.K.C. Weeks, Lieut., 4th Fla. Inf.
R.H. List, Citizen
F.F. Cooper, Capt., 52 Ga., Inf.
John J. Cobeau, Lieut., 10th Miss. Inf.
Hugh Cobble, Private, 5th Ky.
P.J. Rabenan, Capt., 5th Ala. Inf.
Unknown
Unknown
Unknown
Unknown

A gap in the trees provided a view to the water's edge, and across the bay, clearly visible above the trees, were the top sections of some of taller rides at the Cedar Point amusement park—the upper arc of a ferris wheel, the highest twists and turns of the monster roller coaster, the fulcrum from which the chairs of the Flying Scooter fan out. In the summer when the park is in operation, someone standing in the cemetery can probably pick up the squeals and shrieks of teenagers hurtling around the rails and being swept high into the air, kids not much younger than the lieutenants and captains and occasional privates buried here. Born at another time, they might have been the ones yelling with laughter instead of lying in the cold ground of a tiny island in a northern lake.

This was a day when the South kept rising again. After leaving the island we stopped at a restaurant to decide over a cup of coffee where to go next, and in the newspaper rack the headline of the *Cleveland Plain Dealer*, five columns across the top of the front page, read: "Forty-six Per Cent of Alabamans Headed for Hell, Church Survey Shows." That was all it took to convince 100 percent of Sobols that it was time for a break. Gulping down our coffee, we started toward home by the quickest route available, and ten free-ways later we were back in Toronto, where a substantial percentage of the population probably doesn't even believe in Alabama, never mind the place where almost half of its citizens are slated to end up.

PART THREE

The Western Basin

Chapter Sixteen

Back home we studied our slightly dog-eared Ontario map, took a deep breath and prepared to set out for that shallow western basin mentioned many times earlier. By now the glove compartment was stuffed with enough local maps to fill an atlas, each emphasizing a different place. On one, all roads seemed to lead to Port Stanley; on others, that community had shrunk to a barely visible dot and the centre of the universe had moved over to Dunnville, or Ashtabula, or Chatham, or Huron County.

Nights had been chilly for the last two weeks, and the trees were already beginning to turn red and orange. So, oddly enough, was the ground; as we approached Leamington on Colonel Talbot's road, everywhere we looked the earth seemed to be covered with red spots. Tomatoes are the primary cash crop in this part of Essex County. They filled up the fields, teeming baskets of them rested on the counters of numerous roadside stands and every third vehicle on the highway was a tomato-transporter.

We soon found ourselves stuck behind a slow-moving, three-part conveyance—a tractor with two carts hooked on behind it—and flinching as at every bump in the road a few juicy red ones tumbled over the side. "Ecokillers!" they seemed to cry as they were squashed under our tires. But as much as we value all life forms on the planet, we value some, notably ours, more than others, and we didn't feel like risking an accident by swerving abruptly in order to spare a few tomatoes. So we squished uneasily along, hoping that no one would take down our licence plate number and report us to our vegetarian daughter.

At the next intersection the asphalt ran red with vegetable roadkill. For an instant it looked like a rural recapitulation of the St. Valentine's Day massacre, and only after we had jammed on the brakes in alarm did we come to the realization that a tomato truck must have overturned here earlier in the day.

Until you have spent a prolonged period interacting with tomatoes you don't begin to notice their peculiarly assertive character. A popular Monty Python sketch involved the group bursting into cocktail parties and other unlikely situations dressed in cardinals' robes and claiming to be the Spanish Inquisition. "Nobody expects the Spanish Inquisition" was their stock reply to indignant complaints that they really hadn't been expected. We felt the same way here. Nobody expects tomatoes, but there they were. Millions of them.

Of course, if you grow up around Leamington (pop. 14,000) you probably expect nothing else. This is ketchup country. Taking advantage of the mild growing conditions in this southernmost county in Canada, Heinz put up a factory here in 1905 and gradually added to it over the years until it became the world's largest tomato-processing plant. Leamington bills itself as the Tomato Capital of Canada and holds a yearly Tomato Festival over which reigns a Tomato Queen and her Tomato Princesses.

Even as we entered the city limits the pungent aroma of condiment assailed our nostrils. (Although this turned out to be less a regular feature of the local atmosphere than the result of a giant warehouse fire which had destroyed three million dollars' worth of stock a day or two earlier. Tomato products apparently burn, and a ketchuppy haze hung over Leamington during our entire stay.)

Soon after we turned onto Erie Street we passed a man actually carrying a case of ketchup bottles on his shoulder, and a few blocks farther along found ourselves driving under pedestrian walkways connecting the grey buildings of the original plant to newer ones on the other side of the road.

Only along the waterfront could you escape the red menace. The breeze here cleared away the odour, and the sight of hundreds of boats bobbing at anchor claimed all our attention. Servicing the steady stream of Michiganders and Ohioans who fetch up every day in Leamington is another major source of employment. After all, these people need somewhere to take their expensive craft, and once they get here they naturally need to gas up and locate amenities like showers, food and drink and souvenirs. All summer there's non-stop action at the crowded 340-berth public marina; boaters begin arriving with the first robin and don't leave until crusts of ice begin to form in the puddles along the shore.

One terminus of the Sandusky ferry is here (there is another at Kingsville), and when we first pulled into the marina parking lot we found yet another Tall Ship taking up the whole side of a pier. This was a graceful, three-masted lake schooner, built by a wealthy hobbyist from Ottawa, which was gradually making its way to Put-In-Bay to join our old friend the non-historic brig *Niagara* in the planned recreation of the Battle of Lake Erie. We knew all this because near Erieau we had run into a chatty woman who, as a member of a prominent Kent County seed family, had been invited on board for drinks and had told us all about it.

At the Home Suite Home Bed & Breakfast back on Erie Street, a slight, grey-haired, distracted-looking woman wearing a flowered apron answered the doorbell, asked us to take off our shoes, then led us upstairs to a comfortable room that felt like a homespun version of one of the many greenhouses we had noticed in the area. Roses and peonies were growing up the walls (paper ones, that is, on the wallpaper) as well as on the curtains and lampshades and the pillowcases, sheets, throw cushions and coverlet. There were paintings of flowers on the wall, drawings of flowers on the plastic shower curtain and artificial flowers in vases on the dressers. It sounds cloying but somehow wasn't; this just felt like the home of someone who loved flowers.

When we came downstairs, the floraphile's husband was just returning from work. Retired tomato ranchers, Aggie and Harry Tiessen had handed the farm over to one of their children and moved into town eight years earlier. They looked like people who had worked incredibly hard all their lives but had remained youthful in spite of (or perhaps because of) it. Nowadays Aggie keeps busy running the bed-and-breakfast while Harry runs a small trucking business. "Yeah, I run it. Run it right into the ground sometimes," he told us ruefully. It was his truck that had caused the scene of vegetable carnage we had encountered on our way into town; a load of tomato tailings he was taking to the dump had somehow spilled out. "What a mess," he grimaced, then burst out laughing.

The Tiessens are Mennonites. Guillaume Apollinaire once wrote a poem about a Mennonite woman with whom he was desperately in love. She emigrated to this side of the Atlantic, where she lived in

> *Un grand jardin tout plein de roses*
> *Il contient aussi une villa*
> *Qui est une grande rose*

He might have been describing Aggie's house, except for the fact that Apollinaire's girlfriend had taken off in 1903 and Aggie wouldn't be born for another thirty or so years. Her particular Mennonite subset was descended from a group recruited by Peter the Great back in the early 1700s to cultivate unused land in the Ukraine, where they remained until the Bolsheviks chased them out after the 1917 revolution. But Apollinaire was dead on in associating them with flowers.

We were getting hungry. "Jordan's is a good place to eat," Aggie ventured, and Harry nodded. We didn't say "Oh yeah?"

even though we thought it; we'd heard that one before. But they were right. It was the first real food we'd tasted anywhere on the lake. When in Leamington, eat at Jordan's. In fact, when anywhere west of Toronto and east of Winnipeg, eat at Jordan's. And don't fail to start your meal with their cheese and cabbage soup, worthy winner of the 1993 Essex South Heart and Stroke Soup Kitchen People's Choice Award for best soup in all of Leamington.

Later we set out to discover what was going down after dark in the Ketchup Capital—besides, of course, watching the bottles fill up over at the plant. Since Leamington is basically strung out along the axis of the intersection of Highway 3 and Erie Street, it didn't take long to cover the downtown district and to ascertain that, besides a lot of confusion caused by road repairs, not much was happening. The stores were closed, the sidewalks were deserted, the bus station had shut its doors, and in Mac's Milk they weren't even bothering to change the coffee more than every couple of hours.

The only sign of life beyond an occasional car zipping through on its way to somewhere else was a rectangle of erratically blinking coloured lights surrounding the two words "Live Entertainment" in the window of the International Hotel. This utilitarian brick hostelry, whose exterior was coated by what looked like a century or so of grime, sat defiantly on the corner of Erie and Mill Streets just south of the main intersection daring passersby to come in. But our tour of Leamington had made it clear that if we rejected this opportunity we weren't likely to find another.

So we pushed open the windowless grey door and stepped into one of the grottiest taverns we had ever seriously considered buying a drink in. The large, gloomy room, decorated mostly in raw wood, contained a number of rickety tables and chairs and an off-centre pool table. At the bar a half dozen or so people of various ages stared morosely into space. A few others were crashed in chairs with their heads on the tables or propped against the wall. As our eyes became accustomed to the darkness we were able to make out on the wall next to us some black-and-white framed photos of several regulars, labelled "Mixed Snowballs Champions," and of some slightly wild-eyed local rockers. A rudimentary bandstand stood against the far wall.

Conversation could only be called desultory; in this bar everyone concentrated on the essentials. "What do you have on tap?" we asked the bartender. "Blue," he replied. "What else?" "Blue." We ordered a couple of glasses of Blue. But despite the decor, the atmosphere wasn't mean-spirited or particularly rough. On the contrary, the International Hotel felt downright homey and oddly welcoming.

Not only that, every Wednesday, the barman told us, the place featured a special promotion. But twenty-something trendiness didn't seem to have reached Leamington; instead of gimmicks like Sumo Wrestling, what they featured at the International Hotel every Wednesday was a Meat Draw. A dollar bought you five tickets and a chance to win a monstrous, bloody, twenty-five-pound slab of beef fresh from the slaughterhouse. (Wrapped in plastic, of course.) Second prize was a generous hunk of spare-ribs. Given the current level of unemployment in this town, a meat raffle probably made more sense than a bad country singer's newest CD or a twenty-dollar gift certificate at the nearest Stedman's.

The owner waved the prizes around in front of the regulars and cajoled newcomers like us into handing over a loonie or two (though what we would have done with the prize had we won was hard to say) and gradually the jar filled up with tickets. Finally a relative of the owner was asked to reach in and pull out a winner. A jovial, middle-aged regular named Nellie held the lucky coupon. But the law of averages, like the pool table, seemed to be out of kilter here, since the same patron had also won the week before, and twice before that. She looked embarrassed and even unsuccessfully tried to give back her ticket and allow someone else a chance. But besides us and the owner, Nellie and Mr. Nellie seemed to be the only other people who had noticed the big draw taking place at all. Second place was won by a woman who had just stopped in a moment earlier and at first didn't have any idea what they were congratulating her for, though when she did figure it out she looked happy enough.

The band wasn't scheduled to perform for another hour so we peeled our backs off the chairs and stepped outside for some air, our departure unremarked by all. Mill Street forms one side of a triangular block; at the apex, with entrances on both streets, stands the old customs house. We could see some kind of meeting taking place inside and, curious to see what was going on, we crossed the street and climbed the steps. Inside the brightly lit room a confident-looking, casually dressed man in his late forties was addressing a crowd of perhaps one hundred twenty mostly middle-aged people. A couple of younger men in suits with their arms crossed observed the goings-on from the side.

Spanking new red-and-white posters informed us that this was a Liberal Party riding association meeting. And it wasn't just any coffee and doughnuts get-together—the federal election had just been called and we had wandered into the campaign's organizational meeting. Key volunteers were being filled in on how their leaders planned to elect a Liberal member of Parliament in the riding of Essex-Kent. It was the candidate himself (and sitting member of Parliament), Jerry Pickard, who was holding the floor. A couple of people glanced at us quizzically and one of the suits nodded, but no objections were raised when we sat down in a back row to watch. We weren't surprised; after all, this was small-town Ontario, where most people are too reticent to even dream of asking a stranger his business.

Over the next forty minutes we listened to lots of vague talk of strategy, lots of addressing by first names and references to specific villages in the riding by the candidate, lots of verbal pats on the back for individuals who had worked hard on the last campaign, usually followed by the immediate suggestion that they might be willing to donate an equal amount of their valuable time to the new crusade.

Finally Pickard, geniality itself, got around to asking

whether anyone had any questions about Liberal Party policy or important points they felt needed discussion. Maybe now we would get a sense of what these people hoped to accomplish and what instincts for public service had drawn them into the campaign, how they felt about Jean Chrétien's potential liabilities and how best to counteract them, the possibility of a minority government, opinions on divisive questions such as crime and immigration or any of the other important issues crying out to be aired.

All that followed, however, was a long silence. Eventually the Reform Party was brought up, which made several people mutter grouchily. ("A lot of countries find two parties are enough.") But it was the mention of the Bloc Québécois that finally got them going. "Breaking up the country like that, isn't that treason?" one man asked, looking around for support. "Right, they should take them out and shoot them," agreed another.

The energy level in the room began to pick up. "Give them the Louis Riel treatment!" cried a third man. "Yeah, he didn't cause much trouble after that," chipped in someone in the next row, to general laughter.

They were cooking now. The offer to start a lottery based on which date the first brick would go through the front window of the local NDP headquarters brought a new ripple of merriment and was followed by a few practical suggestions on how it might be accomplished, and a lot more laughter. Finally, having dissected every party's policies and character except their own, someone declared the meeting over and people started heading for the door.

Outside in the fresh air, we recalled a chorus from a Proclaimers' song:

> I can tell the meaning of a word like serene
> I got some "O" grades when I was sixteen
> I can tell the difference 'tween margarine and butter
> I can say "Saskatchewan" without starting to stutter

⌐ But I can't understand why we let someone else rule
       our land
    Cap in Hand

Good question.

Needing a drink badly, we retraced our steps back down the
block to our threadbare oasis on Erie Street. Earlier in the
evening, it would have been hard to imagine that the
International Hotel could look good to us, but after forty
minutes of simultaneous forelock-tugging and power-thirst-
ing in the bosom of the Essex-Kent Liberal Party, the scruffy
place almost felt like home.

It wasn't long before we were reminded that this wasn't
quite our natural milieu, either. A request for a gin and tonic
stopped the waitress dead in her tracks; apparently no customer had ever before ordered a mixed drink in these
precincts. "I don't think we have any," she told us haltingly.
We thought she was referring to tonic, but she actually meant
gin. After checking at the bar, she returned to say that though
that was indeed the case, they might be getting some soon.
We ordered two more Blues.

A few additional patrons had wandered in during our
absence. Others we recognized from our previous visit had
managed to shift themselves slightly and were now leaning
against the wall at new angles. But although the band had
arrived and was lethargically taking out their instruments and
tuning up, the mood remained resolutely downbeat.

At one point a slow-moving, vacant-eyed gentleman who
looked as if he had spent the last twenty years ingesting every
white powder and coloured capsule known to drug science
decided to make a move on a woman seated alone at a nearby
table. Duded up in black cowboy boots, black jeans, a chain
belt from which hung a ring with dozens of keys and an off-
white, wide-collar Elvis shirt, he rose, adjusted his jewellery,
ran a comb through his lank hair and started across the room
with the exquisite slow-motion tread of a man permanently

ten feet underwater. He was just carefully lowering himself into a chair next to the woman when her boyfriend returned and scared him away.

That small drama over, all eyes turned for a moment toward the stage, where the band had taken up their positions and looked ready to begin. The lead singer wore a ponytail and a leather vest; the two sidemen were a shade more casual in red T-shirts, faded jeans and haircuts that looked reminiscent of mid-sixties Brit groups like the Animals or the Dave Clark Five. All were the same height and build—a stocky five-foot nine. The drummer just looked like a drummer, and the four collectively were billed as "Three Hits and a Miss." The name had a certain what-the-hell-is-that-supposed-to-mean appeal until the lead singer explained that there was a real Miss and that she was their regular drummer, though tonight a substitute was sitting in.

We weren't expecting much, but as soon as they launched into their first song—in tune, on key—it became obvious that T. H. and an M. were a solid, hard-rocking bar band. Not that their audience noticed. One enthusiastic patron kept up a steady demand for "Maggie May" even after the band capitulated and played it, but overall this crowd (a few young farm couples, six loud members of a local softball team, an obese, drunken woman who alternately flirted and traded insults with the table of ballplayers, her skinny, hapless husband, the semi-conscious regulars, and us) was not likely to boogie the place down. Finally one youngish couple in western outfits stepped out on the floor and launched into their own private line dance. They had their moves down pat, repeating the same finger-snapping lunge-forward/drop-back/move-to-the-side step over and over until it became a contest between them and the band to see who could keep it up the longest. The musicians eventually conceded defeat and went for their break.

"We've played here before. You can't get these people to do anything," Mike Bruce told us as he polished off a beer over at the bar. "I mean, if they really get into it, they might tap a toe." The three front men were brothers, the Bruce brothers from Windsor, which explained why they looked so much alike and perhaps why their playing was so tight. Mike, aged twenty-eight, was the middle one; there was seven years difference between him and the other two, in both directions.

"My real goal is to become a chef," Mike went on. "I'm a short order cook now. But I'll never stop doing the music. I've got two kids, so does my brother, the older one. During the day I'm Mister Mom, when my wife works. We're getting five nights here, a hundred dollars apiece each night, that's not too bad. The drummer, he's from London, he's a great rock drummer, he quit and was a Maytag repairman for like nine years, got divorced and now he's back."

Around midnight we struggled to our feet and passed out the door of the International Hotel for the second and last time that night. As before, no one noticed our departure. Our car was parked under a streetlight across from the Leamington Baptist Church, where the announcement board on the front lawn proclaimed the subject of next Sunday's sermon: "Can we be happy in Leamington?"

The question was probably directed at the town citizens, or perhaps only the congregation, but it had a truly existential ring that seemed to include us all—freelance writers, other tourists, the barflies, the band, the tomato-pickers, the sadsack politicians and anyone else who happened to be passing the evening in town. Our answer was "Part of the time"; if you want to know the others' opinions you'll have to ask them yourself.

The next morning we remembered the three-masted schooner and hurried down to the harbour, but the captain had proved too nimble a naval strategist. He and his Tall Ship had slipped silently away in the night, and we couldn't even find anyone who remembered the vessel's name. Maybe this was his answer to the minister's question.

Chapter Seventeen

KS: At 4:45 a.m. I pulled up and parked on the muddy strip of bare, wet ground that runs along the Kingsville waterfront. Most of the twenty-odd commercial fish tubs based in this port town six miles west of Leamington had already chugged out of the harbour into the lake, and the rest were making preparations to leave. Only the *Edith Marie II* was still dark and untended as it rocked gently at its mooring. "There's no rush. The fish are getting up later these days," Captain Gary Penner had told me over the phone the previous day when we'd made arrangements for me to go along.

Gary is Harry and Aggie's son-in-law, which is how I came to be shivering in the early-morning darkness waiting for the crew to show up. Having never been out on the boat, Aggie had wanted to come too, if Julie would. What made them hesitate and ultimately decide to pass up the opportunity was not only the cramped quarters but the fact that the trip might easily last twelve hours or more, depending on how the fish were running, and there were no toilet facilities. "My daughters just climb up on the roof of the cabin and pee in a pot up there," Gary had offered helpfully. (Of course Edith and Marie are something like ten and twelve years old.)

Not long after five, the crew straggled down to the dock, and soon afterward the captain showed up, introduced himself and took me aboard to drink coffee while the others made ready to get underway. Forty years old, sandy-haired, blue-eyed, with a Zapata moustache, Gary looks something like a Mennonite Marlboro man, or a fish cowboy. Commercial fishing captains are classic independent contractors, small entrepreneurs who prefer wide-open spaces and as much elbow room as possible. They live by their wits, or rather by their instincts. The incomes of everyone on board depend on the captain's ability to predict where in the lake the fish will be running at any given moment.

The process is simple enough: if you put your nets down in the right place you catch the fish, if you guess wrong you come up empty. There are certain variables, however, which include air temperature, water temperature, wind velocity, whether the day is overcast or sunny, shifting water currents, time of year, time of day, depth of water at any given point, at what depth to set the nets (some fish are bottom-feeders, others swim near the surface), size of net opening, length of nets, colour of nets (different species respond to different colours), proximity of other boats, proximity to the U.S. border (Canadian boats are forbidden to fish in U.S. waters), where the fish were found yesterday, where they might be tomorrow, how long to leave the nets in the water and where you are in your yearly quotas. That's all, give or take a few more minor considerations. I asked Gary how he actually decides where the fish are and he was stumped for an answer. "I just know," he said finally.

"Except when he doesn't know," interjected Jed, a crew member.

"The thing is, 10 percent of the lake holds 90 percent of the fish," Gary went on. "The problem is the 10 percent keeps shifting. It's a gambler's profession."

Gary is an unlikely gambler. After receiving a B.A. in history from the University of Windsor, he set out to find a teaching job. Not having much luck, he ended up working for his father, a well-regarded engineer on lake boats who also owned a commercial fishing licence. The licence, which allows its holder to take in whatever is that year's quota for the various species in the lake, is the key to prosperity in the commercial fishery. The catch is sold at fixed rates to local fish plants; the crew, including the captain, divides 45 percent of the gross and the rest goes to the owner.

Because the Penner family holds two licences, their boat is considered a highly desirable berth, and except for one new-comer the rest of the five-man crew has been on board for years. In an average year they can expect to bring home around $40,000, augmented by performing other odd fish jobs, which were explained to me but which I utterly failed to understand.

The crew is classically Canadian in make-up; two, like Gary, are local boys of Mennonite origin who tell Mennonite jokes and laugh about their wealthy "old order" co-religion-ists, the ones who drive around in "Cadillacs without chrome" ordered that way directly from the factory. The remaining three are Portuguese immigrants, none of whom had ever had anything to do with fish or fishing back home; one was a waiter, one a steward on a cruise ship, the third in the army and then a bullfighter of sorts. Arriving in Canada they discovered the one saleable skill all Portuguese were pre-sumed to possess was commercial fishing, so with a Latin shrug each had adapted himself to his new home, declared himself to be an expert fisherman and in the ensuing years had indeed become so.

The boat on which the men spend their working days resembles a large banana that has been hollowed out, painted white and flattened at the bottom. Sixty feet long, eighteen wide, with a five-foot draft, it does a steady nine to ten knots and is perfectly adapted to dodging between the numerous islands and reefs of Erie's western end.

The tub is divided into three compartments. Up front under the bow are stored plastic crates that look like large recycling boxes. These hold the nets and later will hold the fish, along with ice-boxes, pails, rain gear, life-saving equip-ment and so on. Two steps take you up to the bridge, which, in addition to the usual equipment, contains a scattering of the latest electronic gear—a depth-indicator, a cellular phone, a radio and the LORAN (Long Range Navigation) computer that enables Gary, with the flick of a dial, to plot out distances and the time and speed necessary to reach any particular spot. Behind the bridge, taking up the rest of the boat, is a large, open work area.

Perhaps five feet behind the wheel in the bridge compartment a bench has been built into the wall. Above this, extending back six or seven feet over the stern area, is a dark, slot-like compartment, two feet high at most, covered with four foam rubber mattresses. "That's where the guys stretch out," Gary told me, and almost before he had gotten the words out the three crew members not needed on deck had dived in. By the time we passed the outer breakwater they were fast asleep. I don't know if "snoring like a Portuguese sailor" is an old saying, but it should be.

Forty thousand pounds is a good week's catch, but you never know how any given day or week will turn out. One week a few years ago Gary hit a mother lode of yellow perch, the highest-paying species, and within a few days they had brought in 15 percent of the year's quota. The most they've ever done in a single sortie is fourteen thousand pounds, and Gary looks both exhausted and triumphant remembering that particular day. That's a lot of fish. Looking around the small space I picture them chin-deep in them, clinging to the roof to keep from disappearing under the pile.

Today we were headed toward the American border, marked by a series of buoys zigzagging through the two dozen or so islands of the western basin. Most of these islands are uninhabited; many are mere smudges of reef sticking up above the surface. A few slightly larger ones on the American side are owned by private hunt clubs or sporting millionaires. Only five of the islands are big enough to sustain permanent populations; four of these are American, but making up for the numerical imbalance, the Canadian Pelee Island covers more area than all the rest combined.

Once in a while the fish tubs out of Kingsville drift over the boundary line, either by accident or in sly pursuit of a wandering school of fish that refuses to identify its citizenship. American radar picks them up, and the next day when they return to pull up their nets they may find a ticket stuck onto one of their net markers, addressed to an "Unknown person fishing in these waters…" Gary does not recall anyone ever paying the fine, however.

By seven-thirty or eight the sun was starting to warm the air and burn off the few clouds. I was lucky—I'd chosen a nice day. Before the *Edith Marie II* reached the border Gary had intuited that we'd reached a promising spot to put down the nets, and the crew began releasing the size he'd chosen out the open back. We put down what looked like miles worth (they come in detachable forty-yard lengths, each with flag buoy attached), then changed course and headed toward an area in which nets had been left the previous day. It's all precisely plotted on the LORAN; there's no guesswork involved here.

We were now just about halfway across the lake. Looking around, I could see Pelee Island, still shrouded in mist, to the east. Kelley's Island, the largest on the American side of the border, loomed directly south of us, and then continuing around the compass several others appeared to the south-west. The tall pillar of the Perry monument at Put-In-Bay stood out above the trees. Occasionally, between the islands, the Ohio shore came into view, a low, dark line dominated by the pair of ominous white cones of the Davis-Besse Nuclear Facility. No other structures rose to anything approaching their height, and seen from the water they gave the impression of having sucked the lifeblood out of the rest of the shoreline. I asked Gary if he had ever been over to the American mainland; after all, he spends every working day in sight of it. He shook his head but allowed he might go some day. On the other hand he has a tendency to stay put; in the seventeen years he's been fishing he has only once been east of Pelee Island.

In the morning hours, activity on the lake is usually minimal, and today was no exception; the rest of the Kingsville fishing fleet, fifteen or twenty dashes of white against the blue water, was spread out haphazardly around us. A few sport fishermen were anchored off the islands, a freighter was making its way through Pelee Passage, and that was all. We reached the overnight nets and began hauling them in, but Gary's instinct had betrayed him this time: a few yellow perch and pickerel clattered aboard, along with a lot of useless shad and an occasional catfish, but there was barely enough to fill one crate. "Nice going, Gary," the crew ragged him. "At this rate we'll be here until Christmas." The captain took it with a manly shrug.

Some of the nets appeared to be in tatters. They last about a month, Gary said. Gill nets are called that because once the fish swim into them they are caught around the gills and held fast. Different species demand different-sized holes. Yellow perch are short and wide but pickerel are long and thin, and because of their long sharp teeth they are always caught by the mouth.

Except for whitefish, which demand special treatment, the other species that turn up in the nets are more trouble than they are worth. The fish plants pay a little for white perch, but not enough to make it a profitable fish to catch.

I was starting to feel like a Jonah. We had been out all morning without pulling in enough to supply a day's worth of fish fingers at a fast-food shack.

Around eleven we anchored for lunch off East Sister, a slender island about half a mile long on the Canadian side. The province bought it when it went up for sale recently to protect the few acres from development, and it has been designated a wildlife reserve. Cormorants, gulls, herons and other waterbirds line the shore and perch in the trees, which are all a curious silvery colour, almost as if they were coated with ice. The guys laughed when I asked what kind they were. "Birdshit trees," someone said. The nature reserve program has been too successful; so many birds have made East Sister their home that all the flora is coated with excrement and is consequently dying.

The waterfowl population in general has expanded enormously in the last few years, according to Gary, who gets a daily, close-up view of the lake's fauna; it sounded like an echo of Jim Allen's description of blossoming bird life on the Grand River to the east. Certain fish species, pickerel in particular, have also increased substantially, a phenomenon that Gary and the two or three of his crew who had joined the conversation agreed might be ascribed to the generally despised zebra mussels, which they feel the pickerel feed on.

Great flocks of bluebills and cormorants, tens of thousands at a time, have been showing up lately; even the loons have been returning in substantial numbers. Gary pointed out a small island that seemed to be composed of some kind of black rock—except that it wasn't rock at all, the entire surface of the island was solid with black cormorants.

After lunch we returned to one of the spots where we had put down nets earlier in the day, and suddenly perch and pickerel were pouring on board at a mind-boggling rate. Everyone was working flat out. The fish-filled nets were cranked swiftly aboard into the lifter, a winch about the size and shape of an old-fashioned wringer washer, located midships. As they came up, Jed guided them rapidly around a central wheel, unhooked each forty-foot length, deposited it with the still entangled catch in a crate and swiftly slid the crates back into the stern. This job is known as "tailing the lifter" and demands total concentration; even a moment's inattention can result in scaly chaos and some heavy-duty cursing.

Back in the stern, the rest of the crew sat on their stools and picked fish, which meant running through the nets by hand, removing the catch with a little hook, identifying each fish and either tossing it into the proper ice-filled crate or flinging it over the side if it turned out to be a junk fish like shad. This is a stop-start process. If Gary's guessed right, they can be at it furiously for hours at a stretch; if the fish have declined to swim where he's put down the nets, they might have time to get to know personally each of the occasional specimens coming up.

Today many of the fish coming up into the lifter flopped around agitatedly, a good sign because the fresher the better is the working rule and their liveliness indicated that these had just swum into the nets. Watching the constant stream of fish emerge from the water, perhaps two or three hundred a minute, I had a sudden sense of the vast complication of life that must exist below the dark surface of the water. There must be hundreds of millions of creatures down there, a whole universe that has nothing to do with life on land.

Eventually things slacked off and the guys got a chance for a break. The wind had picked up. Crew members kept sticking their heads through the door to the bridge to see if I had gotten seasick yet, although I'd assured them that I never do. Carlos, the former bullfighter, entertained me with a graphic, well-acted story about a colleague of the ring who during a visit to Canada had come out with him on a fish tub, started throwing up in the harbour and didn't stop all day. But I felt fine. I was so absorbed with the fish I had hardly noticed the heavy waves until they'd pointed them out.

I can see what a killer this job must be when the weather turns truly bad. On a cold, stormy, November day, for example, with water crashing over the open sides, fish flying all over the place, crates sliding and overturning, nets getting tangled up with everything, they must wonder if there isn't an easier way to earn a living. Especially since those famously compact waves on Lake Erie can provide a real jolt, and we were really in shallow water. (At no time during the day had the depth-indicator registered more than thirty-eight feet.) "I once saw a guy picked up over my head and sent flying to the other side of the boat," Gary said. "You get some good storms out here."

Around mid-afternoon we finished putting down the overnight nets and turned for home. That late strike had brought the total up to around five thousand pounds, not a great day but not too far below average. Now all that remained was tying up at the dockside fish plant where the crates of fish would be weighed and recorded under the watchful eye of a fisheries official. As I stepped onto the pier

I felt as if I were leaving a way of life, not simply a fishing vessel. I can understand why people brought up as commercial fishermen fight so strenuously to keep the fishery alive.

JMS: The Penners had invited us to come by for a fish dinner, so on the appointed day I found myself in their kitchen watching Cathie peel apples. Gary's wife was a few years younger than her husband, with short, curly brown hair and a direct manner that reminded me of her mother. Like Aggie she also favoured flowered-print dresses.

After weeks on the road and evenings spent talking to strangers in smoky bars and noisy waterfront restaurants, it felt good to have a relaxed conversation with another woman in her own house. We spoke about our children, and that got Cathie started reminiscing about the days when Gary was courting her. "Once when we just started dating, I was helping sort fish when one flew over my head from Gary's direction, and I looked straight at him and said, 'Did you throw that at me on purpose?'" She smiled to herself.

"I used to go out in the boat with him all the time before we had the kids," she told me. She's too busy for that now. Besides their four kids, there's the company she and Gary started to produce high-quality whitefish caviar from a small processing plant attached to the house. They market 1,000 kilograms annually. And since Gary is occupied with the boat much of the time, Cathie has become the foreperson of an up-and-coming fish factory. It's a role she never envisaged while growing up on her parents' tomato farm.

"The first year the oldest of our kids was eight, the youngest three. That was a hard year. We didn't really know what we were doing." She paused thoughtfully. "Now we're coming into our fourth season. I hire six women to help me with the work, neighbours who also have kids, it's great." I told her that the way she described it, it sounded sort of like a quilting bee and she nodded, "That's right, it's really fun. We all kinda know each other, support each other. If I have to go and pick up roe, for example, someone will always help out.

"Come on, I'll show you." She put the apple crisp in the oven and led me down a short flight of steps into a large, brightly lit room where a row of six tiny sinks that looked as if they were meant for six dwarves lined one wall. Next to them stood an L-shaped table, and along the other walls were arranged two stainless-steel cold lockers, shelves lined with boxes of jelly jars and upside-down stacks of pails and colanders, and three larger sinks under which sat bottles of bleach and Mikroklene.

"We have a six-week production schedule. Each lot takes about three days," Cathie explained. "We're after a very pure product. First we hose away any membranes, then the eggs drain for a day before salt is added, then they're put through the colander again and then into the cooler. Every now and then we find little tiny zebra mussels that have got from the fishes' stomachs into the eggs, and those have to be discarded. Red eggs, too. The next day we use our dental vacuum on them." She laughed. "We got it from the States. When we brought it through customs they thought we were dentists. We told them we weren't, but they charged us a big duty anyway."

Cathie asked how we got started writing together, and I told her it just sort of happened after the kids got older and I had more time. "I know what you mean," she said. "Right now I like being able to work at home and building it up gradually." She looked around the gleaming room. "But the ultimate goal is full time. For both of us. We have lots of ideas, for mechanization, for example. We'd like a conveyor belt, but that means a bunch of stainless steel, and it's so expensive. Right now we're working with a federal grant for a year and a half, that's helping us quite a bit. The paperwork is the problem; we had to fill out a thirty-five page application. Everything takes time, it took us two months just to research all the regulations, and then we had to build the room. And it will take a while to build up the market, to educate Canadian buyers to pay more. Sales and that stuff, that's more Gary's department. External Affairs sends quite a bit of business our way, you know, for big receptions and that kind of thing."

Later, at supper, the couple said grace in German, then translated for us before passing around the Pelee Diamond, their top variety. And then, when we were leaving, they insisted we take two more jars of the best stuff with us, even though we had several days of travel ahead of us. "Just put it in your ice bucket," Cathie suggested. They seemed so eager that we hadn't the heart to tell them we had no ice bucket and that even if we did, we would never remember to keep it filled. The next day we met a caviar-loving woman farther down the coast who was delighted to have the tasty delicacy passed on to her.

John Karry lives a couple of blocks over from the Penners. He went to high school with Gary and, like him, started out working on dry land before being irresistibly drawn toward the lake and its mysteries. But while one man spends his days bobbing around on the surface, the other plunges right in and heads directly for the bottom. As the president of the Windsor chapter of Save Ontario Shipwrecks, he is, not surprisingly, an underwater heritage fanatic.

At the moment John is agitating for the province to create a diving park in the area at Point Pelee, like the one up at Tobermory in Georgian Bay. The typical visitor there shells out a daily average of $150, or so the tourist people claim, and with 30,000 divers a year coming to the underwater park that's no small boost to the Tobermory economy.

"But that's nothing," John sniffed, as we sat drinking coffee in his living room early one morning. "We've got much greater potential here. We're closer to the population centres. Our water is warmer. And there's more wrecks—fifty-one confirmed sites within easy distance of Leamington, mostly in Pelee Passage, and maybe another hundred not identified yet. We could put up marker buoys and plaque the wrecks. It would be community education and a great tourist attraction combined. Heritage is wonderful, but heritage that makes money is even better."

We asked if he knew of Dave Stone's exploits, and he cautiously admitted he had heard about him. "But the stories around here are just as dramatic as anywhere," he was quick to add. "There's the *Anthony Wayne*, the *Willis*, the *George Stone*, the *Star of Hope*, the *Tasmania*. The last manned life-saving station on the lake was here.

"We get fifty-foot visibility at forty feet down. That's better than it used to be because of the zebra mussels filtering the water. In the summer they've increased visibility by 200 percent. I know they get all over the wrecks sometimes, but the thickest encrustation you'll see is two inches, and don't forget they only have a life span of three years, after that they lose their grip. Also, because it's so shallow around here, the ice forming on the surface actually reaches down and scrapes them off in places."

John was studiously vague about the locations of certain of the wrecks. Like other Canadian divers all along the lake he frets about Yanks with expensive equipment rushing in to strip them. "Americans have no preservation ethic. They'll take anything." He shook his head. "Ohio is the pits. They don't care at all.

"Really, the whole lake should be a protected area. Michigan does better, in fact it's miles ahead of the other states. Their state archaeologist, John Halsey, is very progressive. They even prosecute looters if they can find them. The RCMP tipped off the Michigan state police and U.S. Customs and they raided this guy in Monroe, Michigan, who'd ripped off this old wooden stock anchor from the *Tasmania*, had it hanging on his rec room wall. The cops loved following it up, they thought it was like a holiday— usually they're chasing drug-smugglers."

John was full of shipwreck stories and was eager to relate one in particular, a sort of worst-case scenario for anyone thinking of running away to sea. "Let me tell you about the

George Stone, 1906. Left Detroit, hit a big storm off Point Pelee. They let out the anchor somewhere around Grubb's Point but a coal lamp tipped over and the ship caught on fire. Most of the crew took to the lifeboats and they were smashed by the waves and drowned, but the few who stayed on board were rescued by a passing steamer at the last minute just before the ship went down. But the steamer took them right back to Detroit, and as soon as they stepped off the boat, they were beaten up by thugs from the Seafarer's Union—there was a strike going on and these guys were non-union. One of the men was thrown back in the water and had to be fished out again. Doesn't seem fair, eh?"

John reached under the television, pulled out a tape, inserted it in the VCR, and suddenly we were down in the depths of the lake with him. Blue water, bubbles, bubble noises, fish swimming casually by some murky shape. "The lake bottom is mostly flat, though there's one sixty-foot-deep hole. Sometimes you come across giant boulders, other places it's gravel or sand or silt. Off Point Pelee it's sheet rock. We rarely see anything man-made, though, trash of any kind."

Now we were staring at the mussel-encrusted timbers of the *Willis* and entering the hold of the ship itself. "This one's the best preserved around here, a steamer that went down in 1872 ten miles east of Point Pelee in seventy feet of water. Except for the wheelhouse, that always collapses first, everything else is still there. Pulley blocks, masthead, belaying pins still in their sheaths, all of it. It's beautiful, beautiful."

"Did you ever hear of something called the rapture of the deep?" Before either of us could say we had thought we'd heard the expression he was already rushing on. "It's a real thing, believe me. Below 170 feet you get nitrogen narcosis. It's like being drunk, you can't judge distance, can't remember what you've seen. Very dangerous. There was a wreck 210 feet down someone wanted me to see but I said no thank you. There's plenty around here to keep me busy."

Chapter Eighteen

Another morning we sat down for breakfast next to a sales rep from Waterloo, Ontario. Kathy was very conscious of being a woman travelling on her own as she hawked her line of gift shop accessories. Whenever she was in this area she always stayed at Aggie's because Home Suite Home felt more secure than an anonymous motel or a hotel with long, bare corridors. With all its repeat customers, the place had something of the feel of an old-fashioned boarding house.

"You know," Aggie told us between popping up and down to run to the kitchen for the next courses, "when we first left the farm and started this business I used to have anxiety attacks every day at sunset, I missed seeing the sun go down so much.

"But I love doing this. It's like having a giant family. We get eight hundred visitors a year, and we've only ever had one problem. That was a man from Montreal. Every time we saw him he had a fancy new set of clothes on, and then one day he took off in a hurry and never came back for his things."

We were thinking that over when two intense-looking women from Clawson, Michigan, came downstairs. One wore a blouse with a bird motif; tiny ducks and geese were flying their way across her chest and down each arm. The women looked at us with a half-pitying, half-envious expression when we mentioned we were preparing for our first visit to the birding paradise of Point Pelee National Park, where the Atlantic and Mississippi migratory flyways converge. "Imagine, the first time," one of them murmured, shaking her head. A retired high school science teacher, she had been coming for years, or perhaps decades. We inquired whether birds winging in on one converging flyway ever accidentally cracked heads with different ones flying unexpectedly up the other, but she failed to catch the joke. The average birder has about the same sense of humour as the average bird.

Point Pelee is a triangular seventeen kilometre sand spit pointing toward Vermilion, Ohio. Even without the birds, its location as the southernmost extension of mainland Canada, on the same latitude as Rome, would give the sand formation a certain cachet among geographers. And unlike Long Point, this peninsula has been almost totally spared from human despoiling. The two small hotels that stood here in the forties are gone, and of the handful of cottages that went up before the point was declared a national park in 1918 only two remain. There are no restaurants or motels, just sandy beaches, woods, an interpretive centre and a kilometre-long boardwalk through the marshes. We decided to try the latter first.

Tall cattails surrounded us, almost forming a tunnel. Water lilies rose just above the surface of the marsh, their slightly softened mirror images reflected in the water below them. Pickerel glided by; herons, ducks and geese puttered about in the shallows. A mysterious shape slithered slowly though the lilies then disappeared, only to glide out from under the other side of the boardwalk. Whatever the thing was, it was large and had a back fin that emerged occasionally, like the periscope on a German submarine in an old black-and-white movie. One of us identified it as a humpback otter, the other as a small walrus. Finally the creature came near enough for us to see it was a huge catfish.

Climbing a viewing platform, we stared out over the water, luxuriating in the silence and the balmy air. But a moment later a group of eight-year-olds and two minders, all wearing T-shirts from a Michigan Bible camp, materialized out of nowhere and clambered up the ladder after us. Two of the girls sang without letup the entire time they were on the platform, and though the tune was obviously "My Bonnie Lies Over the Ocean," the lyrics were harder to make out. They turned out to begin with "Thank God, thank God I'm a Christian," and carried on from there. (No simple trick, as the syllables don't match. "Thank Gaah-odd, thank God I'm a Christian," is the closest you can come.)

We had pretty well gone the whole route by then, so we retraced out steps, got back in the car and headed out to the small interpretive centre, where they provide a free "people mover" to take you within a half mile of the tip.

We were just a bit too early for the main fall flyovers so this wasn't an optimum time for spotting birds (the schoolteacher and her friend were apparently following their own mad hunch about an obscure specimen that just might show up out of season). By pure chance, however, we had arrived at the start of the monarch migration. This is one of the most spectacular mass movements nature has to offer, and probably the most intimate, from a human point of view. Even though the full onslaught was a day or two off, the air was filled with thousands of orange-and-black butterflies. They hung from bushes, covered the surface of the tall Queen Anne's lace, bowed the stalks of goldenrod with their massed weight, lined up on tree limbs, landed on our hair and even our faces. If you moved your arm you could be sure of bumping half a dozen or so.

From minute to minute during the day their numbers seemed to expand exponentially; it was like Biker Day for butterflies, as crowds of newcomers floated in and for all we knew stopped to greet old friends and compare markings before parking themselves on a perch to look over the next batch. The bikes made more noise, and they were driven by a larger and less graceful species of animal life, but not even their colourful array could equal the kaleidoscopic effect of the swirl of winged insects.

Leaving the monarchs back in the trees, we stepped onto the deep sand and started slogging out toward the end of the point in the company of backpacking students, families with young kids, and birders with nothing better to do. It's a curious sensation to stand at the very tip of the country and realize that the entire nation—tundra, prairies, Laurentian Shield, CN Tower and all—funnels in to a point right under your feet. Over to the south-west stood Pelee Island, apparently densely forested, though we knew by now that the deep woods would actually turn out to be a single line of poplars along the shore.

As with the other sand spits up and down the lake, the contours of Point Pelee are constantly changing; the point is really the top of another giant sand pile that goes down seventy feet in places, all of it resting on a limestone ridge. Without a single tree or even a shrub to anchor it, the sand gets pushed around continually by the powerful offshore currents and winds.

That day the prevailing wind had been out of the east, so the sand was pointing more toward Toledo than Cleveland. Convincingly worded signs informed you that swimming here, particularly on the eastern side of the tip, was more than foolhardy; in fact, they more or less guaranteed you instantaneous death by undertow. Even standing safely on shore, the terrain under our feet had a precarious feel. One moment we were standing on dry land, or at least dryish sand; the next we found ourselves ankle-deep in the lake.

Before turning back we stooped down to pick up what at that precise instant were the southernmost pebbles in mainland Canada. This being the province of Ontario, pocketing pieces of the landscape was probably against some bylaw, but we got safely back to the car with our booty without attracting the attention of the park rangers. Unfortunately the pebbles quickly got mixed up with a collection of less significant stones scattered about the floor, all of which we swept out a few days later.

"They've completely lost any of the original island culture," the Pelee Island old-timer told us disdainfully when the subject turned to the American islands just to the south. But then his tone turned slightly envious as he went on to murmur, "I hear some of those bars over on South Bass are taking in a million a year in profit." Pelee Island probably hasn't taken in a million of anything, except perhaps sea birds and pieces of driftwood, in its entire history.

Other than a pheasant hunt in the autumn and fishing most of the year, peace and tranquillity is basically what the Canadian island has to offer. A lot of peace and tranquillity. An excess of it, in fact, from the point of view of economic survival. The islanders are hoping that the spanking new forty-car, four-hundred-passenger ferry, which makes a stop at Pelee as it crosses the lake between Sandusky and Kingsville, will increase the tourist trade considerably. But not too much: as in other communities on the Canadian side, the idea is to find a balance somewhere between all-out development and near-ghost towns where there are no jobs for the young people. It's a fine line.

Shaped like a trapezoid leaking at the corners, Pelee is the northernmost outpost of the twenty-one-island archipelago that skips across the lake and guards the entry to the western basin. (The early explorers imagined the chain looked like a rattlesnake, and well into the eighteenth century it was designated *Isles des Serpents Sonnettes* on French maps.)

Roughly 275 hardy people live here year round, a number which, if you divide it into Pelee's 10,000 acres, works out to 0.0275 inhabitants per acre, or just about three metric islanders per square kilometre. In summer the population triples. If you're the kind of person who needs his or her own space, this is the vacation spot for you. There is one grocery store and no doctor; a daily clinic staffed by nurses looks after medical needs. Once the ice closes in some time in December, small planes or the always risky snowmobiles are the only means of bringing in supplies. Or of getting off the island.

Sixty miles of roads, mostly paved, circle and criss-cross the island. There is a small primary school with thirty-five students, three teachers and, this being Canada, a controversy over whether the French language should be part of the curriculum. After grade eight, students who want to continue their education must board with families on the mainland. Once they have left, many will never return; even if jobs were plentiful on the island, which at the best of times they aren't, a lot of kids would find it difficult to readjust after sampling the sophistication of Leamington (or if they have really taken a walk on the wild side, Windsor). What Reeve Bill Krestel describes in the official tourist brochure as the "peace and quiet uniquely ours" is likely to look to an eighteen-year-old like a permanent near-death experience.

Of course that is exactly what many visitors come for—especially Canadians, who have started landing on Pelee Island in increased numbers recently. You hear them saying, "You know, this place is just like [wherever they originally came from] thirty or forty years ago." It's a statement that would only make sense to a Canadian. Very few Americans can remember anything like Pelee; real rural memories have long since disappeared from the American consciousness. In any event, the two national imaginations operate on quite different aesthetic principles. The American view of the countryside is based on a vision of lush fullness, while the Canadian outback is seen (by non-natives, anyway) as spare and empty; one must be sorted through, the other filled in.

More than any other characteristic, the irrepressible ruralness of the Canadian imagination is what really keeps the national character intact in the face of global villaging and cable superstations. The empty Canadian countryside is so powerful an image, in fact, that even immigrants like us begin to feel that our roots were in someplace like Pelee.

Although spear points dating back over 9,000 years have been uncovered here, for at least 8,800 of them the spot seems to have been nothing more than a temporary fishing camp. Or, as Stephen Leacock put it at the beginning of one of his tales, "Synopsis of Previous Chapters: There are no Previous Chapters." The island does not really enter recorded history until the late eighteenth century, when the local Chippewa chiefs were probably only too happy to unload it on a speculator named Thomas McKee for three barrels of corn annually.

McKee and his descendants logged the abundant red cedar, which was then cut into cedar posts and exported. Farmers arrived, planting grapes, then tobacco, and in more recent years soya beans and corn. In 1834 the island acquired a lighthouse, and with it a lighthouse keeper. His personal light did not shine very long, however. The next year a young West Point graduate by the name of Robert E. Lee was sent north to survey the Michigan-Ohio boundary; the keeper apparently objected when Lee tried to climb the lighthouse. A fight broke out which came to an abrupt conclusion with the death of the keeper.

Lee protested his innocence to the authorities by pointing out that they should have known better than to put a "d——d Canadian snake...irascible and full of venom," in charge of the place, adding in his report that the light had not been properly tended, anyway. You wouldn't think that this was the most diplomatic way for a young officer in a foreign country to explain himself after causing the demise of a local citizen, but since nothing more was heard of the incident, maybe most people agreed with his assessment of the keeper's character.

Two years later more blood was shed when the island was seized during the 1837 rebellion by a couple of hundred Patriot sympathizers, many of them Americans. The rebels had crossed the treacherous early spring ice from Sandusky, but a militia troop hurried over from the Canadian mainland and defeated them in what is generally referred to in history books as a brief skirmish. That designation seems a bit offhand, since more than thirty people died in the fighting.

You get a real sense of the slightly not-of-this-world life here from the *Pelee Island Grapevine*, a photocopied weekly newsletter. The Police Blotter for 1993, summarized in the September 1 issue, included the information that:

> Tragic was a way to describe this weekend in 1992, it was then that a traffic accident took the life of a visitor to this calm and partially peaceful Island. Well this year the weekend went from the sublime to absolutely ridiculous.

It may be said that with all the people who found their way to Pelee to participate in one or more of the happenings, that the lid just had to blow off the place.

When a child visiting with his family from New York was almost swept away by the undertow and a relative tried to save him, they both

> ...came close to the edge of death. Fortunately several people were able to reach the pair and remove them from the undertows [sic] grasp.

But that was just the tip of the dramatic iceberg. In the opinion of the writer, Pelee Island was on its way to hell in a handbasket:

> Violence in T.V. seems to be the normal pace... But in a baseball game, and on Pelee Island! After what should have been a challenging day of pitting skill against skill, some ball players found that the game did not end on a friendly sporting note. An investigation is underway into how and why a visiting player was struck on the head with a bat. This taking place long after the games were over.

Such outbreaks of temper are probably an inevitable feature of a place as cut off as Pelee Island. By early spring cabin fever must, at certain moments, overcome even the most serene and self-reliant. (An Ohio man who grew up on South Bass Island recounted to us how in his youth he and his pals could always expect a fight when they dropped in at Pelee.)

In spite of being almost within sight of much of America's industrial heartland, not to mention heavily populated southern Ontario, the islanders have somehow managed to remain oblivious to it all. Ron Tiessen, for example, rarely makes it back to Leamington, though he was born and raised there. Ron is a cousin of Harry and Aggie, but since he married a seventh-generation islander and moved offshore he rarely sees his relatives. "When I visit Leamington, I don't like sitting in traffic or looking for a place to park." That sounded about right.

Ron reminded us of an acquaintance from central Labrador when he left his home for the first time. We met Harris at the Montreal airport, but while we were waiting for his luggage he disappeared. After a search we found him outside on the departure ramp, counting the vehicles in the parking lot. "That's more cars than I've seen people in my whole life," he told us.

Like many rural people we'd met around the lake, Ron exuded the quiet self-assurance of a man who knew where he wanted to be. He helps his wife, Lynn, run a bed-and-breakfast (it seems to be a family occupation) and oversees the Point Pelee Heritage Centre, a long name for a small and interesting museum.

When we asked which of the local history books sold by the museum Ron would recommend, he picked up a copy of "A Bicycle Guide to Pelee Island" and handed it over, adding the brief comment, "You can't go wrong with this one." It was only after we had put down our money and were back in the car that we noticed that the author was one Ronald Tiessen.

We drove along West Shore Drive with the lake on one side, occasional houses and farmers' fields on the other, as far as Fish Point Nature Reserve on the southernmost tip of the island. According to Ron's book, about 10 percent of the island has now been returned to protected parkland. And, the guide also informed us, if we were lucky we might come across a Kentucky coffee tree, or a fox squirrel, or even possibly a blue racer snake. All are unique to this particular, pristine example of Carolinian forest. Unique this side of the lake, that is.

We kept a sharp lookout as we strolled through the reserve. All around us blue racers and fox-faced squirrels peeked out from trees laden with coffee beans. Or so we imagined, anyway. We didn't actually see any, but as Hemingway might have said, it was fine just knowing they were there. A quarter mile or so along the winding path brought us to a miniature cove, one of many indenting the shoreline. A heron was just landing on a twisted piece of driftwood, and strangely gnarled trees that might have been hackberries dipped their limbs in the quiet water.

Islanders scoff at mainlanders' claims for Point Pelee as the tip of Canada, and if you want to be technical, they're right. *This* is the very southernmost piece of habitable land within the true north strong and free; the spot where we were standing lies a good twelve miles closer to the equator than the national park and felt like twelve hundred. You could build a small cabin here and laze away the rest of your days, almost imagining that you were way down south in Dixie, until the first blizzard of the season swept away any illusion that these Carolinian woods were actually in the Carolinas. On the other hand, you wouldn't have to worry about cottonmouths.

As the ferry back to the mainland left the dock, the sun shone through a slight mist. Fisherpeople fished from the pier and watched the boat pull out. A water-skier buzzed around the harbour. The lake was calm, it was just another pleasant fall day. We climbed the stairs to the top deck and found a large group of fellow passengers already up there enjoying the fresh air.

As we sunned ourselves, one of the travellers pointed out a tiny dark cloud low on the horizon to the north-west. We noted its approach, commenting casually on its speed. Faraway thunder rolled, a long, low rumble, then flashes of lightning appeared all around. A few people (the ones who knew what to expect) moved quickly to the stairs; the rest of us remained on deck. The storm burst upon us no more than ten minutes after we had weighed anchor, and those passengers like us caught at the rail got soaked before they could scramble down the stairs to cover.

A few moments of heavy seas and pelting rain and the tempest had passed. In another short space of time we were back to the placid weather with which we had started the voyage. But the episode made us appreciate once again why you had better always stay alert on Lake Erie.

Chapter Nineteen

After a short rest break, we headed south and approached the American islands from the American side. Only three other vehicles joined ours on the short ferry ride to South Bass Island from Catawba Point on the Ohio mainland; one was a dusty pick-up driven by a middle-aged man wearing a fisherman's cap, the second a Ford carrying an elderly couple and the last a late-model Pontiac that held five men in their thirties, who spent the entire twenty minutes or so of the crossing discussing how quickly, how thoroughly and by what means they intended to get drunk. We couldn't quite figure out why they had chosen a small island, especially off season, for their binge, but we didn't give the matter a lot of thought at the time.

Maybe we should have. We didn't realize it on the ferry, of course, but South Bass Island would provide a dismayingly clear demonstration of a disturbing theme that we had found running through almost every aspect of life on the southern shore of Lake Erie. We're talking about the relentless fragmentation of American life in the last decades of the twentieth century, the constant dividing of the population into *them* and *us*, the coalescing into exclusive interest groups that consciously insulate themselves from the rest of the community—indeed, often the absence of community altogether.

America remains the home of a marvellous variety of odd, amusing, brilliant, fascinating, innovative individuals; we met many such people along the lakeshore. But in this new world of anything goes self-interest, where the practice of thinking beyond your particular situation to the good of society as a whole has become barely a memory, their painfully-arrived-at visions appeared morally and philosophically adrift. Ardent environmentalists would reveal themselves as enthusiastic gun freaks, and we encountered super-patriotic left wingers, patently racist social reformers, and others who in their attempts to make sense of the world were holding on to what anywhere else would be considered completely antithetical views.

The incoherence of American public life leaves everything up for grabs. For one thing, although it's rarely acknowledged, the very act of suppressing concern about a large and historically mistreated segment of the population, which lives right next door and whose striking pigmentation makes them impossible to ignore, can't help but distort and make hollow the white majority's occasional attempts at creating a real community. Increasingly rigid political extremism, new forms of religious intolerance, and the gut fear of economic decline also figure into the dismal equation. For anyone seeking a concise example of this trend to mull over, South Bass Island is as good a place as any to start.

Vineyards and a small airfield bordered the paved perimeter road that led toward the village of Put-In-Bay. Turning off onto a quiet lane toward the bed-and-breakfast where we had reserved a room, we were passed by three electric golf carts filled with cavorting retirees. "They rent them in the village," Mark Barnhill told us when we arrived at his rambling Victorian house. "This is nothing. In the summer sometimes they're bumper to bumper on the road." As if to confirm his words, another cartload pulled into his driveway, peered for a few moments at the house and then, their curiosity satisfied, backed out again.

Mark shook his head, asked if we'd like to sample the local viniculture and led us through an old-fashioned parlour into a sunroom overlooking a wide lawn which was surrounded by grape fields and groves of trees. Ensconced in plush easy chairs, our glasses filled with wine from the very vineyards outside our window, we sank into a genteel, turn-of-the-century lassitude. Mark's wife had just left on a three-week trip to visit friends on the other side of the world, and he was ready for conversation.

They had inherited this pleasant example of nineteenth-century good taste, complete with original furnishings, from an aunt with whom Mark's wife had spent her summers as a child. After his retirement from the armed forces with the rank of colonel, they came to live here full time and turned the place into a bed-and-breakfast. We would have guessed his background even if he hadn't mentioned it; one glance at the trim, ramrod-straight, crew-cut man in his fifties, not to mention the military neatness of the house, and you automatically started to salute.

He was interested in Canada, even though he had once cut short a visit to Montreal because he felt the people there were rude. But despite living a few miles away he professed to comprehend little about it. "I watch the Canadian news sometimes, but it's hard to follow when you don't understand the political system."

We asked how he liked his change of occupation, and like Aggie he said he loved it, particularly the opportunity to meet so many different types of people. "But we have one rule. We only take couples," Mark informed us. This was not because they had anything against unpartnered people, just their way of protecting themselves from the six-to-a-room gangs of revellers like the carload that had crossed over with us. When we remarked that it was lucky for us we'd come in September and missed all that, he looked at us narrowly for a moment but decided not to comment, and then went on explaining his rental philosophy. "I do make one exception," he said. "These three Russian Jews, three guys, right off the boat, or they were then, anyway. We accidentally took their reservation, and we didn't have the heart to turn them away, so now they come back every year. By now they're old friends. But they're the only ones."

Eventually we hauled ourselves up out of the deep chairs and set out to have a look at the rest of the island. Just after returning to the main road we came to the "Perry's Victory International Peace Memorial," the leading tourist attraction. Close up, the effect was startling. More than twice as high as Nelson's Column or the Arc de Triomphe, taller even than the Buffalo City Hall, sheathed in a strangely mustard-coloured stone that resembled heavy shower-curtain material, the 350-foot pillar dwarfed everything around it, like one of those pointlessly immense towers in a Chirico painting. We resisted the impulse to ask the innocent-looking college student manning the information booth how a single monument could be dedicated to peace and victory simultaneously, and in what sense it was an "international" memorial, since no other country to our knowledge had anything to do with it. (You do get a spectacular view of the entire western basin from the observation platform, however. And on the day we came to South Bass, of a steady stream of power boats cruising up the inner passage toward the municipal docks.)

We couldn't find the village of Put-In-Bay, or rather we found Put-In-Bay, but not a village. The business district consisted almost exclusively of very large bars, fast-food outlets, pinball and video arcades, ye olde sweete shoppes and souvenir counters. Except for the plastic fish, anchors and other nautical symbols featured in most of their decorating schemes, this could almost be the "Street of Fun" at Niagara Falls.

We were surprised by the number of people walking up and down the lanes, and the quantity of boats in the marina and the fact that more people all the time seemed to be piling in off the incoming ferries. The season was over, wasn't it?

Asking a salesclerk that question, the answer we got was a resounding no. The State of Ohio permits municipalities to hold two fund-raising gambling weekends a year, and Put-In-Bay devotes one to a no-holds-barred blowout in early fall before the weather turns nippy and the lake too dangerous. That was the reason for the strange buzz in the air.

The main action wasn't scheduled to start until tomorrow, so after a quick lunch we got back in the car and continued our tour of the island. Not far from town we pulled over to admire a three-storey Queen Anne house (one of many left over from more refined nineteenth-century days) whose vast frame exterior was painstakingly being painted by one man. From the looks of the place, he had been at it for months, moving his extension ladder and paint can a few feet over each day, and he still had at least half of his work ahead of him.

Driving past the house on our way back we caught him in the middle of lunch, and like Mark Barnhill he seemed happy to chat—not only about his work, but also about his life, which it soon became apparent pivoted on his tour of duty in Vietnam. Twenty-five years might have passed since then, but, like several other veterans of that conflict we'd come across on our travels around the lake, he returned frequently to his war experiences. It was as if he had never managed to come to terms with what had happened to him over there, and knew he never would manage to, but had to keep trying. "I still think about it. For sure. It really sucked, you know?" But then he stopped for a moment, perhaps at a loss as to how to continue, perhaps all at once off on some private tangent. We couldn't tell.

Neither he nor any of the half dozen or so other former soldiers we'd met had ever been leftist radicals; on the contrary, as young men they were all politically conservative, or even distinctly right-wing, and remained so today. But they shared one thing with the deserters and dodgers: the war had messed up their heads and their lives just as thoroughly. More, perhaps, because these were men who hadn't allowed themselves to think about the obvious moral bankruptcy of American policy, who in fact often didn't even have the vocabulary to frame the questions.

"I got married, got divorced. Don't see my kid much. He's out west somewhere," he told us matter-of-factly. "During the summer I pick up carpentry and renovation jobs here on South Bass, but then when the snow starts I'm gone, I head out where its warm, work on a ranch." He stopped again, looking slightly puzzled at how his life had worked out. You had the feeling it wasn't what he had planned.

"I don't know. That damned war," was about all he could say when we pressed him.

Even older, more settled career soldiers like Mark Barnhill found it hard to express their deep feelings about the war. Just a few hours earlier, for no particular reason that we could see, he, too, had turned the conversation in that direction: "I just couldn't get used to the Oriental way of life," he had confided, with a tone of baffled frustration in his soft-spoken voice. "I went over there with the best of intentions, but I gave up after a while. I just couldn't get used to it."

JMS: Two lists were scrawled on the chalkboard:

Mouth	Gills
Anus	Heart
Fins, dorsal, adipose Liver	
Barbels	Gall bladder
Scales	Spleen
Lateral line	Stomach—food in it?
Pelvic axillary process	

Reading them over, I was immediately transported back to Mr. Bachur's high school biology class. When the heavy-set, bearded, still young but curiously grave instructor wearing a red T-shirt, stained jeans and a baseball cap stared piercingly around the room and demanded, "Come on, kids, just look at the scales and you'll be able to tell what this one is," I felt as if the command were directed straight at me. Although by now I knew a pickerel from a perch, I didn't have a clue what the small, silvery fish he was holding up might be. Someone did, though; when a boy answered tentatively "Fresh water drum?" the teacher nodded and looked pleased.

Several people had mentioned Ohio State University's Stone Lab school to us. Their courses are popular throughout the state because of the rare opportunity they provide for teachers to bring students into direct, hands-on contact with the lake and its marine life. When I had asked Lab Director John Hageman over the phone whether it was possible to drop in he had invited me to come on down and take a look at what they were doing.

Easier said than done. I arrived at the appointed spot on South Bass to be picked up and ferried across a brief stretch of water to tiny Gibraltar Island, where the school is located, only to find the dock deserted and no boat in sight. Eventually I hitched a ride over with Lisa, the dining hall manager, just in time to join a group of sleepy-looking sixth-graders from southern Ohio who were halfway through the first morning session.

John placed a tray of half a dozen dead fish on each table, causing perfunctory squeals ("Ooo, Yuck, Gross") from the four girls nearest me, but a moment later they were deep into identifying the species. An eager-looking, slightly bossy girl in a blond ponytail demanded, "The thing is, does this one have pelvic fins?" They decided it did, making it, according to a second girl, a black bass. "No, a sunfish," said the ponytail firmly, and when she turned out to be right the other girl shrugged her shoulders cheerfully: "Whatever." Within fifteen minutes, the girls had identified all but one, which John told them was a tiny smelt. "Five out of six, that's not bad." The others, he confirmed, were a trout perch, a baby walleye ("See, those rough fins are ptenoids"), a white perch ("These came into the lake through the Seaway") and a catfish ("This one's so small it doesn't have scales").

Dissection time. Groans. John gave the kids a quick run-down: "We'll look at the gills, they're very important, and the internal organs. The liver's the largest, the heart will still be beating. The air bladder's sort of like a balloon, it can expand in order for the fish to rise." Then he glanced at me, as if suddenly worried I might be one of those militant Canadian anti-ichthyosectionists, seemed reassured when I remained silent, and went on to tell the class, "There's a lot of word out there that dissections are abusive, as if we should study them by just saying, 'How's it going, fish?' But this is the only way we can look at the overall health of a species—parasites, cancers, infections, all that. And unlike the ones in preservatives, this way the organs are all there in living colour." Having made that point, he took a live perch from the ice water that served as an anaesthetic and with one swift motion cut clean-ly through its brain stem.

At my table, the ponytailed girl wondered out loud whether she had come across the heart, then answered her own question. "No, I think it's the liver." The others gave their opin-ions: "Yeah, that's the liver." "It looks like the liver to me." "It's shaped like the liver." Four votes for the liver. A few more minutes of poking around inside the fish's entrails, then one of them called triumphantly across the room to a table of boys, "You guys, we found the heart!"

Later that morning I joined a second group for an open-air class in limnology (limno = fresh water) on the lab's thirty-seven-foot trapnet boat. Bob, the instructor, part dedicated biologist, part Ohio State beach boy (his T-shirt read "All-Greek Softball/Sigma Delta Tau"), joked and chattered with the class as we headed out onto the lake, past assorted small islands, under a warm September sky.

We put down anchor just off Rattlesnake Island, a small, pri-vately owned fish and game resort with its own airstrip. (In the summer the runway is often blanketed with wild turkeys, in the winter with ice, both circumstances leading some inexperi-enced pilots to skid off the low cliff and end up in the water.)

Bob passed around some data sheets. "Can anyone name the five Great Lakes? How were they formed? What's this?" He opened a box and help up one of many strange-looking gadgets. "An anemometer, of course. Right? Right. For measuring wind speed."

One of the girls was set to work operating it: from the north-east at 1.4 miles per hour; we all duly noted it on our data sheets. After another student checked the air temperature (21 degrees C./70F.), all our heads craned upwards as Bob asked us to estimate the proportion of blue sky to cloud. I guessed fifty-fifty, trying to factor in the height of the clouds above the horizon, but in my adult way I was over-complicating things; the correct figure was sixty-forty, he told me.

"Oh, cool," the kids exclaimed as Bob reached into his box and took out a neat-looking plumb line and explained its purpose. "Any more questions?" "Yeah," a girl with long red hair mumbled. "Why do we have to wear these dumb life jackets?" After someone measured the lake depth at ten metres plus a bit, Bob pulled a metal disk with a line attached to it from his box, looked around at the kids and demanded, "Okay, what needs sunlight to live down there?"

"Fish. Plants. Organisms. Plankton," they called out. "Right, right, right, right," he agreed. "Now we're going to find out exactly how far down the light reaches."

Two boys were assigned to lower the disk, painted in black and white quarter segments, and to call out the exact point at which they lost sight of it glimmering in the depths. This is known as photic depth and was the most popular experiment so far: "I can see it, I can see it, I can still see it. Now I can't see it," they chanted. After the boys hauled it out, measured the length of the heavy wet cord and multiplied by 2.7, Bob called over to a girl who was pouting because she hadn't had a chance yet. "Kim, I heard you say you liked math, so why don't you do the repeat for us." She jumped up eagerly and got to work, coming up with almost the same figure.

It didn't seem to matter that no one knew exactly why they

were doing all this. You could see from their faces that they were beginning to register the fact that the lake beneath us had a life of its own. Eureka! or exclamations to that effect. This was the same landlubberish Gestalt that Ken had spoken about experiencing on the *Edith Marie II*. Now I knew what he'd been talking about.

One more measurement, this time of dissolved oxygen. "Most fish need a reading of six or seven to live, but carp can manage at four." The surface of the lake where we were anchored measured nine, but a few feet down it was only three. Bob remarked non-committally, "That's low." He didn't seem alarmed, however.

During a brief pause in the action a couple of the kids closed their eyes and nearly drowsed off in the warm sun, but when Bob, ever the performer, called out "Party time" they snapped back to attention. The moment had arrived to examine the actual physical contents of the lake. A student hauled up a mouthful of grey mud from the bottom of the lake in a small dredge. "Ek-cell-ent. We've got benthos. There's a lot of silt down there because they keep diking the rivers, and also a lot of dirt runs off from farms and construction along the shoreline. Lots of leeches means poor water quality, but mayflies would be good news." He passed around a few tiny bloodworms and leeches. "Don't everybody go ill, now."

Which brought us to the grand finale that Bob had been building up to. Filling a tin washtub with water, he took one end of an otter trawl and tossed it into the water. The kids jumped out of the way as several yards of rope uncoiled rapidly, and a couple of mysterious minutes later he started pulling it in. He had to tug hard. "We've got something heavy here. Could be a dolphin."

No dolphins, but along with a few tiny perch and some sawbellies and cheapheads, an absolutely enormous carp that must have weighed fifteen pounds crashed out of the net and into the tub. Everybody screamed as the monster thrashed around, slapping the water with its tail and getting all of us drenched. A debate soon evolved about what to do with it.

"Let's dissect it." "No! Throw it back in." "Let's take it back and show it." In the end the carp, judged too good a specimen to waste, was donated to the lab.

Back on South Bass Island, in the school's administrative building, John Hageman talked about the lake. "This area has its share of problems, of course. Too many boat accidents, for example. Two weeks ago a Scarab rammed a small boat, three or four people killed. And living on an island like this means dodging tourists all summer. You get used to it but you can't wait for the tourons to leave." ("Tourons" is local usage for summer visitors—a combination of "tourist" and "moron.")

The lake is John's lifelong passion. "When I was young my grandmother had a cottage on the water. As a kid I didn't care what I would do when I grew up as long as it was on Lake Erie. And now here I am, surrounded by it."

He is surprisingly optimistic about the current condition of the lake. "It's true, when the central basin ran out of oxygen back in the late sixties, it was a struggle for some species. Some of them died out, like blue pike and some of the herrings. But it's improving all the time. The real nasty heavy metals are gradually being covered by sediments. A lot of the factories and steel mills are closed. Detroit has the best sewage treatment plant in the country, and that's crucial since most of our water comes down through the Detroit River. Toledo, Cleveland, working on it. It's the river mouths that are the big problem today, like Monroe in Michigan where they do a lot of car painting and it ends up in the Raisin River. But the good news is this lake is so shallow it flushes itself naturally every two to six years. Then it's Lake Ontario's problem.

"Zebra mussels remove plankton, that's a worry, but they may be cannibalizing their own. Hard to tell yet. The real estate developers are a lot worse. They don't understand anything. They just want to drain every marsh in sight for marinas. It's all about money."

I asked him to quantify his judgment of the lake's health,

based on a scale of one hundred at the time just before European settlement. "Today, seventy-five," he said thoughtfully. "Back in the seventies I would have said twenty." That was the best news I'd heard in a long time.

Another couple had booked in at the Barnhills and we met them briefly before going to bed. One was a pleasant, mild-mannered young doctor by the name of Wagner, who resembled an Edwardian aesthete, with his longish blond hair parted down the middle and white linen slacks. Originally from Cleveland, he now had a practice in Columbus that specialized in abused and tortured children. His companion was tall and sweet looking, also somehow old-fashioned in appearance, so slender that she looked as if a stiff wind would blow her back to the mainland. Still in university, she was also preparing to work with children. They seemed perfect for each other.

At breakfast the next morning we discovered that they had reached the same conclusion. "We got engaged last night," they told us shyly between the orange juice and the brown toast. We joined Mark Barnhill in congratulating the happy couple. Unfortunately, so much time had passed since we had heard anyone make a formal declaration of "engagement" that we forgot you were supposed to ask to see the ring. (In fact it never occurred to us that people still gave them out; when we got home we asked our son, who had recently announced that he was getting married, whether he had bought Annie an engagement ring, and after a long pause he replied warily, "You're joking, right?")

So we take this opportunity to offer our apologies to the Wagners, or whatever they now call themselves, and to assure them that had we actually noticed the ring, we would certainly have admired it greatly.

We now moved directly from the sublime to the ridiculous, or if you prefer from the dewy-eyed to the drink-sodden.

Back in the village, signs of the impending blast were every-where. Among the crowds on the sidewalk a fair number of the type that Raymond Chandler once described as "ferret faced, foxy men who looked like the male half of a second rate dance team" walked arm in arm with heavily mascara-ed female companions who glanced around vacantly, as if their minds were focused wholly on the upcoming chance to break the bank.

As they drifted up and down the village streets waiting for the action to start, these Las Vegas *manqués* blended into the hordes of beefy jocks wearing Cleveland Browns or Fighting Irish or Bulls caps and jackets who had come mostly just to drink, gawk and half-heartedly look for women (halfhearted-ly because there were six men for every unattached woman). The general atmosphere resembled a monster beer bash at some third-rate state university in a small, economically depressed city. The drinkers were the fraternity boys and the gamblers the townies.

"It gets pretty grim," a local woman told us. "Although it's better now than it was in the sixties, when this place was really wide open, before they started enforcing the open container law. But it's getting back that way now. Sometimes the jet boat from Port Clinton runs up to four-thirty in the morning, and I mean, on one of these big weekends you can get fifteen thou-sand people coming onto the island, all drinking like fish."

Party-seeking power boaters from around Lake Erie and the Detroit area also added their own particular flavour to the mix. By late afternoon the piers were clogged with them, five or six abreast at each berth in a technique called "rafting."

We strolled the length of an L-shaped dock, gawking at the opulence of the multi-level floating rec rooms in which mid-dle-aged men and women clustered to guzzle endless amounts of alcohol. As at Bemus Point, all were white and many were well on their way to oblivion. "How long did it take you to get here?" one man called out to a new arrival, whose boat was registered in Cleveland. "About a six-pack," came the shouted reply.

They avoided looking directly at anyone not on their own boat. Such camaraderie as did exist felt uneasy, as if each new arrival was more a potential threat than a fellow partyer. Two or three made vaguely hostile wisecracks as we passed by and then snickered loudly to let the others in their party know how clever they'd been. More than once we had to push our way through clots of them on the narrow walkway; nobody was making *them* move until they were good and ready.

But nothing expressed the sour, out-of-joint-with-the-wider-world aura they gave off better than the names they had chosen for their boats. Very few children's or family names were stencilled on the sterns of these costly craft. Instead we noted the *Adrenalin*, the *My Way*, the *Never Enough*, the *Breakaway*, *Off Duty*, *Alkie's Den*, *Old Spice*, *Beefeater*, *Need More*, *Sip n' Dip*, *That's Extra*, *Party Hardy*, *Carpe Diem*, *Panacea* and so on down a long list of sophomoric longings. They were almost all descriptions of things their owners coveted, and almost never evidence of satisfaction with what they had.

Chapter Twenty

After our dip into the sinkhole of the human spirit that is South Bass Island on a big weekend, we rolled down the ferry ramp and back onto the northern Ohio mainland feeling so glum about humanity that the only way left was up. By the time Route 163 had carried us into the centre of Port Clinton, its small but active downtown appeared a positively idyllic version of small-town life. None of the townspeople on the sidewalk were pouring beer down their throats as they staggered along, normal kids played ball in a normal schoolyard, a woman in the post office smiled and asked us if it felt like rain outside and didn't go on to make a stupid joke about how it sure was raining alcohol inside. This might not appear like much when you look at it from a wider perspective, but after the last few days Port Clinton seemed a dead ringer for Avonlea or Our Town. At least on that particular fall morning.

A scaled-down version of the drawbridge Leroy Waite stands guard over in Port Stanley crossed the Portage River not far from the centre of town, and further on we found an absolutely splendid 1899 courthouse, the best small-town municipal building we'd seen anywhere on the lake. This well-proportioned, Romanesque revival limestone structure had it all: gracefully arching windows, friezes and sculptures in abundance, a central bell tower and four separate entrances, each a variation on the general pattern in design and dimension.

A plaque outside the courthouse informing us that we were in Ottawa County came as something of a surprise, until we remembered that the Ottawas were another one of those nations driven off their lands, in their case north of Lake Huron, during the Iroquois wars. Some had retreated further north to the Superior shore, but others had joined the southern flight of the Neutral, Huron and Tobacco, crossed Lake Erie and set up camp around Sandusky Bay. The fact that white settlers had named the county after them indicated the strength of the Ottawa presence in the area.

An infant born in an Ottawa camp some time around 1720 grew up to become the great chief Pontiac. In 1763 he led a native alliance in a widespread rebellion against the British, which, had it been successful in its siege of the key regional control point of Detroit, might have resulted in the creation of a genuine Indian nation in the west and changed both American and Canadian history. In the long run, the Europeans would have overwhelmed them, of course, but subsequent native–white relations might have taken a very different course had the whites been forced to deal on a basis of equality.

A few decades after Pontiac's rebellion, Ottawa County, along with the whole of Huron and Erie Counties just to its east, became the homeland of a second set of refugees. In 1781, the British and their Loyalist allies under Benedict Arnold invaded Connecticut, burning New Haven, Danbury, Groton, Fairfield and New London to the ground. It seemed only logical, then, that after the war ended the state legislature would set aside part of its distant wilderness along Lake Erie as compensation for those who had lost their homes. These 500,000 acres at the far end of the Western Reserve became known as the Firelands, or, more eloquently, the Sufferers' Lands, after the cause of the migration.

West from Port Clinton along Route 2 the terrain turned marshy. In the lagoons and inlets, great white egrets stood out against the green rushes. Waterfowl skimmed the surface of an ancient canal that ran parallel to the highway. The land was flat and saturated looking, and it merged so gradually into the grey waters of the lake that we couldn't tell where one stopped and the other took over.

It's a pleasantly relaxed, even dreamy sort of topography, but one that's becoming scarcer every day. When Etienne Brûlé landed his canoe somewhere along here on All Saint's Day (November 1) in 1615, an estimated 300,000 acres of wetlands, averaging two miles in width, lined the south-western shore of the lake. Since that time 90 percent have been drained, the first batch by practical-minded German immigrant farmers in the mid-nineteenth century and the remainder in our time by developers and marina owners. This short stretch between Sandusky and Toledo is one of the few places on the American side of the lake where you can get an occasional sense of what has been lost.

Ironically, unless some brilliant research scientist figures out a way to control a phenomenon known as isostatic rebound, nature may eventually reclaim its losses in this part of the world. The unstable lake bed is still resettling after the retreat of the last glacier, and the coastline along the south-western part of the basin is sinking at an overall rate of two feet every hundred years.

We had plans to hike through Crane Creek State Park, assuming that it didn't give a sudden lurch and disappear under several feet of water as we stepped out onto the boardwalk. But yesterday's cloudy weather had by now turned into a cold, steady downpour, so we contented ourselves with a visit to the park's Sportsmen Migratory Bird Centre.

This is a museum dedicated to marsh ecology, waterfowl preservation and hunting. This list of elements seemed contradictory, but the Ohio Department of Natural Resources sees as one of its main goals the satisfaction of hunters; alongside the stuffed ducks, geese, owls and hawks glaring at us from their glass display cases was a collection of antique guns and decoys.

On the other hand, important work beyond the killing of birds is being accomplished here. Under the North American Waterfowl Management Plan signed a few years ago, the United States, Canada and Mexico are attempting a hemispheric approach to preserving wetlands, and this small research station is one of many participants. The Lake Erie Marshes Project has recently completed the restoration of one thousand acres of wetlands at Pickerel Creek in Sandusky County.

We also learned that the federal government has voted Ohio an award for running "the most successful goose production project in the nation," a program that is run out of Crane Creek. Using special techniques to encourage nesting, they raise seven to nine thousand baby Canada geese yearly, many in artificial nests. It was nice to know that the State of Ohio was for once doing something helpful for the environment, although their success in increasing the population of a species that is overrunning half the beaches in North America may not be celebrated everywhere.

Then suddenly, after leaving Crane Creek, around a curve the huge, ominous cooling towers of the Davis-Besse Nuclear Facility, which Ken had seen from the *Edith Marie II*, loomed up just along the highway, blotting out everything else. Up close they appeared almost casually, or perhaps boastfully, near to the roadway. Only a cyclone fence stood between the public and the Facility, and you could park your car on the shoulder and just about hit one of them with a stone.

That night we stayed in Jerusalem Township, at a motel so new the second coat of paint for the walls was still in the can. The side road on which it was located was bordered mostly by cattails. Despite our just-opened travel lodge, and here and there a house under construction, you didn't get the impression that this was an area about to undergo a boom. In fact, in the thirty-odd miles between Port Clinton and the outskirts of Toledo on Maumee Bay, our map showed a total of three villages along the lakeshore: Bono, Curtice and Camp Perry.

The clerk behind the front desk told us she always went to Judy's Tavern for a night out, so we followed her example and wandered down a deserted road on the edge of the marsh. On an overcast night with no moon or stars to provide light, the only breaks in the inky blackness were an intermittent string of lights along what must have been the edge of the lake in the distance somewhere to our left.

Finally we came to a lone, wooden, one-storey building at a dark intersection. In contrast to the bleak outside, the brightness of the large single room dazzled our eyes, and on looking around, we sensed that this was somehow not quite your typical rural bar. To begin with, it was noticeably clean and tidy, almost cheerful. There were no sports posters on the wall— just a few colourful neon signs, a couple of video games in one corner and a scattering of humorous placards. The one directly behind the centrally located bar announced "Free Beer Tomorrow" and another read "I can go from bimbo to bitch in 3.4 seconds." Most noticeably, everyone in the place, from the bartender to the customers to the cook taking a break from kitchen duties, belonged to the same sex.

Rural Ohio seemed an unlikely setting for a lesbian bar, or for any business catering to alternative lifestyles, and of course it wasn't anything like that. "There's plenty of bars for men," Judy told us. Judy was fifty-one years old, blond and bubbly, a short, sturdy woman who clearly knew her own mind. "I just wanted to start a place where a woman by herself would feel comfortable dropping in, like a family bar." As if to prove her point, a few minutes later a twentyish version of the proprietor stopped by, gave her mother a quick hug, picked up some french fries and then ran out the door again.

Feminism has not made enormous strides in this part of northern Ohio, but Judy seemed to be doing her best to redress the balance. She laughed good-naturedly about certain of her customers, invariably men, who take the "free beer" sign seriously, and when a male customer who had

ᛰ come in with his girlfriend brought up the subject of PMS, she quickly put him in his place: "Yeah, right, PMS. You mean Putting up with Men's Shit, don't you?"

Judy's quirky personality was evident everywhere. She seemed to have convinced local businesses to buy advertising space on her ceiling, where various panels urged you to get your bait here, or your hair cut there. And instead of a playoff game, the TV above the bar was tuned to a made-for-TV movie involving child molesting and courtroom custody disputes. The sound had been turned off, so over the heads of the customers a parade of fashionably blazered young lawyers, morally reprehensible mothers (you could tell because they smoked constantly), idealistic social workers (you could tell because they didn't), shiftless-looking husbands, untrustworthy psychiatric experts, world-weary sheriffs and stupefied children flickered silently and wretchedly on all evening.

By now the bar was filling up, and the late arrivals included several more of that less discerning, sign-believing sex. The subject of hunting, a popular avocation around here, was raised. According to a man in his forties, we had just missed the squirrel season. "What do you do with them after you shoot them?" we asked. "Eat 'em, of course," he replied. "You never heard of squirrel stew?"

"Course you have to skin 'em first," Judy dead-panned. "That hair can really tickle going down." The legal limit is four, by the way, in case our description has tempted anyone to take up the sport.

Somehow the subject of Vietnam made its way into the conversation once again; maybe it was the gun connection. The hunter was yet another one of those veterans who kept referring obliquely to the war, then quickly veering away from the subject if you took him up on it. In the swirl of chatter, we never did get his story clear, just the fact that somehow because of the war he had undergone years of various types of therapy, physical and psychological, but still found himself unable to work and having to survive on a small pension.

As the evening wore on, the gloomy marshes beyond the door receded more and more into the background and Judy's brightly lit tavern became the centre of its own universe. This must be a bit like what the isolated rural inns that once serviced stagecoach routes felt like. The convivial conversation brought home the fact that Judy's world was bounded by the limits of Jerusalem Township, with occasional extensions a few miles in either direction; when someone mentioned a man whose interest in fireworks had led to two of his sons being accidentally blown up and who was currently running for some local office, Judy asked us in all seriousness, "You know him?"

"Let's talk about something else," she said a moment later. "So are they ever going to widen Route 2?" We told her they were starting tomorrow, which got a general laugh.

Eventually we bid everyone goodnight, rolled back down the empty country road without seeing another car and lurched to a halt next to a boat-trailer carrying a full-size cigarette boat. A small notice taped to the stern read "For Sale. Call Owner" and listed a telephone number. Out of the water, the monstrous craft looked as large as a moon rocket, and as practical. The clerk behind the motel counter thought the owner was asking something like $80,000 for it, practically a fire-sale price.

The next morning we unfolded the map again. A large yellow splotch marked the city of Toledo not far ahead, but we discovered that by cutting south before reaching it we could pick up the Maumee River and retrace the route followed by Julie's father sixty years earlier, when he had taken time out from his round-the-lake canoe trip for a side excursion up the Maumee to Grand Rapids. Which was, of course, what we decided to do. For one thing, one of us had had her fill of the other's eastern Ohio childhood memories; now that we were getting into her part of the Midwest she didn't intend to let the landmarks pass unnoticed. Perhaps we would even find the *Tri-County News* still publishing and stop by for our own chat with the current editor.

Only a few houses cluttered the view along Route 65, a narrow country road, as it followed each curve of the Maumee. Formed by the junction of two already fairly substantial streams across the border in Indiana, the river gains speed as it flows north-east before emptying into Maumee Bay just at the point where the state of Michigan takes over the lakeshore. It must be three or four hundred feet across here; the Grand and the Cuyahoga were mere creeks in comparison. John Macfie had been more of an outdoorsman than we'd realized.

JMS: When we reached the village of Grand Rapids, I headed down a dirt path toward the water, the tall, wet weeds scraping against my jeans as I descended the bank. I tried to picture my father as a young man, hauling his canoe up along these flat, grey rocks, stopping to look around and take in the same scene I was looking at now, perhaps thinking the same thoughts. He was something of an artist, coming home sometimes from the factory with a bracelet for me that he had made from a piece of scrap metal, or shaping pots on a basement potter's wheel with mud he'd dug up from the creek. I could imagine him here in this beautiful, quiet spot, bursting into a wild Dionysian cry (as long as no one could hear him) or one of his off-key renditions of "Mandalay" or some other Victorian song of adventure.

Now that I was here, I realized I had had another reason for wanting to make this side excursion. My parents had retired to North Carolina and died there, so I haven't been able to pay occasional visits to their gravesites. Spending a few minutes on this riverbank, to which one of them had travelled before I was born while the other was at home minding my seven-month-old sister and trying not to worry about storms and dangerous travelling companions, made up a little for that lack and provided a badly needed connection to the past.

We walked down the long block that makes up the Grand Rapids business district, following in what would have been John Macfie's footsteps. The old buildings looked fresh and well kept, but instead of a newspaper office, barber shop, drug store, dry goods emporium, dentist and doctor's offices and so on, they were tenanted by Critter Caboose & Willowview Antiques, Olde Red Wagon Antiques, River Barn Antiques and Auction, River's Edge Antiques, Riverside Gift Galleria, Silhouettes-on-the-River, The Apple Tree, By Hand & Heart, The Brickyard Collection & Lo Jo Creations, Cabbages and Kings, Crafts by Janet, Dandy's Lane & Grand Rapids Fudge Factory, The Front Door, Four Seasons Gift Shop, Nan-tiques & Nan-tiques Dolls and the Olde Gilead Country Store.

We could also rent a canoe, tour a restored grist mill or take a ride on a restored steamboat, gather with the rest of the county for the annual Flood Watch days or next summer attend a Muster on the Maumee, to which "Buckskinners, muzzleloaders, collectors, Native Americans, genealogy folks, artists, writers, and others" were all invited.

The *Tri-County News* had ceased publication so long ago that the town librarian had never even heard of it, but she was happy to take on the role of its editor and chat about the town. "In the seventies almost everything downtown was empty, things were pretty depressed. Then an entrepreneur from Toledo bought in and that started the renovating. It's all taken off since then. There's the stores, of course. And tourist buses. And lots of people come to the campgrounds, they're along the water. And they're always travelling up and down the river in autumn to see the leaves." We tried to get her to express an opinion on this radical restructuring of the town's economy, not to mention its character, but she wasn't talking.

Retracing our path downriver, we found ourselves on Anthony Wayne Trail. That was a name we knew from grade school history classes. Mad Anthony Wayne was the impulsive and irascible hero of various Revolutionary War campaigns; when, a decade after the war's conclusion, the natives kept resoundingly defeating every by-the-book commander sent to clear them out of western Ohio, and it looked as if they might make their domination of the area permanent, President Washington in desperation called the unorthodox old troublemaker back from retirement. In 1794, in the battle of Fallen Timbers on the edge of what is now Toledo, Wayne beat the natives at their own game by concealing his troops amid a field of trees uprooted by a recent tornado, killed a large number of them and forced the chiefs to give up any rights they claimed to the area. This opened up the western part of the lake for settlement, permitting, among others, various of Julie's great-great-grandparents to leave New England and seek a new life in the territories.

Entering Toledo we noticed an exceptional number of billboards lining the roads. One set shrieked the virtues of various competing hospitals and wellness plans (More maternity beds! Advanced Technology with a Personal Touch! 239 private rooms, no extra charge! Quicker service! Complete coverage!) and another much more temperately demonstrated the pleasures of cigarette smoking. In open stretches of highway the two types would often alternate, so that your eyes would run along a cadenza of contrasting Cancer/Marlboros/Prenatal/Winston/Diseases of Aging/Benson & Hedges visuals until you began to feel that the whole thing had been designed by Lewis Carroll.

Arriving at our destination, we found the Toledo media in near hysteria over the four murders and numerous rapes, stabbings, maimings, beatings and robberies that had taken place in the city in the space of the previous seven days. Three of the murdered citizens had been black and one Hispanic, and most of the other victims fell into those categories as well. The import of the reporting, however, was to turn that fact around and by implication cast all blame for the crime wave on the uncivilized nature of the black and

Spanish communities themselves.

Once more we heard the breathless drugs/guns/single-mothers/family-breakdown/blood-on-the-sidewalks/he-had-his-whole-life-in-front-of-him story lines while teenagers made faces at the camera in the background and bereaved parents sobbed. These speakers were followed by middle-aged white men in expensive suits or epauletted uniforms reasserting their dedication to the eradication of crime and vowing ever more severe punishments. "Animals" was one word mentioned frequently.

The next day we went to have a look at what all the fuss was about. Ward One was certainly bleak-looking enough— lots of litter and boarded-up buildings, small Pentecostal churches with apocalyptic-sounding names and stores with signs reading "Food Vouchers Accepted Here." But somehow the mood wasn't nearly as hopeless or as angry as on Main Street in Buffalo or in Cleveland's East Side. For one thing there seemed to be considerably more mixing of the races.

Maybe it was mostly a question of population; at 330,000, Toledo is a more manageable size than the larger cities, and it's harder to isolate one group. (Toledo and Buffalo proper are actually almost identical in size, but Buffalo's surrounding communities are five times larger. Here Toledo is basically all there is.) A forward-looking, generous-spirited civic administration might still have a chance to pull this neighbourhood back from the brink before it truly becomes another country.

Unfortunately, the Toledo city fathers have already tried and failed at the vision thing, in the process blowing the rehabilitation budget permanently, or at least until the memory of the fiasco they sponsored has subsided, probably some time in the twenty-second century. We found the details of the affair in an incisive recounting by Stephen Phillips in the Business column of the March 1991 issue of *Ohio Magazine*. The results of the debacle are open to inspection by anyone, however. In fact, you can't avoid them; they take up the entire downtown waterfront.

The usual rust belt syndrome of declining industry, racial

divisions, flight to the suburbs and so on hit Toledo after World War Two. When John Denver sang "Saturday night in Toledo, Ohio / is like being no place at all," the town entered middle-of-the-road pop music as a symbol for futility. So the local movers and shakers got together and came up with a plan.

Not just a plan, but a "vision." (And not just a vision, but a fantasy, someone might say in hindsight.) They tore down much of the waterfront and created a sprawling post-modern world of luxury hotels, parks, a couple of forty-storey office towers, colourful, upscale shops, convention centres and condo complexes. "Portside" was to become a beacon of progress that would enable Toledo to outshine all the other cities around the lake. Conventions would compete to convene here, head offices would relocate, and travel agencies would make it a must-see. Projections for 1984, the first full year of operation, were for five million visitors. *Five million.*

They completed their city of dreams on schedule, at the cost of unfathomable millions, cut the ribbon and waited. And just as at Cleveland's Terminal Tower complex and Detroit's Renaissance Centre, both much more modest projects given their relative sizes, nobody came. This was Toledo, for crying out loud. Within a few years the condos, one of the soaring office towers, many of the stores and the two luxury hotels had all gone into receivership. The other skyscraper had been taken over by a bank, which was now essentially its only occupant. In 1990 Portside was officially put out of its misery and shuttered. Toledo's new downtown had managed the remarkable feat of going bankrupt at the height of the prosperity of the 1980s.

Today, downtown Toledo is a ghost town, its streets virtually empty. Looking around, we found the fancy department store closed, its display windows fitted with black glass and many of the older warehouses boarded up. Several prewar-style pillared and gingerbreaded banks looked as if they might still be in operation, but it was hard to tell, since we couldn't see any customers.

The sidewalks were deserted as well. Near a small park where the Ten Commandments were engraved on a large rock, we passed a lone bagperson pulling his green plastic carryall behind him. Further along a long-haired young courier hurried around a corner, and after he had disappeared a drunk wandered casually across the street just in front of our car to greet a pal. And no one else—not even a single example of the window-washing derelicts, mentally disturbed talkers-to-themselves or potential muggers common in most urban downtowns; you couldn't even get harassed here.

For one of the few times ever we had our choice of parking spaces on a main street. We selected one of the several occupied slots in front of a Woolworth's, one of the few stores that still seemed open for business. Strolling over to Summit Street, we went into the sumptuous Marriott Hotel in search of a newspaper. The time was two o'clock on a business day; at the desk a middle-aged couple was checking out, and when they left we became the only non-staff people in the entire lobby.

Apparently a few guests were expected, because the roster of events posted for the day announced the schedule of the "Ohio Government Risk Management Plan." This devil-may-care group of bureaucrats had started with an 8:30 "eye opener" and was to follow that up several hours later with "1:00 p.m. Register" and then "2:00 p.m. Meet." That was it for the day's events, although another board announced the identity of the "Whatever It Takes" employee of the month next to a snapshot of a serious-looking young man with a Spanish name.

The business élite responsible for the Portside fiasco has long since bailed out, leaving this gleaming Pruitt-Igoe of the eighties in its isolated splendour on the banks of the Maumee. The few Toledoans who have found work here seem almost cheerfully resigned to life in the furthest reaches of post-industrial desolation. Across the street from the hotel, in a post-modern complex spread out over most of a block, the guard at the information desk was eager to have someone to talk to. He shrugged when we asked him who had their offices here at Seagate. "Basically, nobody," was his reply. "It's a disaster."

Outside a smaller building on a side street we found a couple of women grabbing a smoke. They were both employees of a brokerage firm. "You can't do anything when you're caught in a corporate buy-out," was the way one of them put it, shrugging cheerfully. It seemed a strikingly fatalistic view of life for someone in their profession, but typical of Toledo.

It's a pity the financial projections of the Portside project proved so overblown, because architecturally the overall scheme isn't bad. Some of the more picturesque factories and warehouses have been retained, and open passages give sight lines from the streets to the river. We sat down in a waterside park with flowing fountains, terraces and largish sculptures. On a side wall we noticed a large, bright-red button marked "Press Here for Help." We weren't sure of its purpose, but whatever it was, it was too late.

Glass is to Toledo's self-image what cars are to Detroit's. The Henry Ford of the glass industry was Edward Drummond Libbey, one of the late-Victorian manufacturing geniuses who helped raise the swampy, mosquito-ridden community known as "Frogtown" to a bustling commercial centre. Libbey also founded the Toledo Museum of Art and donated to it his splendid glassware collection, which is worth a trip in itself.

Perhaps inspired by all that varicoloured art nouveau refraction, we decided to drop in at the on-site shop at Libbey Glass and see what they were up to these days. Decades had passed since either of us had been to a genuine factory outlet, although in the immediate postwar years many Depression-hardened families, the Sobols prominent among them, had pursued the practice of periodically hurtling several hundred miles down obscure highways in search of bargains at such places. Factory outlets were spoken of in the same reverent tones as designer shops are today, and the outlet at Libbey

Glass was as well known in the upper Midwest as the House of Chanel in Paris.

Outside the museum we found a stout, red-faced Colonel Blimp look-alike, probably a board member, deep in conversation with the parking lot supervisor. The two elderly men collaborated on explicit, unmistakable directions that sent us straight downtown and onto a one-way street heading toward southern Indiana. Finally we realized that we had misplaced our trust and managed to flag down a woman getting into her car, who in great detail pointed us in a completely different direction. We followed her instructions to the letter only to end up in a cul-de-sac somewhere in the north end. Luckily, after more aimless wandering, we spotted the factory water tower poking up over the trees in the distance and eventually found our own way there.

We were soon happily wandering among long shelves of incredibly cheap discontinued lines and seconds. They weren't museum quality, but they were certainly well designed enough for our cupboards. In fact, something like bargain fever seized us—what you might call the rapture of the cheap—and at the check-out counter we discovered that we were about to lug home a lifetime's supply of heavy cobalt-blue glasses of varying sizes, beginning with large and going up, as well as a representative sampling of other styles, plus a pair of sausage-shaped ceramic salt and pepper shakers. The whole bill came to forty-seven dollars and a few cents, and for a moment we basked in what would have been the approbation of long-gone penny-pinching family elders. We could hear them saying, "I think Kenny and Julie must be managing their money better these days. Maybe they're finally getting some sense."

Reality set in by the time we got to the parking lot, and although we actually use some, and have foisted off as many as possible of the others on reluctant children ("No more, that's all, our shelves are full, thanks anyway, stop!"), we still have three or four boxed sets left in the cupboard in case anyone is running short.

Chapter Twenty-One

Another dismal, pelting, off-and-on downpour began as we crossed into the last state that bordered the lake and began the final leg of our journey. The twenty-five-mile-long heel of Michigan that comprises the western shore of Lake Erie seemed like something of an afterthought in the greyness of the morning, another tag end of sparsely populated marshland like the one surrounding Judy's Tavern.

Route 125, also known as Old Dixie Highway, offered a little bit of everything; auto parts dealers, an abandoned airstrip, fields of dry cornstalks, fragile-looking fishing shacks dating from the days when large numbers of men made their living on the lake, streets with French names, run-down beach villages, chemical slagheaps, duck blinds, odd, self-contained lakeside condo developments at the end of obscure side roads. The low, dampish topography and the wildflowers along the shoulder—blue cornflowers and pickerelweed and yellow daisies—were all that tied these disparate elements together visually.

In a few minutes we arrived at the outer malls of Monroe (pop. 23,000), the only city on the Michigan shore. We wondered what there could be left to say about one more small, industrial lake port the approximate size of Ashtabula—or of Fort Erie, or Sandusky or Port Colborne for that matter. But the city's diligent historical association has put up so many informational plaques that before we knew it we had absorbed an entire crash course in the area's early days. So, for what it's worth, we pass on the following pieces of information, in case you ever find yourself in Monroe, Michigan. 1. This is an old town. 2. It was originally French. 3. The Raisin River flows through it. 4. General Custer got married here.

Once known as Frenchtown, thus completing the alliterative series that includes Fishtown (Sandusky) and Frogtown (Toledo), this soggy corner of the world was settled by Québécois farmers and trappers before the end of the eighteenth century. That makes Monroe the oldest American town along the western basin, with more than the usual amount of heritage architecture—another good stone courthouse, some nice ornamental brickwork, neat rows of frame, federal-style houses. Today there are still Gallic names in the telephone book, and we were told that one man, a Mr. Navarre, even speaks the language of his ancestors, although it was never clear whether that was because he grew up hearing it at home or because he had taken a French course at university.

There's also a respectable amount of history here; before Europeans arrived this was an important native gathering place. Later, during a bloody battle in the War of 1812 known as the Raisin River massacre, an American force was annihilated (literally, down to the last man) by the British and their native allies. "Remember the Raisin River!" became a rallying cry of vengeance-bent American troops for the remainder of the conflict, the first in a series of similarly phrased slogans ("Remember the Alamo!" "Remember the Maine!") that resonate through American military annals. And a few years later, in 1835, the small stagecoach stop halfway between Toledo and Detroit was the focal point of a boundary dispute between Ohio and Michigan known locally as the Toledo War.

But the event this city has picked out to memorialize is an occurrence of absolutely no historical significance—the marriage of General George Armstrong Custer to a local girl,

Elizabeth Bacon, over at the Presbyterian church. Not only is there a General Custer Historic Site somewhere in Monroe celebrating the life of the vain, arrogant show-off who got himself and all his men slaughtered at the Battle of the Little Big Horn, but in the local museum you can also gaze upon his bathrobe. (After his death his widow returned to Monroe and devoted the rest of her life to glorifying his memory through a series of myth-making memoirs, which is why he got so much attention here. Her family and neighbours were almost honour bound to put up some sort of monument.)

Today, Monroe is struggling. To begin with, the local car-painting plants have been discharging toxic poisons into the harbour for decades; at 10,000 parts per billion of PCBs, the mouth of the Raisin River today may well be the most chemically contaminated pool of water letting out into the lake. Two pieces of advice to keep in mind when holidaying in Monroe: don't swim in the harbour and don't fish in it, either.

There's also another large nuclear plant just down the road that keeps casually dumping its waste water into the lake without warning. Back in the sixties it came close to having a Chernobyl-type meltdown and very recently there was a serious fire, both quickly hushed up. Maybe it's just having to overlook the fact that every day your house is sinking slowly but inexorably into the swampy soil. For whatever reason, the townspeople we met in Monroe seemed to share Toledo's strangely detached view of life. When we asked the good-natured waitress in Zorba's Restaurant in the heart of the city centre (pink-and-black booths under large posters of Elvis and James Dean) about the high proportion of empty buildings, she stared as blankly as if we had asked her to explain to us once and for all just why it is that E equals MC squared. Then she commented, "Oh, yeah, the downtown's going, that's for sure," in an upbeat tone before going on to ask, "You want your tea hot or iced, hon?"

As for politics, on the day we passed through the editorial writer of the *Monroe Evening News* was taking a line on the Clinton health plan so reactionary that even a Pat Buchanan or Newt Gingrich might have felt it needed a touch of humanization. He assailed the health plan not on the basis of cost or curtailment of choice or creation of additional bureaucracies, but on motivational grounds. Allowing poor or unemployed people access to health insurance would be giving them the wrong message; see, the way to get them off welfare and unemployment is to make sure the penalties for being in their position are so severe they will be desperate to better themselves and so go out and find jobs.

The *Monroe Evening News* also featured the cavalier approach to time typical of many small-city American newspapers today; the front page announced that a federal election had been called in that other country across the lake, even though in real time the Canadian campaign was nearly half finished and the circumstances described in the article had changed so radically that it might as well have been a description of Brazil.

When you leave some places you just know you will never be back; Monroe was one of those. We debated simply hopping on the freeway and heading home for good, but instead turned off a few miles farther up the road into the parking lot at Goose Droppings State Park (not its real name, of course, although it should be), for one more look at the lake. There, ignored by entire flocks of Canada geese, we carefully picked our way down a guano-covered nature trail bordered by a cyclone fence marked "Keep Out, Combustible Materials" at the far edge of which we came out at an isolated little U-shaped cove.

Standing at the very bottom of the U, where a few pieces of driftwood and traces of almost delicate-looking zebra mussels were scattered on the sandy beach, we could see across to where the Detroit River ended and the Ontario shoreline curved eastward. Except for the absence of an urban skyline (Detroit's skyscrapers were too far away to make out), the spot where we were standing was the mirror image of Erie Beach opposite Buffalo. This was where the water from the upper lakes entered Lake Erie; Erie Beach was where it flowed out on its way to Lake Ontario.

It seemed a long time ago that we had started out—more like centuries than just a dozen or so weeks—which in a sense it was, if you added in the lifespans of all the various characters we had encountered on the way. Mr. Dittmar, Lourdes Iglesias, the Allens, Dr. Troyer and Mrs. McMichael, the sentimental bikers, John Yarish, Mary Ann Rutherford, lonely migrant workers, Leroy Waite, assorted members of the extended Tiessen family, the hard-rocking Bruce Brothers, John Hageman, the newly engaged couple, Judy and her customers, Mad Anthony Wayne, *et al*: living or dead, they had crowded into our consciousness, hardly leaving room for anything else.

The rain, which had conveniently slacked off long enough to allow us this brief chance to contemplate the westernmost point of the lake, now picked up again. So we scrambled quickly back to the car, scraped off our shoes, climbed back in and cruised slowly through the park, past deserted picnic tables and empty baseball diamonds and a stretch of water where half the shorebirds in the Midwest seemed to be congregating. A single glance took in herons, egrets, several varieties of ducks, sandpipers, the ubiquitous Canada geese and even a thick-bodied bittern herky-jerking its way in and out of the tall grass.

Beyond the park we passed through a couple of villages still resolutely holding onto their marshy rural roots, but then the outer edges of greater Detroit began to swallow up the landscape. Soon enough the great, grimy metropolis itself surrounded us, but I-75 carried us quickly through the city and let us out not far from the river; from the freeway exit you only have to pass through a few blocks of total slum bombardment before you're safely on the Ambassador Bridge, soaring over the freighters and tugboats far below and eventually gliding along the edges of Windsor and on through the green fields of Essex County once again.

Back home we put our feet up, decanted our last bottle of Watso's white, drank a toast to ourselves and mused about the world of Lake Erie we had set out to find. Was there such a thing?

We decided that there was. Or rather that there was, then there wasn't, and now there was starting to be again. During the nineteenth century a vast number of vessels sailed the lake, putting in at the dozens of bustling ports all around it. Cargo and passengers crisscrossed the water, holidayers from one side made day trips to resorts on the other, ships were built in one country and sold in the other, fishermen of both nations pulled in their catches and took them to the nearest drop-off point. Many of Ontario's first white settlers drifted up from the States, and family ties remained strong. There were Rockefellers on the north shore and Backuses on the south, and Edisons all over the place. For Abigail Becker's heroics to have been celebrated all around the lake was nothing out of the ordinary, because in those days Erie was a whole wide world unto itself.

By the beginning of this century industrial and transportation patterns were rapidly changing. Immigrants no longer arrived by water. The farmland on the American side was pretty much gone, replaced by the crowded cities and pollution-spewing foundries and factories which would eventually give the lake the reputation of a sewer. The fishery had started its century-long decline and with it the once thriving small towns on the Canadian side had begun to falter; some packed up shop completely. The resorts lasted a little longer, but the handwriting was on the wall.

By the Great Depression, the excursion boats had stopped coming by, mutant fish began to litter the beaches, and soon the lake had dropped from the general consciousness. Erie just wasn't very important any more.

It was quite a disappearing act.

But as Jim Allen pointed out, everything circles back eventually. We kept running into people who were starting to think again about what a large body of water can mean to the lives of anyone lucky enough to live near it.

As a commercial artery Lake Erie no longer plays as crucial a role as it did a century ago, but the lake's natural assets—the pure pleasure it offers of being able to gaze out over the changing surface, or swim, or fish, or bob around in a boat, or dive beneath the surface, or just be a small part of a monumental work of nature—are increasingly valuable in a crowded world where man's works are all too obtrusive. (Ironically, the abandonment of many of the most harmful factories due to industrial obsolescence has even given us a chance to undo some of our earlier damage to the environment.)

This emerging consciousness is at best a fragile thing; even with fax machines and computers, there's still too little knowledge shared between the two sides of the lake, too much rivalry, too many conflicting objectives. The fact that jurisdiction is divided among two countries, four states, one province, a dozen or so counties, scores of municipalities, and more than sixty assorted supervisory boards and agencies, doesn't help. In places the old shoot-the-moon greed and extravagance still ride high in the saddle, and the old battles against overdevelopment must be refought time and time again.

But you have to start somewhere. An hour spent with the kids on one of Stone Lab's teaching boats or observing a skilled commercial fisherman at work or listening to a diver enthuse about his excursions on the floor of the lake or just sitting on a rock watching the sun set over the water is all that's necessary to bring you back to this vision of the lake as a living organism.